Prentice Mulford's Story

Life by land and sea

Prentice Mulford

Alpha Editions

This edition published in 2024

ISBN 9789362091123

Design and Setting By

Alpha Editions

www.alphaedis.com

Email - info@alphaedis.com

Contents

CHAPTER I.

SHADOWS OF COMING EVENTS.

ONE June morning, when I was a boy, Captain Eben Latham came to our house, and the first gossip he unloaded was, that "them stories about finding gold in Californy was all true." It was "wash day" and our folks and some of the neighbors were gathered in the "wash house" while the colored help soused her fat black arms in the suds of the wash tub.

That was the first report I heard from California. Old Eben had been a man of the sea; was once captured by a pirate, and when he told the story, which he did once a week, he concluded by rolling up his trousers and showing the bullet-scars he had received.

California then was but a blotch of yellow on the schoolboy's map of 1847. It was associated only with hides, tallow, and Dana's "Two Years Before the Mast." It was thought of principally in connection with long-horned savage cattle, lassoes, and Mexicans. Very near this in general vacancy and mystery was the entire region west of the Rocky Mountains. What was known as the Indian Territory covered an area now occupied by half a dozen prosperous States. Texas was then the Mecca of adventurers and people who found it advisable to leave home suddenly. The phrase in those days, "Gone to Texas," had a meaning almost equivalent to "Gone to the ——." Then California took its place.

The report slumbered during the summer in our village, but in the fall it commenced kindling and by winter it was ablaze. The companies commenced forming. It was not entirely a strange land to some of our people.

Ours was a whaling village. Two-thirds of the male population were bred to the sea. Every boy knew the ropes of a ship as soon if not sooner than he did his multiplication table. Ours was a "travelled" community. They went nearer the North and South Poles than most people of their time and Behring Straits, the Kamschatkan coast, the sea of Japan, Rio Janeiro, Valparaiso, the Sandwich Islands, the Azores and the names of many other remote localities were words in every one's mouth, and words, too, which we were familiar with from childhood. Many of our whalers had touched at San Francisco and Monterey. There had recently been a great break down in the whale fishery. Whale ships for sale were plentiful. Most of them were bought to carry the "'49" rush of merchandise and men to California.

By November, 1848, California was the talk of the village, as it was all that time of the whole country. The great gold fever raged all winter.

All the old retired whaling captains wanted to go, and most of them did go. All the spruce young men of the place wanted to go. Companies were formed, and there was much serious drawing up of constitutions and by-laws for their regulation. In most cases the avowed object of the companies, as set forth in these documents, was "Mining and trading with the Indians." Great profit was expected to be gotten out of the California Indian. He was expected to give stores of gold and furs in exchange for gilt watches, brass chains, beads, and glass marbles. The companies bought safes, in which to keep their gold, and also strange and complex gold-washing machines, of which numerous patterns suddenly sprang up, invented by Yankees who never saw and never were to see a gold mine. Curious ideas were entertained relative to California. The Sacramento River was reported as abounding in alligators. Colored prints represented the adventurer pursued by these reptiles. The general opinion was that it was a fearfully hot country and full of snakes.

Of the companies formed in our vicinity, some had more standing and weight than others, and membership in them was eagerly sought for. An idea prevailed that when this moral weight and respectability was launched on the shores of California it would entail fortune on all belonging to the organization. People with the lightning glance and divination of golden anticipation, saw themselves already in the mines hauling over chunks of ore and returning home weighed down with them. Five years was the longest period any one expected to stay. Five years at most was to be given to rifling California of her treasures, and then that country was to be thrown aside like a used-up newspaper and the rich adventurers would spend the remainder of their days in wealth, peace, and prosperity at their Eastern homes. No one talked then of going out "to build up the glorious State of California." No one then ever took any pride in the thought that he might be called a "Californian." So they went.

People who could not go invested in men who could go, and paid half the expense of their passage and outfit on condition that they should remit back half the gold they dug. This description of Argonaut seldom paid any dividends. I doubt if one ever sent back a dollar. Eastern shareholders really got their money's worth in gilded hopes, which with them lasted for years. But people never put such brilliant anticipations on the credit side of the account; and merely because that, at the last, they are not realized.

As the winter of "'48" waned the companies, one after another, set sail for the land of gold. The Sunday preceding they listened to farewell sermons at church. I recollect seeing a score or two of the young Argonauts thus preached to. They were admonished from the pulpit to behave temperately, virtuously, wisely, and piously. How seriously they listened. How soberly were their narrow-brimmed, straight-up-and-down, little plug hats of that period piled one atop the other in front of them. How glistened their hair with the village barber's hair oil. How pronounced the creak of their tight boots as they marched up the aisle. How brilliant the hue of their neck-ties. How patiently and resignedly they listened to the sad discourse of the minister, knowing it would be the last they would hear for many months. How eager the glances they cast up to the church choir, where sat the girls they were to marry on their return. How few returned. How few married the girl of that period's choice. How little weighed the words of the minister a year afterward in the hurry-scurry of the San Francisco life of '49 and '50.

What an innocent, unsophisticated, inexperienced lot were those forty odd young Argonauts who sat in those pews. Not one of them then could bake his own bread, turn a flapjack, re-seat his trousers, or wash his shirt. Not one of them had dug even a post-hole. All had a vague sort of impression that California was a nutshell of a country and that they would see each other there frequently and eventually all return home at or about the same time. How little they realized that one was to go to the Northern and one to the Southern mines and one to remain in San Francisco, and the three never to meet again! What glittering gold mines existed in their brains even during the preaching of that sermon! Holes where the gold was put out by the shovelful, from which an occasional boulder or pebble was picked out and flung away.

The young Argonaut, church being dismissed, took his little stiff, shiny plug and went home to the last Sunday tea. And that Sunday night, on seeing her home from church for the last time, he was allowed to sit up with her almost as long as he pleased. The light glimmered long from the old homestead front parlor window. The cold north wind without roared among the leafless sycamores and crashed the branches together. It was a sad, sad pleasure. The old sofa they sat upon would be sat upon by them no more for years. For years? Forever in many cases. To-day, old and gray, gaunt and bent, somewhere in the gulches, "up North" somewhere, hidden away in an obscure mining camp of the Tuolumne, Stanislaus, or Mokelumne, up in Cariboo or down in Arizona, still he recollects that night as a dream. And she? Oh, she dried her eyes and married the stay-at-home five years after. A girl can't wait forever. And besides, bad reports after a time reached home about him. He drank. He gambled. He found fair friends among the señoritas. And, worse than all, he made no fortune.

By spring most of the Argonauts had departed. With them went the flower of the village. Their absence made a big social gap, and that for many a day. The girls they left behind tried for a time to live on hope, and afterward "took up" and made the most of the younger generation of boys. They remembered that after all they were not widows. Why should their mourning be permanent? 'Twere selfish for the departed Argonaut to demand it. And who knew how these Args might console themselves on arriving in San Francisco?

After many months came the first letters from San Francisco, and then specimens of gold dust and gold pieces. The gold dust came in quills or in vials, mixed with black sand. But this dust was not always dug by the moral Argonauts, from whom the most was expected. It was often the gathering of some of the obscurer members of our community. Fortune was democratic in her favors.

In the course of two years a few of the "boys" came straggling back. The first of these arrivals, I remember, walked up our main street, wearing on his shoulders a brilliant-hued Mexican serape. It created a sensation. All the small boys of the village "tagged on behind him" a sort of impromptu guard of honor. The serape was about all he did bring home. He talked a great deal of gold and brought specimens, but not in sufficient quantity to pay all outstanding bills. The next of the returned was a long, gaunt, yellow case of Chagres fever. He brought only gloom. Along in 1853-54 came a few of the more fortunate who had made a "raise." Two returned and paid up their creditors in full who had been by creditors given over. But few came to remain. They "staid around" home a few weeks, turned up their noses at the small prices asked for drinks, cigars, and stews, treated everybody, grew restless and were off again. Relatives of the not returned beset them with inquiries which they found it difficult to answer, because there was an idea prevalent in the village that a man in California ought to make money, and why didn't he?

Up to 1860 a "returned Californian" was an object of curiosity and of some importance if he brought any money with him, or rather as long as the money he brought with him lasted. But "the war" wiped them out in this respect. The California fortune of that time was a mere pimple compared with the fortunes made by the war. A generation now exists to whom the whole Argonaut exodus is but an indifferent story.

Sometimes on visiting my native village I stand before one of those old-fashioned houses, from whose front door thirty-four years ago there went forth for the last time the young Argonaut on his way to the ship.

There is more than one such house in the village. The door is double, the knocker is still upon it, the window panes are small, the front gate is the same and up to the door the same stones lie upon the walk. But within all are strangers. The father and mother are past anxious inquiry of their son. The sisters are married and live or have died elsewhere. A new generation is all about. They never heard of him. The great event of that period, the sailing of that ship for California, is sometimes recalled by a few—a few rapidly diminishing. His name is all but forgotten. Some have a dim remembrance of him. In his time he was an important young man in the village. He set the fashion in collars and the newest style of plugs. Oh, fame, how fleeting! What is a generation? A puff. A few old maids recollect him. What a pity, what a shame that we do all fade as a leaf!

What a sad place; what a living grave is this for him to return to! Where would he find the most familiar names? In the cemetery. Who would he feel most like? Like "Rip Van Winkle." Who are these bright and blooming lasses passing by? They are her grown-up children—she with whom he sat up that last Sunday night in the old-fashioned front parlor on the old-fashioned sofa. Where is she? That is she, that stout, middle-aged woman across the street. Is she thinking of him? No; she is thinking whether there shall be cabbage or turnips for dinner. Who is that codgery-looking man going up the street. That is the man she didn't wait for and married. Should the Argonaut return home if he could? No. Let him stay where he is and dream on of her as she was, bright, gay, lively, blooming, and possibly romantic. The dream is solid happiness compared with the reality.

The recollections treated in this chapter are to me as a commencement and an ending of the shadows of a series of coming events.

CHAPTER II.

GOING TO SEA.

EIGHT years later I shipped "before the mast" on the A 1 first-class clipper *Wizard* bound from New York to San Francisco.

When I made up my mind to become a sailor, I had tried several of this world's callings and seemed to find none suitable. I had asked counsel of several elderly gentlemen in my native village as to the best way of securing all things needful during my sojourn in this world. They said many wise and good things. They looked wise and good. But really the wordy help they offered was unsatisfactory. So I cut the knot myself and said I would be a sailor. I explained to my male and female friends that I felt myself destined for a maritime career. I needed more excitement than could be got out of a shore humdrum life. The sea was the place for enterprising youthful Americans. The American merchant marine needed American officers and sailors. All heard me and agreed. No doubt it was the best thing. And I talked on and they agreed with all my arguments. How people will agree with you when it's all one to them what you do! I was eighteen and in most respects a fool, including this—that I did not know it.

The *Wizard*, on which I shipped with five other boys from my native town, was a first-class clipper. She was a fine thing to look at from a distance, either as she lay at anchor, the tracery of her spars and rigging in relief against the sky, or speeding along under studding sails rigged out on both sides. But once on board and inside her symmetrical lines, things were not so beautiful. Those white, cloud-like sails tore men's fingers as, hard and heavy with ice or snow, the sailors tried to furl them. Those graceful tapering yards, supporting the studding sails, strained and half-crushed men's backs when lowered and toted about the deck. There were wooden belaying-pins, iron marline-spikes and other miscellaneous things to fling at men's heads by those in authority. Those cobweb-like ropes had hard, thick ends lying coiled on deck to lash men's bodies.

We, the six boys, were obliged to leave our native heaths because there wasn't room for us on them to earn our bread and clothes. We were not clearly aware of this at the time, though an unspoken sentiment prevailed there, as it does in most of the older settled States, that the young man must move away to "seek his fortune." Ten years previous we should have entered the whaling service. But the whale fishery had utterly failed. Once it was the outlet for nearly all the brawn and muscle of our island.

The Captain of the *Wizard* was from our native town. Therefore myself and the five other boys had shipped under him, expecting special favors. A mistake. Never sail under a Captain who knows your folks at home. You have no business to expect favoritism; he has no business to grant it.

I was the last of the six young lubbers to leave the town for New York. On the morning of my departure the mothers, sisters, and other female relatives of the five who had gone before discovered many other things which they deemed necessary for the urchins to carry on the voyage. So they bore down on me with them, and I bade most of these good people an earthly farewell, loaded down, in addition to my own traps, with an assorted cargo of cakes, sweetmeats, bed quilts, Bibles, tracts, and one copy of "Young's Night Thoughts" for the boys.

I ate my last dinner as a free man at a Broadway restaurant, and then I went to the wharf where the ship lay. Already the tug was alongside, preparatory to hauling her out in the stream. I went up the plank and over the side. A gentleman in authority asked me, as I stepped on deck, if I belonged to the ship. I said I did. "Take off those togs, then, put on your working duds and turn to, then," he remarked. The togs went off. I put on my canvas pants and flannel shirt, the garb of sea servitude. Henceforth I was a slave. The ship just then was not a Sunday-school nor a Society for Ethical Culture. It was a howling pandemonium of oaths and orders. Fully one-third of the able seamen had not recovered from their closing-out shore spree, and had tumbled into their berths or were sprawled on deck drunk. Cargo in cases, bales, boxes, and barrels was still rattled over the bulwarks and into the hold. Everybody seemed to be swearing—first, each one on his own, private account, and secondly, all in one general chorus for mutual purposes. Many people seemed in command. I couldn't distinguish the officers of the ship from the stevedores. Still officers continued to turn up everywhere, and each officer ordered me to some particular and separate duty.

The world looked pretty black to me then. I wished there was some way out of it. On shore the period between the foremast hand and the position of Captain was only the duration of a thought. Here it was an eternity. Day dreams are short, real experience is long. But all this is often in youth a difficult matter to realize.

There came along a short, stout man with a deeper voice and more sonorous oath than anybody else. This was the fourth and last mate. It was a relief to find at last the end of the mates and to know the exact number of men legitimately entitled to swear at me. This gentleman for a season concentrated himself entirely on me. He ordered me with a broom and scraper into the ship's pig-pen, which he argued needed cleaning. This was my first well-defined maritime duty. It was a lower round of the ladder than I had anticipated. It seemed in its nature an occupation more bucolic than nautical. I would have preferred, also, that compliance with the order had not been exacted until the ship had left the wharf, because there were several shore visitors on board, and among them two of my intimate friends who had come to see me off. There they stood, in all the bravery of silk hats and fashionably-cut attire, conversing on terms of equality with the first mate. They could talk with him on the weather or any subject. I, by virtue of my inferior position, was not at liberty to speak to this potentate at all.

I jumped into the pig-pen. Thus destiny, despite our inclinations, forces down our throats these bitter pills. The fourth mate was not more than a year my senior. He stood over me during the entire process and scolded, cursed, and commanded. My shore friends looked on from afar and grinned. Already they saw the great social chasm which yawned between me and them, and governed their actions accordingly. Already did they involuntarily patronize me. It requires a wise man to detect the wickedness and deceit in his own nature. Probably I should have similarly acted had our positions been reversed. The mate was very particular. He made me sweep and scrape every corner with an elaborate and painful accuracy. He sent me into the pig's house to further perfect the work. I was obliged to enter it in an almost recumbent position. The pig ran out disgusted. I scraped his floor in a similar mood. Thus commenced life on the ocean wave.

But I got even with the mate. Destiny made me my own involuntary avenger of the indignity put upon me. By indignity I don't mean the cleaning of the pig-pen. That was an honorable, though menial occupation—at least in theory. Cincinnatus on his farm may have done the same thing. But I do mean the scurrility and abuse the young officer bestowed on me, while I did my best to execute his bidding.

I hauled the young man overboard about three minutes afterward, but he never knew I did it, and I never allowed myself to think of the occurrence while on shipboard, for fear the powers of the air might ventilate the matter. It came about in this way: A line was passed through a hawse-hole forward to the tug, which was puffing, fretting, fuming, and churning with her screw the mud-ooze and garbage floating in the slip into a closer fusion. My friend the mate stood on the fore-chains with the end of the heavy rope in both hands, trying to pass it to those on the tug. This line running through the hawse-hole aft was lying near where I stood. Some one called out: "Haul in on that line!" I supposed that the order referred to me and the hawser lying at my side. So I hauled with all my might. I felt at first some resistance—something like a tugging at the other end. I hauled all the harder. Then something seemed to give way. It hauled easier. I heard, coincident with these sensations, a splash, loud cries, much swearing and the yell of "Man overboard!" I raised my head over the bulwarks and there was my mate, floundering amid dock ooze, rotten oranges, and salt water. It was he who held the other end of the line, and my hauling had caused the centre of gravity in his short body to shift beyond the base, and in accordance with a natural law he had gone overboard. He was the general cynosure of all eyes. They fished him out, wet and swearing. There was a vigorous demand for the miscreant who had been hauling on the line. I was as far as possible from the spot and kept myself very busy. Bluster went below and changed his clothes. I was avenged.

CHAPTER III.

GETTING MY SEA LEGS ON.

WE were towed into the stream and anchored for the night. To look at New York City, with its many lights and its thousands amusing themselves in various ways, from the ship's deck, without the possibility of joining them, was to feel for the first time the slavery of marine life. Emerging very early next morning from the "boys' house," I found everything in the bustle and confusion of getting under way. A long file of men were tramping aft with a very wet hawser. As I stood looking at them my ear was seized by our Dutch third mate, who accompanied the action with the remark, "Cooms, I puts you to work." He conducted me in this manner to the rope and bade me lay hold of it. I did so. I could have done so with a better heart and will had it not been for the needless and degrading manner in which he enforced his command. Most men do their work just as well for being treated with a certain courtesy of command due from the superior to the inferior.

At noon the tug cast off. The Highlands of Navesink sank to a cloud in the distance. The voyage had commenced. All hands were mustered aft. The Captain appeared and made them a short speech. He hoped we would all do our duty and that the voyage would be a pleasant one. It was not a pleasant one at all. However, that was all in the future. The first and second mates then chose the men for their respective watches, commencing with the able seamen, then picking out the ordinary seamen, and finally descending to the boys. Of course the best of all these grades were picked off first. I think I was among the last of the boys who were chosen.

The first night out was fine. The *Wizard* slightly bowed to the ocean, and the sails seemed great black patches, waving to and fro against the sky. The six boys, so soon to be miserable, gathered in a cluster on deck. Jed Coles proposed that we "spin yarns." It was the nautically correct way of passing the time. So we "spun yarns," or at least Jed did. He had a batch ready for the occasion. He sat on a tub, put an enormous chew of tobacco in his mouth, hitched up his trousers and felt every inch a sailor. I noticed the second mate, that incarnation of evil and brutality, hovering about us, dark as it was. I saw his fiendish grin and the glare of his greenish eye. A precious lot of young fools we must have seemed to him. A little after our yarn spinning was interrupted by shrieks and cries of distress proceeding from the forward part of the ship. We had then our first exhibition of the manner of enforcing American merchant-service discipline. The second mate was beating Cummings, a simple being, who, having sailed only in "fore-and-aft" coasting vessels, had made the mistake of shipping as an ordinary seaman on a square-rigged craft, and was almost as much at sea in his knowledge of the ropes as the "boys." This officer had singled out Cummings for his awkwardness as the proper man to "haze." He was showering upon him blows, thick and fast, with the end of one of the fore braces. It was the first time I had ever seen a man beaten by one in authority. The cringing attitude, the cries, sobs, and supplications of a full-grown man, and the oaths and terrible ferocity of his castigator, were inexpressibly shocking to me. The incident, which was often repeated during the voyage, broke up our amateur yarning and made us very thoughtful.

Jedediah Coles was not at all nautically loquacious the next night. Then the Gulf Stream gave us a touch of its tantrums. All during the afternoon the sky grew more and more threatening. By dark it was blowing hard. The lighter sails one by one were stowed. Then it blew harder. The mate swore the harder. The Captain came on deck and swore at everybody. One of the "boys" asked him if he thought it would be stormy. He considered himself privileged to ask the Captain that question. He was a native of the same village. His father and the Captain were friends, and his mother and the Captain's wife visited each other. So he deemed it advisable to establish himself on a sociable footing with the Captain at the commencement of the voyage. Poor boy! Never again during the trip did he consult the Captain meteorologically. He learned speedily the great gulf which yawns between the cabin and the forecastle.

It grew dark, the waves became bigger and bigger, and the ship seemed taxed to her utmost trying to clamber them one after another as they presented themselves. The mates came out in their oilskins. The order was given to reef topsails. Gangs of men ran hither and thither, pulling here, hauling there, and running straight over us whenever we got in their way, and it seemed impossible to get out of their way. Everything became unsettled and uncomfortable. The ship would not keep still. New complications of ropes and hauling-gear were developed. The capstan in the waist was manned, and round and round went the sailors, while the deck they trod was inclined in all manner of uncomfortable angles. Tackle and great blocks were hooked to ringbolts, and a vast amount of what seemed to me fruitless hauling went on. Barrels of water swashed over the bulwarks, knocking us down and drenching us. Wet and shivering we clung to belaying pins or anything within reach, of no earthly use to anybody, thinking of the cheerfully lit, well-warmed rooms and comfortable tea-tables even then set but so few miles away on the shores of Long Island.

When the order came to reef, and I saw the men clambering up the fore and main rigging, I added myself to their number, though I felt I should never come down again—at least in one piece. It was my debut aloft off soundings. Many a time had I clambered about the rigging of the old whalers as they lay at the village wharf, but they were not roaring, kicking, and plunging like this vessel. Heavy seamen's boots kicked me in the face as I followed their wearers up this awful ascent; other heavy boots trod on my fingers; they shook the ratlines, too, in a most uncomfortable manner. The mast strained and groaned fearfully. Somehow, after climbing over some awful chasms, I got on the yard with the men. I dared not go out far. The foot rope wobbled, jerked, and gave way under me at times with the weight and notion of the men upon it. The great sail seemed in no humor to be furled. It hauled away from us, bellied, puffed, and kept up a gigantic series of thundering flaps. Laying over on the yard the men would gather in as much of the hard, wet, wire-like canvas as possible and then together haul back on it.

This I objected to. It was risky enough to lay out on an enormous stick sixty feet in the air, while the wind tore our voices from us and seemed to hurl the words far away ere they had well got out of our mouths, and the white-topped waves, dimly seen below, seemed leaping up and snatching at us. But at that height, and amid all that motion, to balance one's body on the stomach, grasp with outstretched arms a hard roll of struggling, wet canvas, while the legs were as far extended the other way and the feet resting only against a rope working and wobbling and giving way here and there from the weight of fifteen hundred pounds of men unequally distributed over it, was a task and seeming risk too great for my courage. I dared do nothing but hold on. The conduct of the maintopsail was desperate and outrageous. It seemed straining every nerve—supposing, for the sake of forcible expression, that it had nerves—to pull us off the yard and "into the great deep." I found myself between two old sailors, who lost no time in convincing me of my complete and utter worthlessness aloft. I concurred. They bade me clear out and get down on deck. I was glad to do so. Reefing topsails in reality was very different from reefing them in books or in imagination. On reaching the deck I concluded to lie down. All through the evening I had experienced an uneasy sensation in the stomach. I argued with myself it was not seasickness—something did not agree with me. But when I lay down in the scuppers I admitted being seasick. Then I only cared to lie there. Life was too miserable even to hope in. The tumult went on as ever. The sailors trampled over me. Being in the way, they dragged me aside. I cared not. Finally some one bawled in my ear, "Sick! go below." I went. The five other boys, all similarly affected, all caring naught for life or living, lay in their bunks.

The boys' house was about the size of a respectable pig pen—a single pig pen. There was room in it for two boys to turn at once, providing they turned slowly and carefully. On going on board we had bestowed such of our outfit as could be brought into this pen in the manner in which boys of sixteen bestow things generally on first commencing to "keep house." Everything was arranged on a *terra firma* basis. We made no calculation for the ship's deviating from an even keel. When she did commence to pitch everything fell down. Clothing fell on the floor; plates, knives, forks, cups and bottles rolled from shelf and bunk; bread, meat, and the molasses kegs fell; plum and sponge cake, pie and sweetmeats fell; for each boy had a space in his sea-chest filled with these articles, placed there by kind, dear relatives at home. It was intended that we should not refer to them until the ship was far advanced on her voyage. But we never had such large supplies of cake and sweetmeats at hand before; so we went for these things immediately. The house abounded with them the first night out. The roof leaked. We left our sliding-door carelessly open, and a few barrels of the ocean slopped over the bulwarks into the apartment. At midnight our combined clothing, plates, mugs, knives, forks, bottles, water-kegs, combs, hair-brushes, hats, pants, coats, meat, bread, pie, cake, sweetmeats, molasses, salt water, and an occasional seasick and despairing boy, united to form a wet, sodden mass on the floor two feet in depth. Above the storm howled and swept through the rigging, with little sail to interrupt it. Six sick and wretched boys in their berths lay "heads and pints," as they pack herring; that is, the toe of one rested on the pillow of the other, for it was not possible to lie otherwise in those narrow receptacles for the living. But the horrors of that second night are not to be related.

No solicitous stewards with basins and tenders of broth and champagne attended us. We were not cabin passengers on an ocean steamer. Barely had the next morning's dawn appeared when our door was flung open. In it stood that dreadful second mate of the greenish eyes, hard, brick-red complexion, horny fists and raspy voice—a hard, rough, rude, unfeeling man, who cried: "Come out of that! Oh, you're young bears—your troubles ain't commenced yet!" Then his long, bony arm gripped us one after the other and tore us from our bunks. How unlike getting up at home on a cold winter's morning, as, snuggling in our warm feather beds, we heard our mothers call time after time at the foot of the stairs: "Come now, get up! Breakfast is ready!" And with the delay prone to over-indulged youth, we still lay abed until the aroma of buckwheat cakes and coffee stealing to our bedrooms developed an appetite and induced us to rise. Out, this dreadful morning, we tumbled, in the wet clothes wherein we had lain all night, weak, sick, staggering, giddy. A long iron hook was put in my hand and I was desired to go forward and assist in hauling along length after length of the cable preparatory to stowing it away. Sky and sea were all of dull, monotonous gray; the ship was still clambering one great wave after an another with tiresome and laborious monotony. All the canvas of the preceding day had disappeared, save a much-diminished foretop-sail and storm staysail. The mates on duty were alert and swearing. The men, not all fully recovered from their last shore debauch, were grumbling and swearing also. The cook, a dark-hued tropical mongrel, with glittering eyes, was swearing at something amiss in his department. It was a miserable time. But a cure was quickly effected. In thirty-six hours all seasickness had departed. With the delicate petting process in vogue with wealthy cabin-passengers it would have required a week. But we had no time in which to be seasick.

Life for us on board this ship was commenced on a new basis. We were obliged to learn "manners." Manners among modern youth have become almost obsolete. The etiquette and formality required from the younger to the elder, and common to the time of perukes and knee-breeches, has now little place save on shipboard, where such traditions and customs linger. We were surprised to find it our duty to say "Sir" to an officer, and also to find it imperative to recognize every order addressed us by the remark; "Aye, aye, sir!" The sullen, shambling fashion of receiving words addressed us in silence, so that the speaker was left in doubt as to whether he was heard or not, had no place off soundings. In short, we were obliged to practice what is not common now to many boys on shore—that is, an outward show of respect for superiors. If business called us to the "West End" of a ship, the quarter-deck, our place was to walk on the lee side of that deck and leave the weather side the moment the duty was done. If sent for any article by an officer, it was our business to find it without further recourse to him.

Petted boys have little patience for hunting for things. At home two minutes is about the limit of time spent in looking for a mislaid poker, and then "Ma!" "Pa!" or "Aunt!" is called on to turn to and do this disagreeable work. The second mate once ordered me to find a certain iron hook, wherewith to draw the pump boxes, and when, after a short search, I returned and asked him where it might be I was horrified by the expression of astonished indignation spreading over his face as he yelled: "Great Scott, *he* expects *me* to help him find it!" I saw the point and all it involved, and never so wounded an officer's dignity again. It is a sailor's, and especially a boy's business on shipboard, to find whatever he is ordered to. It must be produced—no matter whether it's in the ship or not. At all events that's the sentiment regarding the matter. But it is good discipline for boys over-nursed at home and only physically weaned. The "cold, cold world" would not, in some cases, be so cold to the newly-fledged youth first trying his feeble wings outside the family nest, did parents judiciously establish a little of this maritime usage at home.

We soon learned on the *Wizard* how well we had lived at home. Our sea fare of hard tack and salt junk taught us how to appreciate at their true value the broiled streaks, hot cakes, and buttered toast of home tables. The quart of very common molasses served out to us weekly soon became a luxury, and when the steward occasionally brought us "Benavlins" (the nautical term for the broken fragments from the cabin table), we regarded it as very luxurious living, though a month previous we should have deemed such food fit only for the swill-tub.

In about two weeks we had settled down into the routine of life at sea. Sailors are apt to term theirs a "dog's life." I never did. It was a peculiar life, and in some respects an unpleasant one—like many others on land. But it was not a "dog's life." There was plenty to eat, and we relished our "lobscouse," hard tack, salt junk, beans, codfish, potatoes and Sunday's and Thursday's duff. The hours for labor were not exhausting. It was "watch and watch, four hours off and four hours on." Many a New York retail grocer's clerk, who turns to at 5 in the morning and never leaves off until 11 at night, would revel on such regulation of time and labor. So would many a sewing-girl. We had plenty of time for sleep. If called up at 4 every alternate morning, and obliged to stand watch until 8 A.M., we could "turn in" at that hour after breakfast and sleep till noon. Apart from the alternate watches the work or "jobs" occupied about six hours per day. True, there was at times some heavy work, but it was only occasional. Sailor-work is not heavy as compared with the incessant fagging, wearing, never-ending character of some occupations on shore. Skill, agility, and quickness are in greater demand than mere brute strength.

Lobscouse is a preparation of hard bread, first soaked and then stewed with shredded salt beef. It looks somewhat like rations for a delicate bear when served out by the panful. But it is very good. Salt beef is wonderfully improved by streaks of fat through it. These serve the foremast hands in place of butter. I know of no better relish than good pilot bread and sliced salt junk, with plenty of clean white fat. On shore that quart of boiling hot liquid, sweetened with molasses and called tea, would have been pitched into the gutter. At sea, after an afternoon's work, it was good. With similar content and resignation, not to say happiness, we drank in the morning the hot quart of black fluid similarly sweetened and called coffee. It was not real coffee. I don't know what it was. I cared not to know. Of course we grumbled at it. But we drank it. It was "filling," and was far better than the cold, brackish water, impregnated thickly with iron rust, a gallon of which was served out daily. For the fresh water was kept below in an iron tank, and, as the deck leaked, a small portion of the Atlantic had somehow gained admission to it and slightly salted it. It resembled chocolate to the eye, but not to the palate.

CHAPTER IV.

MUCH WATER AND MUTINY.

ON the fourth day out the *Wizard* was found to have four feet of water in her hold. The ship was pumped dry in about four hours, when she proceeded to fill up again. The Captain seemed a man of many minds for the next two or three days. First the ship was put back for New York. This course was altered and her bows pointed for Africa. Then the foremast hands became worried, and going aft one morning in a body, asked Captain S—— what he meant to do and where he meant to go, because they had shipped for San Francisco and they did not intend going anywhere else. The Captain answered, that his own safety and that of the vessel were as dear to him as their lives were to them, and that he intended doing the best for the general good. This answer was not very satisfactory to the crew, who went grumbling back to their quarters. Ultimately it turned out that we were to take the leak with us to San Francisco. At the rate the water was running in it was judged that the bone, muscle, and sinews of the crew could manage to keep it down. So we pumped all the way round Cape Horn. We pumped during our respective watches every two hours. In good weather and on an even keel it took half an hour to "suck the pumps." If the vessel was heeled to larboard or starboard, it took much longer. In very rough weather we pumped all the time that could be spared from other duties. There were two pumps at the foot of the mainmast worked by levers, and these were furnished with "bell ropes" to pull on. Half the watch worked at each lever, and these were located exactly where on stormy nights the wild waves were in the habit of flinging over the bulwarks a hogshead or two of water to drench us and wash us off our feet.

The *Wizard* was a very "wet ship." She loved giving us moist surprises. Sometimes on a fine day she would gracefully, but suddenly, poke her nose under, and come up and out of the Atlantic or Pacific ocean with fifteen or twenty tons of pea-green sea water foaming over the t'gallant forecastle, cascading thence on the spar deck and washing everything movable slam bang up and sometimes into the cabin. This took place once on a washday. Sailors' washday is often regulated by the supply of water caught from the clouds. On this particular occasion the fore deck was full of old salts up to their bared elbows in suds, vigorously discoursing washtub and washboard. Then the flood came, and in a moment the deck was filled with a great surge bearing on its crest all these old salts struggling among their tubs, their washboards, their soap and partly-washed garments.

The cabin bulkhead partly stopped some, but the door being open others were borne partly inside, and their woollen shirts were afterward found stranded on the carpeted cabin floor. One "duff day" we had gathered about our extra repast in the boys' house. The duff and New Orleans molasses had just commenced to disappear. Then a shining, greenish, translucent cataract filled the doorway from top to bottom. It struck boys, beef, bread, duff, and dishes. It scattered them. It tumbled them in various heaps. It was a brief season of terror, spitting, and sputtering salt water, and a scrambling for life, as we thought. It washed under bunks and in remote corners duff, bread, beef, plates, knives, forks, cups, spoons and molasses-bottles. The dinner was lost. Going on deck we found a couple of feet of water swashing from bulwark to bulwark with every roll, bearing with it heavy blocks and everything movable which had been loosened by the shock, to the great risk of legs and bodies. But these were trifles. At least we call them trifles when they are over. I have noticed, however, that a man may swear as hard at a jammed finger as a broken leg, and the most efficacious means in the world to quickly develop a furious temper is to lose one's dinner when hungry, get wet through, then abused by a Dutch mate for not stirring around quicker, and finally work all the afternoon setting things to rights on an empty stomach, robbed and disappointed of its duff. This is no trifle.

Learning the ropes isn't all a boy's first lessons at sea. He must learn also to wash and mend his own clothes. At least he must try to learn and go through the forms. I never could wash a flannel shirt, and how the extraneous matter called dirt, which the washing process is intended to disperse, is gotten rid of by soap and muscle at an equal average over the entire surface of the garment is for me to-day one of earth's mysteries. I could wash a shirt in spots. When I tried to convince myself that I had finished it I could still see where I had washed clean and where I had not. There is a certain system in the proper manipulation of a garment in a washtub which to me is incomprehensible. An old sailor is usually a good washer. It's part of his trade. Those on the *Wizard* would reprove the boys for their slipshod work. "Such a slovenly washed shirt as that," said Conner, an old man-of-war's man, "hung in the rigging is a disgrace to the ship." He alluded to one of mine. The failure was not from any lack of labor put on it. The trouble lay in that I didn't know where to put the labor on. It was easier to tie a shirt to a line, fling it overboard and let it tow. This will wash clothes—wash all the warp out of them in time. The practice was at last forbidden the boys on the *Wizard*. It's a lazy boy's wash. The adage "It's never too late to mend" is not applicable on shipboard. It should there read "It's never too early to mend." Of course a boy of sixteen, whose mother has always stitched for him, will allow his clothes to go until they fall off his body before using his needle. As I did. And I sewed myself up only to rip asunder immediately. I went about decks a thing of flaps, rips, rags, and abortive patches, until they called me the ship's scarecrow. And so would many another spruce young man under similar discipline. It's good once in one's life to be brought thus low.

It was particularly disagreeable at midnight as we assembled at the bell ropes to give her the last "shake-up," and more asleep than awake pulled wearily with monotonous clank. Sometimes at that hour, when our labors were half through, the valves would get out of order. It was then necessary to call the carpenter and have them repaired. This would keep us on deck half an hour or more, for by mutual compact each watch was obliged to "suck its own pumps." Such delays made the men very angry. They stopped singing at their work—always a bad sign—and became silent, morose, and sullen. For the first six weeks all the "shanti songs" known on the sea had been sung. Regularly at each pumping exercise we had "Santy Anna," "Bully in the Alley," "Miranda Lee," "Storm Along, John," and other operatic maritime gems, some of which might have a place in our modern operas of *The Pinafore* school. There's a good deal of rough melody when these airs are rolled out by twenty or thirty strong lungs to the accompaniment of a windlass' clank and the wild, shrill sweep of the winds in the rigging above. But the men would no longer sing. The fact was reported to the Captain. He put on his spectacles, walked out on the quarter-deck and gazed at them mournfully and reprovingly. The mates tried to incite them to renewed melody. But the shipping articles did not compel them to sing unless they felt like it. The pumps clanked gloomily without any enlivening chorus. The Captain went sadly back to his cabin and renewed his novel.

One night the pumps broke down five minutes before 12 o'clock. Our watch was at work on them. The carpenter was called as usual, and after the usual bungling and fishing in the well for the broken valves, they were put in order again. It was then nearly 1 A.M. Meanwhile all the able seamen in our watch had at eight bells walked below. The watch newly come on deck refused to pump the ship clear, alleging it was the business of the others. The watch below were bidden to come on deck and perform their neglected duty. They refused. This was mutiny. The four mates got their pistols, entered the forecastle and stormed, ordered, and threatened. It was of no avail. The fifteen able seamen who refused constituted the main strength and effectiveness of that watch. They were threatened with being put in irons. They preferred irons to pumping out of their turn. They were put in irons, fifteen stout men, by the four mates, who then returned and reported proceedings to the Captain. The men remained shackled until the next morning. It was then discovered that it was impossible to work the ship without their aid. Of course they couldn't handle the vessel in irons. In reality double the number of able men were needed in both watches. The *Wizard* rated over 3,000 tons, and many a frigate of her size would have been deemed poorly off with less than one hundred men for handling the ship alone. We rarely secured the lower sails properly in heavy weather, from the mere lack of physical strength to handle them. So Captain S——— pored sadly at his breakfast through his gold-bowed spectacles, and when the meal was over issued orders for the release of the fifteen men in irons. In this little affair the boys and ordinary seamen belonging to the mutinous watch took no part. They were strictly neutral and waited to see which side would win. I felt rather unpleasant and alarmed. Though not a full-fledged mutiny and a conversion of a peaceful merchantman into a pirate, it did look at one time as if the initiatory steps to such end were being taken.

One of the great aims of existence at sea is that of keeping the decks clean. The scrubbing, swishing, and swashing is performed by each watch on alternate mornings, and commences at daylight. It was the one ordeal which I regarded with horror and contempt. You are called up at four in the morning, when the sleep of a growing youth is soundest. The maniacal wretch of the other watch, who does the calling, does it with the glee and screech of a fiend. He will not stop his "All Ha-a-a-nds!" until he hears some responsive echo from the sleepers. He is noisy and joyous because it is so near the time he can turn in. And these four hours of sleep at sea are such luxuries as may rarely be realized on shore. But the mate's watch is calling us, screeching, howling, thumping on the forecastle door, and making himself extremely pleasant. The old sailors being called gradually rise to sitting postures in their berths with yawns, oaths, and grumblings. If the hideous caller is seen, a boot or other missile may be shied in that direction. Otherwise the prejudice and disgust for his clamor on the part of those called expresses itself in irritable sarcasms such as, "Oh, why don't you make a little more noise?" "Think yourself smart, don't you?" "Say, don't you s'pose we can hear?" To-morrow morning at 12 or 4 these personalities and conditions of mind will be reversed. The awakened irritable grumbler will be the joyous caller, and the joyous caller of this early morn will be searching about his bunk for some offensive implement to hurl at the biped who thus performs the matutinal office of the early village cock.

We are called and on deck, and stumbling about, maybe with one boot half on, and more asleep than awake and more dead than alive. We are in the warm, enervating latitude of the tropics, with every sinew relaxed from the steaming heat. Perhaps there is a light wind aft. We are carrying studding-sails. Studding-sails are beautiful to look at from a distance. But when once you have sailed in a ship carrying them from the royals down and know something of the labor of rigging them out all on one side, fore, main, and mizzen-masts, and then, if the breeze alters a couple of points, taking the starboard sails all down and rigging out the larboard, or perhaps on both sides—and this on a Sunday afternoon, when there are no jobs and you've been expecting plenty of leisure to eat your duff and molasses; or if you have ever helped carry those heavy yards about the deck when the ship was rolling violently in a heavy ground swell, and every time she brought up, sails, blocks, and everything movable was bringing up also with a series of pistol-like reports; or if you have ever laid out on a royal yard trying to pass a heavy rope through the "jewel block," at the extreme end thereof, while the mast and yard were oscillating to and fro with you through the air in a rapidly recurring series of gigantic arcs caused by the lazy swell, in the trough of which your ship is rolling—and at the end of each roll you find yourself holding on for dear life, lest at the termination of each oscillation you be shot like an arrow into the sea from your insecure perch—why in all these cases the beauty and picturesqueness of a ship under studding-sails will be tempered by some sober realities.

It is 5:30 or 6 o'clock. The morning light has come. The cry of "Turn to!" is heard. That is, "turn to" to wash down decks, an operation which will tax the already exhausted resources of an empty stomach until breakfast time at 8 o'clock. The mates have their fragrant "cabin coffee" and biscuit served them on the brass capstan aft; we can smell its aroma, but nothing warm can get into our stomachs for over two long hours of work. The basic idea in this regular washing down decks at sea seems to be that of keeping men busy for the sake of keeping them busy. The top of every deck plank must be scrubbed with a care and scrutiny befitting the labors of a diamond polisher on his gems, while the under side may be dripping with foulness, as it sometimes is. I had the post of honor in scrubbing the quarter-deck. That was the drawing of water in a canvas bucket from the mizzen chains to wash over that deck. The remaining five boys would push wearily about with their brooms, hand-brushes, squabs, and squilgees, superintended by our extraordinary fourth mate (always to me an object of interest, from the fact of the secret carefully hoarded in my breast that I had pulled him into the New York dock), who, with a microscopic eye inspected each crack and seam after the boys' labors, in search of atomic particles of dirt, and called them back with all the dignity of command, and a small amount of commanding personality behind it, whenever he deemed he had discovered any. When this labor was finished I was generally so exhausted as to have no appetite for breakfast. But a sailor's stomach is not presumed to be at all sensitive under any conditions. And above all a "boy"—a boy belonging to a squad of boys who about once a day were encouraged and enthused to exertion and maritime ambition by the assurance conveyed them by one of the mates that they weren't "worth their salt"—what business had a boy's stomach to put on airs at sea? Most landsmen if called up at 4 o'clock on a muggy morning and worked like mules for a couple of hours on a digestive vacuum, would probably at the breakfast hour feel more the need of food than the appetite to partake of it.

Though I followed the sea nearly two years, I am no sailor. The net result of my maritime experience is a capacity for tying a bow-line or a square knot and a positive knowledge and conviction concerning which end of the ship goes first. I also know enough not throw hot ashes to windward.

But on a yard I could never do much else but hold on. The foolhardy men about me would lie out flat on their stomachs amid the darkness and storm, and expose themselves to the risk of pitching headlong into the sea in the most reckless manner while trying to "spill the wind" out of a t'gallant sail. But I never emulated them. I never lived up to the maritime maxim of "one hand for yourself and the other for the owners." I kept both hands for myself, and that kept me from going overboard. What would the owners have cared had I gone overboard? Nothing. Such an occurrence twenty-five odd years ago would, weeks afterward, have been reported in the marine news this way: "Common sailor, very common sailor, fell from t'gallant yard off Cape Horn and lost." The owner would have secretly rejoiced, as he bought his Christmas toys for his children, that the t'gallant yard had not gone with the sailor. No; on a yard in a storm I believed and lived up to the maxim: "Hold fast to that which is good." The yard was good. Yet I was ambitious when a boy before the mast on the clipper which brought me to California. I was quick to get into the rigging when there was anything to do aloft. But once in the rigging I was of little utility.

The first time I went up at night to loose one of the royals, I thought I should never stop climbing. The deck soon vanished in the darkness of a very black tropical night, the mastheads were likewise lost in a Cimmerian obscurity—whatever that is. At last I found the yard. I wasn't quite sure whether it was the right one or not. I didn't know exactly what to do. I knew I had to untie something somewhere. But where? Meantime the savage Scotch second mate was bellowing, as it then seemed, a mile below me. I knew the bellow was for me. I had to do something and I commenced doing. I did know, or rather guessed, enough to cast off the lee and weather gaskets, or lines which bind the sail when furled to the yard, and then I made them up into a most slovenly knot. But the bunt-gasket (the line binding the middle and most bulky portion of the sail), bothered me. I couldn't untie it. I picked away at it desperately, tore my nails and skinning my knuckles. The bellowing from below continued as fiercely as ever, which, though not intelligible as to words, was certainly exhorting me, and me only, to vigilance. Then the watch got tired waiting for me. Thinking the sail loosed, they began hoisting. They hoisted the yard to its proper place and me with it. I clung on and went up higher. That, by the way, always comes of holding fast to that which is good. Then a man's head came bobbing up out of the darkness. It was that of a good-natured Nantucket boy, whose name of course was Coffin. He asked me the trouble. I went into a lengthy explanation about the unmanageable knot. "Oh—the knot!" said he. "Cut it!" and he cut it. I would never have cut it. In my then and even present nautical ignorance I should have expected the mast or yard to have fallen from cutting anything aloft. Only a few days previous I had seen the Captain on the quarter-deck jumping up and down in his tracks with rage because a common seamen had, by mistake, cut a mizzen brace, and the second mate, as usual, had jumped up and down on the seaman when he reached the deck. I feared to set a similar jumping process in operation. Coming on deck after my lengthy and blundering sojourn loosing a royal, I expected to be mauled to a pulp for my stupidity. But both watch and bellowing mate had gone below and I heard no more of it.

CHAPTER V.

SAN FRANCISCO IN 1856.

THE *Wizard* sailed through a great bank of fog one August morning and all at once the headlands of the Golden Gate came in sight. It was the first land we had seen for four months. We sailed into the harbor, anchored, and the San Francisco of 1856 lay before us.

The ship was tied up to the wharf. All but the officers and "boys" left her. She seemed deserted, almost dead. We missed the ocean life of the set sails, the ship bowing to the waves and all the stir of the elements in the open ocean.

The captain called me one day into the cabin, paid me my scanty wages and told me he did not think I "was cut out for a sailor," I was not handy enough about decks.

Considering that for two months I had been crippled by a felon on the middle finger of my right hand, which on healing had left that finger curved inward, with no power to straighten it, I thought the charge of awkwardness somewhat unjust.

However, I accepted the Captain's opinion regarding my maritime capacities, as well as the hint that I was a superfluity on board.

I left the *Wizard*—left her for sixteen years of varied life in California.

I had no plans, nor aims, nor purpose, save to exist from day to day and take what the day might give me.

Let me say here never accept any person's opinion of your qualifications or capacities for any calling. If you feel that you are "cut out" for any calling or that you desire to follow it, abide by that feeling, and trust to it. It will carry you through in time.

I believe that thousands on thousands of lives have been blasted and crippled through the discouragement thrown on them by relation, friend, parent, or employer's saying continually (or if not saying it verbally, thinking it) "You are a dunce. You are stupid. You can't do this or that. It's ridiculous for you to think of becoming this or that."

The boy or girl goes off with this thought thrown on them by others. It remains with them, becomes a part of them and chokes off aspiration and effort.

Years afterward, I determined to find out for myself whether I was "cut out for a sailor" or not. As a result I made myself master of a small craft in all winds and weathers and proved to myself that if occasion required, I could manage a bigger one.

San Francisco seemed to me then mostly fog in the morning, dust and wind in the afternoon, and Vigilance Committee the remainder of the time.

San Francisco was then in the throes of the great "Vigilanteeism" of 1856. Companies of armed men were drilling in the streets at night. In the city's commercial centre stood "Fort Gunnybags"—the strong hold of the Vigilantes—made, as its name implied, of sand-filled gunny sacks. Carronades protruded from its port holes, sentinels paced the ramparts. There was constant surging of men in and out of the building behind the fort,—the headquarters and barracks of the Vigilantes. From its windows a few days before our arrival they had hung Casey for the killing of James King—one of the editors of the *Bulletin*. I saw two others hung there on the sixth of August. Vigilanteeism was then the business and talk of the town. The jail had just been captured from the "Law and Order" men, who were not "orderly" at all, but who had captured the city's entire governmental and legal machinery and ran it to suit their own purposes.

The local Munchausens of that era were busy; one day the U. S. ship of war, *St. Mary's*, was to open fire on Fort Gunnybags; the next, Governor Johnson, backed by twenty thousand stalwart men, was to fall upon the city and crush out the insurrection.

The up-country counties were arming or thought of arming to put down this "rebellion." The "Rebellion" was conducted by the respectability and solidity of San Francisco, which had for a few years been so busily engaged in money making as to allow their city government to drift into rather irresponsible hands; many of the streets were unbridged, many not lighted at night. Cause—lack of money to bridge and light. The money in the hands of the city officials had gone more for private pleasure than public good.

I speak of the streets being unbridged because at that time a large portion of the streets were virtually bridges. One-fourth of the city at least, was built over the water. You could row a boat far under the town, and for miles in some directions. This amphibious part of the city "bilged" like a ship's hold, and white paint put on one day would be lead colored the next, from the action on it of the gases let loose from the ooze at low tide.

There were frequent holes in these bridges into which men frequently tumbled, and occasionally a team and wagon. They were large enough for either, and their only use was to show what the city officials had not done with the city's money.

Then Commercial street between Leidesdorff and Battery was full of Cheap John auction stores, with all their clamor and attendant crowds at night. Then the old Railroad Restaurant was in its prime, and the St. Nicholas, on Sansome, was the crack hotel. Then, one saw sand-hills at the further end of Montgomery street. To go to Long Bridge was a weary, body-exhausting tramp. The Mission was reached by omnibus. Rows of old hulks were moored off Market street wharf, maritime relics of "'49." That was "Rotten Row." One by one they fell victims to Hare. Hare purchased them, set Chinamen to picking their bones, broke them up, put the shattered timbers in one pile, the iron bolts in another, the copper in another, the cordage in another, and so in a short all time that remained of these bluff-bowed, old-fashioned ships and brigs, that had so often doubled the stormy corner of Cape Horn or smoked their try-pots in the Arctic ocean was so many ghastly heaps of marine débris.

I had seen the *Niantic*, now entombed just below Clay street, leave my native seaport, bound for the South Pacific to cruise for whale, years ere the bars and gulches of California were turned up by pick and shovel. The *Cadmus*, the vessel which brought Lafayette over in 1824, was another of our "blubber hunters," and afterward made her last voyage with the rest to San Francisco.

Manners and customs still retained much of the old "'49" flavor. Women were still scarce. Every river boat brought a shoal of miners in gray shirts from "up country." "Steamer Day," twice a month, was an event. A great crowd assembled on the wharf to witness the departure of those "going East" and a lively orange bombardment from wharf to boat and *vice versa* was an inevitable feature of these occasions.

The Plaza was a bare, barren, unfenced spot. They fired salutes there on Independence Day, and occasionally Chief Burke exhibited on its area gangs of sneak thieves, tied two and two by their wrists to a rope—like a string of onions.

There was a long low garret in my Commercial street lodgings. It was filled with dust-covered sea-chests, trunks, valises, boxes, packages, and bundles, many of which had been there unclaimed for years and whose owners were quite forgotten. They were the belongings of lost and strayed Long Islanders, ex-whaling captains, mates and others. For the "Market" was the chief rendezvous. Every Long Islander coming from the "States" made first for the "Market." Storage then was very expensive. It would soon "eat a trunk's head off." So on the score of old acquaintance all this baggage accumulated in the Market loft and the owners wandered off to the mines, to Oregon, to Arizona, to Nevada—to all parts of the great territory lying east, north and south, both in and out of California, and many never came back and some were never heard of more. This baggage had been accumulating for years.

I used occasionally to go and wander about that garret alone. It was like groping around your family vault. The shades of the forgotten dead came there in the evening twilight and sat each one on his chest, his trunk, his valise, his roll of blankets. In those dusty packages were some of the closest ties, binding them to earth, Bibles, mother's gifts, tiny baby shoes, bits of blue ribbon, which years by-gone fluttered in the tresses of some Long Island girl.

It was a sad, yet not a gloomy place. I could feel that the presence of one, whose soul in sad memory met theirs, one who then and there recalled familiar scenes, events and faces, one who again in memory lived over their busy preparations for departure, their last adieux and their bright anticipations of fortune, I could feel that even my presence in that lone, seldom-visited garret, was for them a solace, a comfort. Imagination? Yes, if you will. Even imagination, dreamy, unprofitable imagination, may be a tangible and valuable something to those who dwell in a world of thought.

One night—or, rather, one morning—I came home very late—or, rather, very early. The doors of the Long Island House were locked. I wanted rest. One of the window-panes in front, and a large window-pane at that, was broken out. All the belated Long Islanders stopping at the place, when locked out at night, used to crawl through that window-pane. So, I crawled through it. Now, the sentinel on the ramparts of Fort Gunnybags, having nothing better to do, had been watching me, and putting me up as a suspicious midnight loiterer. And so, as he looked, he saw me by degrees lose my physical identity, and vanish into the front of that building; first, head, then shoulders, then chest, then diaphragm, then legs, until naught but a pair of boot-soles were for a moment upturned to his gaze, and they vanished, and darkness reigned supreme. The sentinel deemed that the time for action had come. I had just got into bed, congratulating myself on having thus entered that house without disturbing the inmates, when there came loud and peremptory rappings at the lower door. Luther and John, the proprietors, put their heads out of the chamber windows. There was a squad of armed Vigilantes on the sidewalk below; and, cried out one of them, "There's a man just entered your house!" Now I heard this, and said to myself, "Thou art the man!" but it was so annoying to have to announce myself as the cause of all this disturbance, that I concluded to wait and see how things would turn out. John and Luther jumped from their beds, lit each a candle and seized each a pistol; down-stairs they went and let the Vigilantes in. All the Long Island captains, mates, coopers, cooks, and stewards then resident in the house also turned out, lit each his candle, seized each a pistol or a butcher-knife, of which there were plenty on the meat-blocks below. John came rushing into my room where I lay, pretending to be asleep. He shook me and exclaimed, "Get up! get up! there's a robber in the house secreted somewhere!" Then I arose, lit a candle, seized a butcher-knife, and so all the Vigilantes with muskets, and all the Long Island butchers, captains, mates, cooks, coopers, and stewards went poking around, without any trousers on, and thrusting their candles and knives and pistols into dark corners, and under beds and behind beef barrels, after the robber. So did I; for the disturbance had now assumed such immense proportions that I would not have revealed myself for a hundred dollars. I never hunted for myself so long before, and I did wish they would give up the search. I saw no use in it; and besides, the night air felt raw and chill in our slim attire. They kept it up for two hours.

Fort Gunnybags was on Sacramento Street; I slept directly opposite under the deserted baggage referred to. The block between us and the fort was vacant. About every fourth night a report would be circulated through that house that an attack on Fort Gunnybags would be made by the Law and Order men. Now, the guns of Fort Gunnybags bore directly on us, and as they were loaded with hard iron balls, and as these balls, notwithstanding whatever human Law and Order impediments they might meet with while crossing the vacant block in front, were ultimately certain to smash into our house, as well as into whatever stray Long Island captains, mates, boat-steerers, cooks, and coopers might be lying in their path, these reports resulted in great uneasiness to us, and both watches used frequently to remain up all night, playing seven-up and drinking rum and gum in Jo. Holland's saloon below.

I became tired at last of assisting in this hunt for myself. I gave myself up. I said, "I am the man, I am the bogus burglar, I did it." Then the crowd put up their knives and pistols, blew out their candles, drew their tongues and fired reproaches at me. I felt that I deserved them; I replied to none of their taunts, conducted myself like a Christian, and went to bed weighted down with their reproof and invective. The sentinel went back to his post and possibly slept. So did I.

CHAPTER VI.

AS A SEA COOK.

I DRIFTED around San Francisco for several months and finally shipped as cook and steward of the schooner *Henry*, bound from San Francisco for a whaling, sealing, abalone curing, and general "pick up" voyage along the Lower Californian coast. My acceptance as cook was based on the production of an Irish stew which I cooked for the captain and mate while the *Henry* was "hove down" on the beach at North point and undergoing the process of cleaning her bottom of barnacles. I can't recollect at this lapse of time where I learned to cook an Irish stew. I will add that it was all I could cook—positively all, and with this astounding capital of culinary ignorance I ventured down upon the great deep to do the maritime housework for twenty men.

When we were fairly afloat and the Farallones were out of sight my fearful incapacity for the duties of the position became apparent. Besides, I was dreadfully seasick, and so remained for two weeks. Yet I cooked. It was purgatory, not only for myself but all hands. There was a general howl of execration forward and aft at my bread, my lobscouse, my tea, my coffee, my beef, my beans, my cake, my pies. Why the captain continued me in the position, why they didn't throw me overboard, why I was not beaten to a jelly for my continued culinary failures, is for me to this day one of the great mysteries of my existence. We were away nearly ten months. I was three months learning my trade. The sufferings of the crew during those three months were fearful. They had to eat my failures or starve. Several times it was intimated to me by the under officers that I had better resign and go "for'ard" as one of the crew. I would not. I persevered at the expense of many a pound of good flour. I conquered and returned a second-class sea cook.

The *Henry* was a small vessel—the deck was a clutter of whaling gear. Where my galley or sea-kitchen should have been, stood the try-works for boiling blubber. They shoved me around anywhere. Sometimes I was moved to the starboard side, sometimes to the larboard, sometimes when cutting in a whale way astern. I expected eventually to be hoisted into one of the tops and cook aloft. Any well regulated galley is placed amidships, where there is the least motion. This is an important consideration for a sea cook. At best he is often obliged to make his soup like an acrobat, half on his head and half on his heels and with the roof of his unsteady kitchen trying to become the floor. My stove was not a marine stove. It had no rail around the edges to guard the pots and kettles from falling off during extra lurches. The *Henry* was a most uneasy craft, and always getting up extra lurches or else trying to stand on her head or stern. Therefore, as she flew up high astern when I was located in that quarter, she has in more than one instance flung me bodily, in an unguarded moment, out of that galley door and over that quarter-deck while a host of kettles, covers, and other culinary utensils, rushed with clang and clatter out after me and with me as their commander at their head. We all eventually terminated in the scuppers. I will not, as usual, say "lee scuppers." Any scupper was a lee scupper on that infernal vessel. I endeavored to remedy the lack of a rail about this stove by a system of wires attaching both pots and lids to the galley ceiling. I "guyed" my chief culinary utensils. Still during furious oscillations of the boat the pots would roll off their holes, and though prevented from falling, some of them as suspended by these wires would swing like so many pendulums, around and to and fro over the area of that stove.

That was the busiest year of my life. I was the first one up in the morning, and the last save the watch to turn in at night. In this dry-goods box of a kitchen I had daily to prepare a breakfast for seven men in the cabin, and another for eleven in the forecastle; a dinner for the cabin and another for the forecastle; likewise supper for the same. It was my business to set the aristocratic cabin table, clear it off and wash the dishes three times daily. I had to serve out the tea and coffee to the eleven men forward. The cabin expected hot biscuit for breakfast, and frequently pie and pudding for dinner. Above all men must the sea cook not only have a place for everything and everything in its place, but he must have everything chocked and wedged in its place. You must wash up your tea things, sometimes holding on to the deck with your toes, and the washtub with one hand, and wedging each plate, so soon as wiped, into a corner, so that it slide not away and smash. And even then the entire dish-washing apparatus, yourself included, slides gently across the deck to leeward. You can't leave a fork, or a stove-cover, or lid-lifter lying about indifferently but what it slides and sneaks away with the roll of the vessel to some secret crevice, and is long lost. When your best dinner is cooked in rough weather, it is a time of trial, terror, and tribulation to bestow it safely on the cabin table. You must harbor your kindling and matches as sacredly as the ancients kept their household gods, for if not, on stormy mornings, with the drift flying over the deck and everything wet and clammy with the water-surcharged air of the sea, your breakfast will be hours late through inability to kindle a fire, whereat the cook catches it from that potentate of the sea, "the old man," and all the mates raise their voices and cry with empty stomachs, "Let him be accursed."

One great trial with me lay in the difficulty of distinguishing fresh water from salt—I mean by the eye. We sea cooks use salt water to boil beef and potatoes in: or rather to boil beef and pork and steam the potatoes. So I usually had a pail of salt water and one of fresh standing by the galley door. Sometimes these got mixed up. I always found this out after making salt-water coffee, but then it was too late. They were particular, especially in the cabin, and did not like salt-water coffee. On any strictly disciplined vessel the cook for such an offence would have been compelled to drink a quart or so of his own coffee, but some merciful cherub aloft always interfered and got me out of bad scrapes. Another annoyance was the loss of spoons and forks thrown accidentally overboard as I flung away my soup and grease-clouded dishwater. It was indeed bitter when, as occupied in these daily washings I allowed my mind to drift to other and brighter scenes, to see the glitter of a spoon or fork in the air or sinking in the deep blue sea, and then to reflect that already there were not enough spoons to go around, or forks either. Our storeroom was the cabin. Among other articles there was a keg of molasses. One evening after draining a quantity I neglected to close the faucet tightly. Molasses therefore oozed over the cabin floor all night. The cabin was a freshet of molasses. Very early in the morning the captain, getting out of his bunk, jumped both stockinged feet into the saccharine deluge. Some men will swear as vigorously in a foot-bath of molasses as they would in one of coal-tar. He did. It was a very black day for me, and life generally seemed joyless and uninviting; but I cooked on.

The *Henry* was full of mice. These little creatures would obtrude themselves in my dough wet up for fresh bread over night, become bemired and die therein. Once a mouse thus dead was unconsciously rolled up in a biscuit, baked with it, and served smoking hot for the morning's meal aft. It was as it were an involuntary meat-pie. Of course the cabin grumbled; but they would grumble at anything. They were as particular about their food as an habitué of Delmonico's. I wish now at times I had saved that biscuit to add to my collection of odds-and-endibles. Still even the biscuit proved but an episode in my career. I cooked on, and those I served stood aghast, not knowing what would come next.

After live months of self-training I graduated on pies. I studied and wrought out the making of pies unassisted and untaught. Mine were sea mince pies; material, salt-beef soaked to freshness and boiled tender, dried apples and molasses. The cabin pronounced them good. This was one of the few feathers in my culinary cap. Of course, their goodness was relative. On shore such a pie would be scorned. But on a long sea-voyage almost any combination of flour, dried fruit and sugar will pass. Indeed, the appetite, rendered more vigorous and perhaps appreciative by long deprivation from luxuries, will take not kindly to dried apples alone. The changes in the weekly bill of fare at sea run something thus: Sundays and Thursdays are "duff days"; Tuesday, bean day; Friday, codfish and potato day; some vessels have one or two special days for pork; salt beef, hardtack, tea and coffee are fluids and solids to fall back on every day. I dreaded the making of duffs, or flour puddings, to the end of the voyage. Rarely did I attain success with them. A duff is a quantity of flour and yeast, or yeast-powder, mixed, tied up in a bag and boiled until it is light. Plum-duff argues the insertion of a quantity of raisins. Plain duff is duff without raisins. But the proper cooking of a duff is rather a delicate matter. If it boils too long the flour settles into a hard, putty-like mass whereunto there is neither sponginess, lightness, nor that porousness which delights the heart of a cook when he takes his duff from the seething caldron. If the duff does not boil long enough, the interior is still a paste. If a duff stops boiling for ever so few minutes, great damage results. And sometimes duff won't do properly, anyway. Mine were generally of the hardened species, and the plums evinced a tendency to hold mass meetings at the bottom. Twice the hands forward rebelled at my duffs, and their Committee on Culinary Grievances bore them aft to the door of the cabin and deposited them there unbroken and uneaten for the "Old Man's" inspection. Which public demonstration I witnessed from my galley door, and when the duff deputation had retired, I emerged and swiftly and silently bore that duff away before the Old Man had finished his dinner below. It is a hard ordeal thus to feel one's self the subject of such an outbreak of popular indignation. But my sympathies now are all with the sailors. A spoiled duff is a great misfortune in the forecastle of a whaler, where neither pie nor cake nor any other delicacy, save boiled flour and molasses sauce, come from month's end to month's end.

In St. Bartholomew's or Turtle bay, as the whalers call it, where for five months we lay, taking and curing abalones, our food was chiefly turtle. This little harbor swarmed with them. After a few hours' hunt one of our whaleboats would return with five or six of these unwieldy creatures in the bottom, some so large and heavy as to require hoisting over the side. Often the green fat under the callipee, or under shell, lay three inches in thickness. I served up turtle fried, turtle stewed, quarters of turtle roasted and stuffed like loins of veal, turtle plain boiled and turtles' flippers, boiled to a jelly and pickled. A turtle is a variously flavored being. Almost every portion has a distinct and individual taste. After all, old Jake, our black boat-steerer, showed us the most delicate part of the turtle, and one previously thrown away. This was the tripe, cleansed of a thin inner skin. When the cabin table had once feasted on stewed turtle tripe they called for it continuously. After many trials and much advice and suggestion, I learned to cook acceptably the abalone. The eatable part of this shellfish when fresh is as large as a small tea saucer. There are two varieties, the white and black. The white is the best. Cut up in pieces and stewed, as I attempted at first, the abalone turned out stewed bits of gutta percha; fried, it was fried gutta percha. Then a man from another vessel came on board, who taught me to inclose a single abalone in a small canvas bag and then pound it to a jelly with a wooden mallet. This process got the honey out of the abalone. The remains of four or five abalones thus pounded to a pulp, and then allowed to simmer for a couple of hours, would make a big tureen of the most delicious soup man ever tasted, every drop of which, on cooling, hardened to the consistency of calves'-foot jelly. When my cabin boarders had once become infected with abalone soup they wanted me to keep bringing it along. The Americans do not know or use all the food in the sea which is good.

I was an experimental cook, and once or twice, while cutting-in whale, tried them with whale meat. The flesh lying under the blubber somewhat resembles beef in color, and is so tender as easily to be torn apart by the hands. But whale meat is not docile under culinary treatment. Gastronomically, it has an individuality of its own, which will keep on asserting itself, no matter how much spice and pepper is put upon it. It is a wild, untamed steed. I propounded it to my guests in the guise of sausages, but when the meal was over the sausages were there still. It can't be done. Shark can. Shark's is a sweet meat, much resembling that of the swordfish, but no man will ever eat a whale, at least an old one. The calves might conduct themselves better in the frying-pan. We had many about us whose mothers we had killed, but we never thought of frying them. When a whaler is trying out oil, she is blackened with the greasy soot arising from the burning blubber scraps from stem to stern. It falls like a storm of black snow-flakes. They sift into the tiniest crevice. Of all this my cookery got its full share. It tinged my bread and even my pies with a funereal tinge of blackness. The deck at such times was covered with "horse pieces" up to the top of the bulwarks. "Horse pieces" are chunks of blubber a foot or so in length, that being one stage of their reduction to the size necessary for the try-pots. I have introduced them here for the purpose of remarking that on my passage to and fro, from galley to cabin, while engaged in laying the cloth and arranging our services of gold plate and Sèvres ware, I had to clamber, wade, climb, and sometimes, in my white necktie and swallow-tail coat, actually crawl over the greasy mass with the silver tureen full of "consommé" or "soup Julien," while I held the gilt-edged and enamelled menu between my teeth. Those were trying-out times for a maritime head butler.

The cook socially does not rank high at sea. He stands very near the bottom round of the ladder. He is the subject of many jests and low comparisons. This should not be. The cook should rank next or near to the captain. It is the cook who prepares the material which shall put mental and physical strength into human bodies. He is, in fact, a chemist, who carries on the last external processes with meat, flour, and vegetables necessary to prepare them for their invisible and still more wonderful treatment in the laboratory which every man and woman possesses—the stomach—whereby these raw materials are converted not only into blood, bone, nerve, sinew, and muscle, but into thoughts. A good cook may help materially to make good poetry. An indigestible beefsteak, fried in grease to leather, may, in the stomach of a General, lose a battle on which shall depend the fate of nations. A good cook might have won the battle. Of course, he would receive no credit therefor, save the conviction in his own culinary soul, that his beefsteak properly and quickly broiled was thus enabled to digest itself properly in the stomach of the General, and thereby transmit to and through the General's organism that amount of nerve force and vigor, which, acting upon the brain, caused all his intelligence and talent to attain its maximum, and thereby conquer his adversary. That's what a cook may do. This would be a far better and happier world were there more really good cooks on land and sea. And when all cooks are Blots or Soyers, then will we have a society to be proud of.

CHAPTER VII.

SIGHTS WHILE COOKING.

St. Bartholomew or Turtle Bay is a small, almost circular, sheet of water and surrounded by some of the dreariest territory in the world. The mountains which stand about it seem the cooled and hardened deposit of a volcano. Vegetation there is none, save cactus and other spined, horned, and stinging growths. Of fresh water, whether in springs, rivulets, or brooks, there is none. Close by our boat-landing was the grave of a mother and child, landed a few years previous from a wreck, who had perished of thirst. Coyotes, hares, and birds must have relieved thirst somewhere, possibly from the dews, which are very copious. Our decks and rigging in the morning looked as though soaked by a heavy shower. Regularly at night the coyotes came down and howled over that lone grave, and the bass to their fiend-like yelping were furnished by the boom of the Pacific surges on the reef outside. To these gloomy sounds in the night stillness and blackness, there used for a time to be added the incessant groaning of a wretched Sandwich Islander, who, dying of consumption, would drag himself at night on deck to avoid disturbing the sleep of the crowded forecastle. Small hope for help is there for any thus afflicted on a whaler. There is no physician but the Captain, and his practice dares not go much beyond a dose of salts or castor-oil. The poor fellow was at last found dead, early one evening, in his bunk, while his countrymen were singing, talking, laughing, and smoking about him. It was a relief to all, for his case was hopeless, and such misery, so impossible to relieve, is terrible to witness on a mere fishing-schooner so crowded as ours. The dead man was buried at sea without any service, much to the disgust of one of our coopers, who, although not a "professor," believed that such affairs should be conducted in an orthodox, ship-shape fashion. Some one, after the corpse had slid overboard, remarked, "Well, he's dead and buried," whereat the cooper muttered, "He's dead, but he ain't what I call buried." I don't think the Captain omitted the burial service through any indifference, but rather from a sensitiveness to officiate in any such semi-clerical fashion.

Some rocks not far from our anchorage were seen covered at early dawn every morning with thousands of large black sea-birds. They were thickly crowded together and all silent and immovable, until apparently they had finished some Quaker form of morning devotion, when they commenced flying off, not all at once, but in series of long straggling flocks. In similar silence and order they would return at night from some far-off locality. Never during all the months of our stay did we hear a sound from them. Morning after morning with the earliest light this raven-colored host were ever on their chosen rocks, brooding as it were ere their flight over some solemnity peculiar to their existence.

The silent birds gone, there came regularly before sunrise a wonderful mirage. Far away and low down in the distant seaward horizon there seemed vaguely shadowed forth long lines one above and behind the other of towers, walls, battlements, spires and the irregular outline of some weird ancient city. These shapes, seemingly motionless, in reality changed from minute to minute, yet the movement was not perceptible. Now it was a long level wall with an occasional watch-tower. Then the walls grew higher and higher, and there towered a lofty, round, cone-shaped structure, with a suggestion of a flight of circular steps on the outside, as in the old-fashioned Sunday-school books was seen pictured the tower of Babel. It would reveal itself in varying degrees of distinctness. But when the eye, attracted by some other feature of the spectacle, turned again in its direction it was gone. A haze of purple covered as with a gauzy veil these beautiful morning panoramas. Gazed at steadily it seemed as a dream realized in one's waking moments. It was sometimes for me a sight fraught with dangerous fascination, and often as I looked upon it, forgetting all else for the moment, have I been recalled disagreeably to my mundane sphere of slops, soot, smoke and dish-rags, as I heard the ominous sizzle and splutter of the coffee boiling over, or scented on the morning air that peculiar odor, full of alarm to the culinary soul, the odor of burning bread in the oven. 'Tis ever thus that the fondest illusions of life are rudely broken in upon by the vulgar necessities and accidents of earthly existence.

There were ten Sandwich Islanders in the forecastle of the *Henry*, one big Jamaica negro, who acted as a sort of leader for them, and no white men. These Kanakas were docile, well-behaved, could read in their own language, had in their possession many books printed in their own tongue, and all seemed to invest their spare cash in clothes. They liked fish, very slightly salted, which they would eat without further cooking, plenty of bread, and, above all things, molasses. Molasses would tempt any of these Islanders from the path of rectitude. When not at work they were either talking or singing. Singly or in groups of two or three they would sit about the deck at night performing a monotonous chant of a few notes. This they would keep up for hours. That chant got into my head thirty-three years ago and it has never got out since. Change of scene, of life, of association, increase of weight, more morality, more regular habits, marriage, all have made no difference. That Kanaka chant, so many thousand times heard on the Southern Californian coast, will sometimes strike up of its own accord, until it tires me out with its imagined ceaseless repetition. It's there, a permanent fixture. Recollection will wake it up.

So unceasing was the gabble of these Kanakas that one day I asked Jake, the negro boat-steerer, who understood their language, what they found to talk so much about. "Oh, dey talk about anyting," said he; "dey talk a whole day 'bout a pin." Whereat I retired to my maritime scrubbery and kitchen and varied my usual occupation midst my pots, pans, and undeveloped plum duffs with wondering if the simpler, or, as we term them, the inferior races of men are not more inclined to express their thoughts audibly than the superior. I do not think an idea could present itself to a Kanaka without his talking it out to somebody.

But some of these simple children of the Pacific isles used to pilfer hot biscuits from my galley when I was absent. In vain I set hot stove covers in front of the door for them to step on and burn their bare feet. I burned myself on the iron I had prepared for my recently civilized, if not converted, heathen brother. Both the superior and inferior races often went barefooted on the *Henry* while in the lower latitudes.

At times, leaving a portion of the crew at the St. Bartholomew's bay station to collect and cure abalone, the schooner cruised about the coast for sea-elephant. Not far from the bay are the islands of Cedros (or Cedars), Natividad and some others. The first we saw of Cedros was her tree-covered mountain-tops floating, as it were, in the air above us on a sea of fog. This lifting, we were boarded by a boat containing two men. They proved to be two Robinson Crusoes, by name Miller and Whitney, who had been alone on the island nearly six months. They, with others, had fitted out in San Francisco a joint-stock vessel and were left with a supply of provisions on Cedros to seal. Their vessel was long overdue, their provisions down to the last pound of biscuits, and they were living largely on fish and venison, for though Cedros is many miles from the main land, deer have got there somehow, as well as rattlesnakes. Their vessel never did return, for their Captain ran away with her and sold her in some South American port. Miller and Whitney joined our crew and made the remainder of the voyage with us. They brought on board all their worldly goods in two small trunks; also, a kettleful of boiled venison, a treat which they were very glad to exchange for some long-coveted salt pork. They reported that a "stinker" was lying among the rocks ashore. A "stinker" in whaleman's parlance is a dead whale. In giving things names a whaleman is largely influenced by their most prominent traits or qualities, and the odorous activity of a dead whale can be felt for miles. They told us, also, that they had nineteen barrels of seal oil stored on the island of Natividad. Natividad is but a bleached-topped, guano-covered rock. We sailed thither but found no oil. The Captain who had stolen their vessel also included the oil. Miller and Whitney proved very useful men. Whitney was a powerful talker. Miller never spoke unless under compulsion. Whether in their six months of Cedros isolation such a pair had been well mated is a matter on which there may be variance of opinion. Perhaps from a colloquial standpoint some if not many long-married men can best tell. Miller was a Vermonter, and had spent seventeen years of his life roaming about among seldom-visited South Sea islands. Could his tongue have been permanently loosened and his brain stimulated to conversational activity, his might have been a most interesting story. Once in a great while there came from him a slight shower of sentences and facts which fell gratefully on our parched ears, but as a rule the verbal drought was chronic. He had an irritating fashion also of intonating the first portions of his sentences in an audible key and then dying away almost to a whisper. This, when the tale was interesting, proved maddening to his hearers. He spoke once of living on an island whose natives were almost white, and the women well formed and finer looking than any of the Polynesian race he had ever seen. Polygamy was not practised; they were devoted to one wife; and their life, cleanliness and manners, as he described them, made, with the addition of a little of one's own imagination, a pleasing picture. Miller's greatest use to mankind lay in his hands, in which all his brainpower concentrated instead of his tongue. From splicing a cable to skinning a seal, he was an ultra proficient. Others might tell how and tell well, but Miller did it. Talking seemed to fatigue him. Every sentence ere completed fell in a sort of a swoon.

In St. Bartholomew's, alias Turtle, Bay, we lay four months, taking abalones. All hands were called every morning at four o'clock. Breakfast was quickly dispatched, their noon lunch prepared, and everybody save myself was away from the vessel by five. That was the last I saw of them until sunset, and I was very glad to be rid of the whole gang and be left alone with my own thoughts, pots, pans, and kettles. The abalone clings to the surf-washed rocks by suction. It has but one outer shell. San Francisco is very familiar with their prismatic hues inside, and the same outside when ground and polished. Heaps of those shells, three feet in height and bleached to a dead white by the sun, lay on the beaches about us. Of unbleached and lively-hued shells we took on board several tons. They were sent to Europe, and there used for inlaid work. The live abalone must be pried off the rock with stout iron chisels or wedges. It was rough work collecting them from the rocky ledges in a heavy surf. Carried to the curing depot on shore, the entrails were cut away and the round, solid chunk of meat left was first boiled and then dried in the sun. An inferior pearl is often found within the body of the abalone. Our one Chinaman, Ah Sam, was *chef* of the abalone-curing kitchen on shore. He was shipped for that purpose. One live abalone will cling to the back of another too tightly to be pulled off easily by hand, and you may in this way pile them on top of one another, and thus erect a column of abalone as many feet in height as you choose to build. These fish were intended for the Chinese market, and the projectors of the voyage expected to get forty cents per pound for them in San Francisco. When some forty tons had been cured we heard from a passing steamer that the English had instituted another of their Christian wars with China, for which reason abalones in San Francisco brought only ten cents per pound. Then we stopped cooking abalones, hauled up our anchor and hunted the sea-lion and the whale.

But while in St. Bartholomew's Bay I was left alone on the vessel all day with no companions save the gulls in the air and the sharks in the water. Both were plentiful. The gulls made themselves especially sociable. They would come boldly on board and feast on the quarters of turtle-meat hung up in the rigging. Once I found one in the cabin pecking away at the crumbs on the table. His gullible mind got into a terrible state on seeing me. I whacked him to my heart's content with the table-cloth. He experienced great trouble in flying up the cabin stairway. In fact, he couldn't steer himself straight up stairs. His aim on starting himself was correct enough, like that of many a young man or woman in commencing life; but instead of going the straight and narrow path up the companionway he would bring up against a deck beam. There is no limit to the feeding capacity of those Pacific-coast gulls. The wonder is where it all goes to. I have experimentally cut up and thrown in small pieces to a gull as much fat pork as would make a meal for two men, and the gull has promptly swallowed it all, waited for more, and visibly got no bigger. They never get fat. Sometimes I tied two bits of meat to either end of a long string and flung it overboard. Barely had it touched the water when the meat at either end was swallowed by two of these bottomless scavengers, and they would fly away, each pulling hard at the latest received contents of the other's stomach. The picture reminded me of some married lives. They pulled together, but they didn't pull the right way.

At low tide the shore would be lined with these birds vainly trying to fill themselves with shellfish and such carrion as the waters had left. It couldn't be called feeding; a Pacific-coast gull does not feed, it seeks simply to fill up the vast, unfathomable space within. Eternity is, of course, without end, but the nearest approach to eternity must be the inside of a gull; I would say stomach, but a stomach implies metes and bounds, and there is no proof that there are any metes and bounds inside of a gull. It was good entertainment to see the coyotes come down and manœuvre to catch the gulls. There was a plain hard beach, perhaps a quarter of a mile wide, between coyote and gull. Of course coyote couldn't walk across this and eat gull up. So he went to work to create an impression in gull's mind that he was thereon other business, and was quite indifferent, if not oblivious, to all gulls. He would commence making long straight laps of half a mile on the beach. At the end of each lap he would turn and run back a few feet nearer gull; back another lap, another turn, and so on. But he wasn't looking for a gull. He didn't know there was a gull in the world. He had some business straight ahead of him which banished all the gulls in the world from his mind. He kept forgetting something and had to run back for it. And the gull on the water's edge, trying to fill its void where men imagined a stomach to be, had no fears of that coyote. It realized the momentous and all-absorbing character of coyote's business. There was no danger. So coyote, getting a little nearer and a little nearer at each turn, suddenly shot out of his lap at a tangent, and another gull was forever relieved of the impossible task of trying to fill itself.

CHAPTER VIII.

WHALING IN MARGUERITA BAY.

MARGUERITA BAY lies on the Mexican coast about 200 miles north of Cape St. Lucas. On arriving the schooner was "kedged" up the lagoons running parallel with the coast fully one hundred miles. This took two weeks. We passed, as it were, through a succession of mill-ponds, filled with low, green islands, whose dense shubbery extended to the water's edge. The trunks of a small umbrella-shaped tree were washed by the tides to the height of several feet, and thickly incrusted with small oysters. When we wanted oysters we went on shore and chopped down a boatload of trees. Is it necessary to remark that the trees did not grow the oysters. The oysters grew on the trees, and they were as palatable as so many copper cents, whose taste they resembled. When cooked, the coppery taste departed. The channel through these lagoons was very crooked. It was necessary to stake out a portion at low water, when it ran a mere creek through an expanse of hard sand, sometimes a mile from either shore. At high water all this would be covered to a depth of six or seven feet. The *Henry* grounded at each ebb, and often keeled over at an angle of forty-five. From our bulwarks it was often possible to jump on dry ground. This keeling-over process, twice repeated every twenty-four hours, was particularly hard on the cook, for the inconvenience resulting from such a forty-five-degree angle of inclination extended to all things within his province. My stove worked badly at the angle of forty-five. The kettle could be but half-filled, and only boiled where the water was shallowest inside. The cabin table could only be set at an angle of forty-five. So that while the guests on the upper side had great difficulty in preventing themselves from slipping off their seats on and over that table, those on the lower side had equal difficulty in keeping themselves up to a convenient feeding distance. Captain Reynolds, at the head of the board, had a hard lot in the endeavor to maintain his dignity and sitting perpendicularly at the same time on the then permanent and not popular angle of forty-five. But I, steward, butler, cook, and cabin boy, bore the hardest tribulation of all in carrying my dishes across the deck, down the cabin stairs, and arranging them on a table at an angle of forty-five. Of course, at this time the rack used in rough weather to prevent plates and platters from slipping off was brought into permanent use. Transit from galley to cabin was accomplished by crawling on two legs and one arm, thus making of myself a peripatetic human triangle, while the unoccupied hand with difficulty bore aloft the soup-tureen. It was then I appreciated the great advantages afforded in certain circumstances by the prehensile caudal termination of our possible remote ancestors. With such a properly equipped appendage, the steward might have taken a close hitch round an eyebolt, and let all the rest of himself and his dishes safely down into the little cabin. It is questionable whether man's condition has been physically improved by the process of evolution. He may have lost more than he has gained. A monkey can well afford to scorn the relatively clumsy evolutions of the most skilful human brother acrobat.

Marguerita Bay was the nursery of the female whales, or in whaler's parlance, "cows." The long, quiet lagoons, fringed with green, their waters warmed by the sun to a most agreeable temperature, were the resort during the spring months of the mother whales to bring forth and nurse their young. The bulls generally remained outside. The cows were killed with tolerable ease in the shoal waters of the bay. Outside they have, on being struck, the reputation of running out all the line a boat can spare and then demanding more. Grant could never have fought it out on one line with a "California Gray." In the lagoons, so long as the calf was uninjured, the mother would slow her own pace, so as to remain by her young. Thus she became an easy sacrifice. If the calf was wounded, woe to the boat's crew. The cow seemed to smell the blood the moment it was drawn from its offspring. The first time this happened—the boat-steerer accidentally slipping his lance into the calf—the cow turned and chased the boat ashore. The tables were turned. The miserable pigmies, who dared strike Leviathan's child, were saved because their boat could float where Mrs. Whale couldn't. She drew at least seven feet of water. A whale is one of the few things read of that is bigger than it looks. The pigmies hauled the boat upon the beach, while the whale for full half an hour swam to and fro where her soundings were safe, and embargoed them. It was, with her, "Come off if you dare." But they didn't care to dare, and finally she went away unkilled. She managed, at the start to give the boat one crack, enough to fill it with water. But whaleboats are made to be broken. A few hours' work and the insertion of a few bits of wood in the light clinker-built sides will restore a whaleboat which, to an inexperienced eye, looks fit only for kindling-wood. A whale is much more of an animal than people generally imagine. There's a great deal of affection somewhere in that big carcass. I have seen them close aboard from the schooner's deck play with their young and roll and thrash about in mammoth gambols. They knew the doors to these lagoons leading out into the ocean as well as men know the doors to their houses. When struck, though miles distant, they made straight for that door, and if not killed before reaching it they escaped, for no boat, when fast, could be towed through the huge Pacific breakers. Pigmy man in such case sullenly cut his line and sulkily rowed back to his crowded little schooner to growl at the cook.

We filled up in six weeks. Our luck was the envy of the eleven other vessels in Marguerita Bay. This luck was mainly due to "Black Jake," a huge Jamaica negro, with the face of a Caliban, the arm of a Hercules and a stomach greater than an ostrich's for rum. When we left San Francisco he had a tier of twenty-five bottles, full, stored under his bunk, and not a soul was ever the wiser for it until all were emptied. He kept his own head level, his own counsel, and lying in his berth in the early evening hours of his watch below, would roll over, turn his back to the noisy, chattering Kanaka audience of the forecastle, and put the bottle, but not to his neighbors' lips. He was king of the forecastle, king of the Kanaka crew, and king of the whaleboat when after a "muscle-digger." He could throw a harpoon twice as far as an ordinary man, and it was to this force of muscle, added to a certain knack of his own in working up to the "grayback," before striking, and managing the boat after, that we owed our successful voyage. Great was his fame as a whale-killer in Marguerita Bay. Many were the offers made by masters of other vessels to bribe him from us. He remained true to us. Hard were the knocks the cows gave their boats and sometimes their crews. One well-appointed schooner lying near us had her boats stove twenty-six times during our stay. Twelve men out of the fleet were more or less injured. "Dese yere whale," Jake would remark to his audiences in the night yarns when one or two other boats' crews from other vessels came on board, "dey aint' like oder whales. Dar ways are 'culiar, and ye got to mind sharp how ye get onto 'em." But nobody ever solved Jake's "'culiar way o' getting onto 'em."

A harpoon was not a toasting-fork to throw in the days when men oftener threw the iron by muscle instead of powder. It is a shod, with a heavy wooden pole five or six feet in length fastened into the socket of the iron barb. This, with the line attached, makes a weight requiring for the cast the use of both arms, and strong arms at that. A man would not care to carry a harpoon more than a mile in a hot day. Its own weight, as much as the impelling force, is depended on to bury itself in the floating mound of seemingly polished India-rubber which constitutes a whale above water. And when it first buries itself, there is for a few seconds some vicious splashing and ugly flirting of fluke or fin. A whale's tail is an instrument of offence of about one hundred horse power, and well adapted to cutting through a boat as a table knife goes through an egg shell. The two fins suggest members between paddles and rudimentary arms. It is also a member very capable of striking out from the right or left shoulder, and striking very hard. When a half-dozen men are within six feet of these weapons, controlled by an enormous black sunken mass, eighty or one hundred feet long, they are apt to look a trifle wild and their eyes have a tendency to bulge. There are stories among whalemen of boat-steerers who have had all the grit permanently taken out of them by the perils and catastrophes of that moment. A New Londoner once had the cap swept from his head by the sweep of the whale's tail over it, and he was too nervous for boat service ever afterward. It is no skulking fight, like shooting lions and tigers from the shelter of trees or rocks. It's a fair standup combat between half a dozen men in an egg-shell of a boat on the open sea, and sometimes on heavy ocean billows, and 500 tons of flesh, bone, and muscles, which, if only animated by a few more grains of sense, could ram the whaleship herself as effectually as an ironclad. As a murderous spectacle the capture and killing of a whale, as seen even by a sea-cook from the galley window, is something ultra-exciting. It makes one's hair stand upon both ends.

There is the whaleboat, the men sitting motionless in their seats, the long oars apeak, shooting through the water, towed by the whale unseen underneath the surface. Sometimes two or three boats hitch on, for the more the whale has to drag the sooner he becomes exhausted. Now they haul in on him and carefully coil the wet line in the tubs. Closer and closer they near him, the passage of the great mass under water being marked by swirls and eddies on the surface. Our herculean king, "Black Jake," is at the bow, the round, razor-edged, long-handled lance lying by him, his back to the crew, his eye on the eddies, his great bare black arms, now the right, now the left—moving first in one direction, then another, as thus he signals to the steersman the direction in which to keep the boat's head; for although we are being towed as a tug would tow a skiff, we must be kept as near as possible in a line with the submerged motive power, and then, with a swash and snort, out of the water six feet ahead comes twenty, may be forty feet of that great black mass! It is astonishing how much there is of him. And he is down and under, with his great gulp of air, in less time than it takes to write or even speak these last twenty words, but not before the lance is out of Jake's hands, driven three feet into his side, and hauled aboard again by the light, strong line attached. Suddenly the whale line slacks. The boat ceases its rush through the water. The eddy and swirl ahead cease. Now look out for squalls. This is one of Mrs. Grayback's peculiar tricks. She is ambushed somewhere below. She designs coming up under the boat's bottom, and constituting herself into a submarine island of flesh, bobbing up like a released cork. She is resolving herself into a submarine earthquake, and proposes to send that boat and crew ten feet into the air, or capsizing them off her India-rubber back. One hundred or five hundred tons of wicked intelligence is thus groping about in the unseen depths for the purpose of attaining the proper position, and, as it were, exploding herself like an animated torpedo. Every seat in the boat is an anxious seat. There is no talking, but a great deal of unpleasant anticipation. Those who have seen the thing done before, await in dread suspense the shock and upset. It's very much like being over a powder-magazine about to explode. To keep up the interest let us leave his particular boat and situation *in statu quo*. Your imagination may complete the catastrophe or not, as you choose. Final consummations are not desirable in a thrilling tale, and this tale is meant to be thrilling. Therefore, if you've got a thrill in you, please thrill.

From the schooner's deck, a mile and a half away, Captain, cook, and cooper—the head, tail, and midriff of the ship's company—we perceive that the white puff of spray from the whale's blowholes has changed to a darker color. "Spouting blood," we remark. The boat is lying quite near by. At intervals of a few minutes a circular streak of white water is seen breaking the smooth surface of the lagoon. He's in his "flurry." He is dying. It is a mighty death, a wonderful escape of vitality and power, affection, and intelligence, too, and all from the mere pin's prick of an implement in the hands of yon meddlesome, cruel, audacious, greedy, unfeeling pigmies. Spouting blood, bleeding its huge life away, shivering in great convulsions, means only for us forty barrels more of grease, and a couple of hundred pounds of bone to manufacture death-dealing, rib-compressing, liver-squeezing corsets from. And all the while the calf lingers by the dying mother's side, wondering what it is all about. Dead and with laborious stroke towed to the vessel, the calf swims in its wake. Made fast alongside, its beautifully symmetrical bulk tapering from head to tail in lines which man copies in the mould of his finest yachts, the body remains all night, and in the still hours of the "anchor watch" we can hear the feeble "blow" of the poor calf, as it swims to and fro.

In the morning the mass which last night was but a couple of feet out of water, has swollen and risen almost to the level of the low bulwark's top, while the gas generated by the decomposition within escapes from each lance puncture with a faint sizzle. With the earliest light the crew are at work. Skin and fat are torn off in great strips and hoisted on board. Round and round the carcass is slowly turned, with each turn another coil of blubber is unwound and cut off. The sharks are busy, too. Monsters (I use the term "monsters" merely for the sake of euphony, not liking to repeat the word "shark" so often) fifteen and eighteen feet long rush up to the carcass, tear off great pieces of the beefy-looking flesh and then quarrel with each other for its possession, flirting the water with nose and fin, and getting occasionally a gash from a sharp whale-spade which would take a man's head off. Amid all this, men shouting, swearing, singing, the windlass clanking, fires under the try-pots blazing, black smoke whirling off in clouds, sharks grabbing and fighting and being fought, the motherless calf still swims about the mutilated carcass, and when cast adrift, a whity-yellowish mass of carrion, swept hither and thither by wind and tide, it still keeps it company until dead of starvation or mercifully devoured by the "monsters." Madame, every bone in your corset groans with the guilt of this double murder.

After a whale had been "cut in," or stripped of his blubber, an operation somewhat resembling the unwinding of a lot of tape from a long bobbin, the whale answering for the bobbin as he is turned round and round in the water, and the blubber for the tape as it is windlassed off, the whity-yellowish, skin-stripped carcass was then cast adrift, and it floated and swelled and smelled. Day after day it swelled bigger and smelled bigger. It rose out of the water like an enormous bladder. It would pass us in the morning with the ebb tide and come back with the flood. A coal-oil refinery was a cologne factory compared to it. Sometimes two or three of these gigantic masses would be floating to and fro about us at once. Sometimes one would be carried against our bows and lodge there, the rotten mass lying high out of the water, oozing and pressing over our low bulwarks on deck. We had a fight with one of these carcasses for half an afternoon trying to pry it off with poles, oars, and handspikes. It was an unfavorable mass to pry against. Of course it smelt. For a dead mass it was extremely lively in this respect. There are no words in which to describe a powerful smell so closely as to bring it to the appreciation of the senses. It is fortunate there are none, for some talented idiot to make his work smell and sell would be certain to use them. The gulls used to navigate these carcasses on their regular trips up and down the lagoons. They served these birds as a sort of edible ferry-boat. You might see forty or fifty feeding and sailing on a single carcass. But they seemed downcast—the dead whale was too much for them. Not that they ever got full of the carrion, but they exhausted themselves in the effort. The supply was unlimited; ditto the void within the gull, but there were limits to his strength.

CHAPTER IX.

OUR BUTTER FIENDS.

IN former days while narrating the events of this voyage, which I have done some thousands of times, I used to say "we whaled." But I never whaled, never went in the boats, never pulled an oar. I had other fish to fry in the galley, and now that I commence to realize what a conscience is, I mention this for truth's sake as well as to give variety to the story. We were boarded occasionally by a few Mexicans. There was one melancholy-looking Don Somebody who seemed always in a chronic state of corn-husk cigarette. When not smoking he was rolling them; when not rolling or smoking he was lighting them. He and his companions were persons of some importance, for which reason Captain Reynolds tendered them the hospitalities of the *Henry* and would ask them to whatever meal was nearest ready. These two Mexicans had enormous stowage for grub. They resembled the gulls. They also seemed unfathomable. There was no filling them. What they did at table they did with all their might, and when they finished, especially when eating by themselves, as they frequently did, there was literally nothing left. "Nothing" in this case meant something. It meant in addition to bread, meat, and potatoes, every scrap of butter on the butter-plate and every grain of sugar in the sugar-bowl. I didn't take the hint the first time they ate with us, deeming the entire absence of butter and sugar at the end of the repast to be owing to my placing a small amount on the table. The second time they came on board I remedied this. But on inspection after they had finished I found left only an empty butter-plate and sugar-bowl. It was so at the third trial. Butter and sugar seem to be regarded as delicacies by the natives of Lower California. Nor do they seem to comprehend the real mission and import of butter and sugar on the table. They regarded both these articles as regular dishes and scooped them in. On discovering this, after a consultation with the Captain, I put them on allowance. These two men would have eaten up all our butter and sugar in four weeks.

However it was comparatively a slight toll they levied on us for carrying off their whale-oil, seal and abalone. We were miles within their legal boundaries taking away the wealth of their waters. Twelve other American whalers lay in Marguerita Bay that season. It was practically an invasion; only the Mexicans didn't seem to know they were invaded or didn't care if they did know. So long as they had plenty of butter and sugar on coming on board and the blubber-stripped carcasses which came on shore they seemed satisfied. These carcasses they cut open when stranded and extracted the fat about the heart, which on being tried out would yield from one to four barrels of oil and about three miles of solid stench. They borrowed from us the vessels wherewith to boil this fat. I was ordered to loan them all the pots, pans, and kettles which could be spared from my culinary laboratory. They never returned them, and I was very glad they did not. No amount of scouring would ever have rid them of the odor of decomposed leviathan. We left them a dozen or so iron vessels the richer. A Mexican, at least on that coast, with a kettle is looked up to as a man of wealth. Beyond serapes, cigarette-lighters, saddles and bridles, the gang of natives on shore had few other possessions. They seemed brilliant examples of contented poverty. The individual Mexican is a more independent being than the citizen of our own boasted "independent" nation. His wants are ten times less. Consequently, he is ten times as independent. Parties who use horses' skulls for parlor chairs, whose wooden bowl wherein they mix flour for tortillas, flint, steel, and a small bonfire constitute their entire kitchen range, won't keep many furniture or stove manufacturers alive.

Some mercantile hopes may hang on the señoras and señoritas. The few we saw wanted calicoes of gay and diverse patterns. The men will eat butter and sugar, but whether they will buy these articles remains to be proved. Perhaps furniture sets of polished and painted horses' skulls might tempt some of the more æsthetic in the matter of household adornment to purchase, if put at a reasonable rate. Such are the conclusions drawn regarding the probabilities of trade with Mexico, at least the fragment of Mexico I saw from my galley. If we wanted any service of them they talked dollars at a very high figure. But they never abated. They showed no anxiety to tempt a bargain or an engagement. They went on just as ever, full to the brim of genuine sang-froid, eternally rolling, lighting, and smoking their cigarettes, and looking as if they felt themselves a superior race, and knew it all, and didn't want to know any more, until we asked them to eat. Then they seemed in no hurry, but clambered lazily down the cabin stairs and lazily set to work to find the bottom of every dish on the table, including the sugar-dish and butter-plate. I learned on that voyage the true signification of the term "greaser," as I fearfully noted the rapidly diminishing butter keg.

CHAPTER X.

GUADALUPE.

TWO hundred miles from the Lower California coast lies the lone island of Guadalupe. Guadalupe is one of the twelve or twenty names which for centuries the Spaniards have been applying to the various geographical divisions of the earth's surface. Each Spanish navigator, explorer, and discoverer, armed with these twelve or twenty "San Joses," "Santa Marias," "Sacramentos," etc., has gone on naming, taking each one in regular order, and as the list was exhausted and more islands, capes, etc., were found, starting again at the beginning of the list and using it all over again. Whitney talked of the plentifulness of sea-elephant on the Guadelupe beaches; I presume the sea-elephant is identical with the sea-lion. They resemble a lion about as much as an elephant. So the prow of the *Henry* was turned toward Guadalupe. While on this trip one morning before daylight I heard at intervals a strange noise, something between a bellow and a creak. I thought it at first the creaking of something aloft, but as it grew lighter I saw a strange-looking head emerge momentarily from the water. It gave forth the same cry, dove, and came up on the other side of the vessel. It was a seal pup, which the sailors said had lost its mother and followed the vessel, mistaking the hull for its maternal parent. I presume that seals have no recognized fathers to look after them. The poor thing, uttering its plaintive but discordant cry, must have followed us to sea forty or fifty miles. I know not whether the sailors' explanation of its conduct be correct. Anyway, it makes the occurrence more pathetic, and were I utterly unprincipled I should make an entire chapter describing how this pup seal followed the *Henry* during the voyage like a dog, being regularly fed, and as it grew up came on board and was taught a number of accomplishments, among the rest that of supplying us with fish. 'Tis thus that a rigid adherence to veracity spoils many an interesting and thrilling tale, and brings to him who practises it more poverty than pence.

Guadalupe on the third day came in sight; a lone, wave-washed, wind-swept isle about forty miles in length. It seemed the very embodiment of loneliness. Some would also say of desolation, as man is ever disposed to call any place he does not inhabit. But though Guadalupe contained not a single representative of the most intelligent animal on the planet, it sustained great herds of goats, sea birds, and a little black and white land-bird, so tame and trustful as to perch and eat from Miller's and Whitney's tin plates during their former visit to the island. All these got along very well without the presence of the talented biped who deems every place "desolate" unless he is there to carry on a monopoly of all the killing of bird and animal deemed necessary to his comfort and existence.

It was our business to murder all the mother sea-lions who had established their nurseries at Guadalupe. A boat full of murderers was quickly sent on shore. We did not see boat or crew again for three days. Most of that period was spent by us in looking for the boat, and by the boat's crew in looking at us. They landed on the first day, found no seal, put off at dusk, lost us in a fog, went ashore, swore at the *Henry's* people for not sighting them, hauled their boat well up on the beach at the mouth of a deep canyon, supped on hard bread and water, and, turning their craft bottom-up, crawled under it for a bed-quilt and went to sleep on the sands. During the night a semi-hurricane, called in those latitudes a "willa wah," came tearing and howling down the canyon. Striking the boat, it rolled it over and over among the rocks, smashed the frail sides, and rendered it unseaworthy. For two days the crew roamed up and down the island, living on shellfish and the fresh water left standing in pools, and trying to signal us by fires built on the mountains. The Captain was in a state of great perplexity at this disappearance. But, having left a portion of the crew at St. Bartholomew's Bay, he had not hands enough to send another boat ashore, and work the vessel. Then he dare not come nearer the island than three miles, fearing sunken rocks and currents setting in-shore. On the third night one of their fires was seen from the *Henry*. Standing in for it, by daylight the missing men were seen making for us in an old yawl. Behind, full of water, was towed the shattered whaleboat. The yawl had been found on the beach, probably left there by former sealers. By stuffing all the clothes they could spare in its sun-warped cracks and constant bailing they managed to keep afloat long enough to reach us. They crawled on board—a pale, haggard, famished lot—and I was kept very busy for a time ministering to their wants. They ate steadily for an hour. Even with this rescue a greater catastrophe than all came near happening. Becalmed and by means of a treacherous current we were being rapidly carried toward an enormous rock, which towered sentinel-like alone a mile or more from the north end of the island. It reached full five hundred feet toward the clouds. Its perpendicular sides seemed built up in artificial layers. Toward this the *Henry* seemed helplessly drifting, and the "Old Man," under the influence of combined anger and despair, jumped up and down in his tracks and howled on the quarter-deck as he saw the voyage approaching such an unfortunate termination. Fortunately a providential or accidental breeze came off the land just in time to give us steerage-way. We trifled no more with Guadalupe, but sailed straight away for our old harbor. As we passed the last of these towering sentinel rocks at dusk, we heard from them the howling and barking of what, judged by the sound, might have been ten thousand seals. It was as the roaring of a dozen combined menageries. Had Virgil of old ever sailed by such a sound, he would have pulled out his stylus forthwith, and written of the Æneid an extra chapter about some classical hell afloat. These seals were howling at our discomfiture. The rock was half veiled in a mist in which we could indistinctly see their countless forms seemingly writhing and tumbling about.

CHAPTER XI.

AT THE GOLD MINES.

AFTER a ten months' cruise we went back to San Francisco with 500 barrels of oil and ten tons of abalones. My share of the proceeds amounted to $250, having shipped on a "lay." Mine was the fifteenth lay, which gave me one barrel of oil out of every fifty and a similar proportion in abalones. Then I looked around for something to do, didn't find it, spent a great deal of my money unnecessarily in so looking for a job, shipped at last as cook on a coasting schooner, was discharged before she left the wharf, my grade of culinary work not reaching to the level of the captain's refined taste.

I resolved to go to the mines. I went. By boat and stage, I got over the two hundred miles intervening 'twixt San Francisco and the "diggings." I had friends on Hawkins' Bar on the Tuolumne River in Tuolumne County. Thither I went. When I "struck" Hawkins' in 1858, it was on its last legs. Still it boasted a store and a dozen houses. Golden hopes were still anchored in the bed of the river. Expensive river claims were then being worked from Red Mountain down to French Bar. But a premature rain and consequent freshet swept the river that season from end to end with the bosom of destruction, and sent for the winter the miners back to their two dollar per day bank diggings. And from that time henceforward the Bar steadily declined. The store was kept open for two seasons with great loss to its proprietor. He was a new man. When he came to the Bar the "boys" held a consultation on a big drift log. They concluded they could go through him in one season, provided he gave credit. But he was a discriminating man as regarded giving credit. So it required two seasons to get through him. Then he moved away forever, and with tears in his eyes at his losses. The Bar lingered on for several years. Steadily it lessened in houses and population. The store was torn down and the lumber carted away. In 1864 I made a pilgrimage thither and found remaining one house and one man. That man was Smith. Alex. Smith, a '49er, a Baltimorean and a soldier during the Mexican war. Smith's house was high up on the hillside and his back yard brought up against the camp graveyard. A score of Smith's old companions there lay buried. And here this man lived alone with the dead and the memories of the last eighteen years. I said to him: "Smith, how do you stand it here? Do you never get lonesome?"

"Well, yes; once in a while I do," replied Smith; "but when I feel that way I go up the hill and bring down a log for firewood."

Smith was a philosopher, and thought that the best remedy for melancholy is physical exertion.

Smith was one of the first settlers at Hawkins' Bar; Smith could remember when it contained a voting population of nearly eight hundred souls; Smith knew every point on the river which had yielded richly; Smith could show you Gawley's Point, where Gawley pitched his tent in '49 and buried under it his pickle jars full of gold dust. The tradition of Hawkins was that Gawley used to keep a barrel of whiskey on free tap in his tent. And that in the fall of 1850 Gawley, warned by the experience of the previous rainy season, determined to lay in a winter's stock of provisions. But Gawley's ideas as to the proper quantities of food were vague. He had never before been a purveyor or provider on a larger scale than that of buying a week's "grub" at the Bar store. He went to the trader and told him what he wanted. "Make out your order," said the merchant. Gawley gave it to him verbally. "I guess," said he, "I'll have a sack of flour, ten pounds of bacon, ten of sugar, five of coffee, three of tea, a peck of beans, a bag of salt and—and—a barrel of whiskey!"

In 1870 I made another pilgrimage to Hawkins' Bar. Smith was gone. Nobody lived there. The fence of the camp graveyard was broken down. The wooden headboards were lying prone to the earth. Some were split in two and most of the inscriptions were being rapidly erased through the action of the sun and rain. But one house was standing. It was the cabin wherein had lived one Morgan Davis, the former custodian of the Hawkins' Bar library. For as early as 1854 or '55 the Hawkins' Bar "boys" had clubbed their funds, sent down to San Francisco and there purchased a very respectable library. It was a good solid library, too, based on a full set of American Encyclopedias and Humboldt and Lyell, and from such and the like dispensers of heavy and nutritious mental food, rising into the lighter desserts of poetry and novels. As late as 1858 the "boys" were in the habit of replenishing their library with the latest published scientific works, novels, and magazines.

But in '70, on my last visit, the library was gone. Morgan was dead. His cabin door had fallen from its hinges: a young oak tree had sprung up and blocked the entrance. The flooring had been torn up. The window sashes had been taken out. A dinner-pot and broken stove were all that remained of Morgan's cooking utensils. Some of the roofing had disappeared. It was a ghostly place. The trails leading to and from the Bar were fading out. Here, they were overgrown with brush. There, the river in some higher rise had swept away the lower bank and left nought but a confusion of rough rock over which was no semblance of a track. It was at Hawkins that I had first "buckled to the mines." My first "buckling," however, was in the capacity of a meat peddler. I became the agent of a firm of butchers up on the mountain for distributing their tough steaks to the Hawkins' Bar miners. Through the instrumentality of a horse, over whose back was slung a couple of huge panniers, I continued the agency for a week. Then one morning the horse kicked up his heels and ran away. As he ran, at every kick a raw and bloody steak would fly out of the boxes, flash in the brilliant morning sunshine, and then fall in the fine red dust of the mountain trail. I followed hard after, gathering up these steaks as they fell, and when the burden became too heavy I piled them up by the roadside in little heaps of dusty, very dusty meat. At last, dusty, perspiring and distressed beyond measure, I managed to catch that villainous horse. For he, after having ejected nearly the whole load of meat, concluded to stop and be caught. I loaded the panniers again with the dusty, carnivorous deposits, led the horse down the steep trail to the river, then muddy and of a rich coffee-color from up country mining sediment. Herein I washed my steaks, rinsed them as well as I could of dust, and, as was then the custom, hung up piece after piece in the gauze-curtained meat-safes at the miner's cabins. I think Hawkins' got its share of grit that day in its beef. Shortly afterward I went out of the beefsteak-distributing bureau.

Then I went into the service of the man who kept the Bar store, saloon, and boarding-house. I was errand boy, barkeeper, bookkeeper, woodchopper, assistant cook and general maid of all work, and possibly worthlessness. One day the storekeeper's horse, packed with miners' supplies, was given into my charge to lead three miles up the river to the camp of the Split-Rock River claim. The load was strapped to a "cross-jack" saddle. It consisted mostly of flour, potatoes, bacon and a demijohn of whiskey. I was advised by the merchant, on setting out, not to let that horse get ahead of me. If he did it was prophesised that he would run away, "sure pop." But I had not gone forty rods from the store when the beast made a rush, got ahead of me, tore the leading halter out of my grasp and set off along the narrow mountain trail at the rate of twenty knots per hour. I followed on a run of about ten knots per hour. Hence the distance between us soon increased. As he ran the motion burst the bag of flour, ditto the potatoes, and then the whiskey demijohn broke. It was a fine sight. The flour rose in the air like a white cloud above the horse, out of and above which flew potatoes, and the whole was interspersed with jets of whiskey. It looked like a snow squall travelling on horseback. When the animal had spilt all the flour, all the potatoes and all the whiskey, he slowed up and allowed himself to be caught. His mission was accomplished. I found remaining the saddle and the empty potato sack. The trail was white with flour for a mile, and so it remained for months afterward. I led the animal back to the store. My heart was heavy and his load was light. The store-keeper gave me his blessing. I did not thereafter long remain in the service of that transportation bureau.

After this I borrowed a rocker and started to washing some river-bank gravel. It took me several days to become in any degree skilled in the use of the rocker. I had no teacher, and was obliged to become acquainted with all its peculiarities by myself. First I set it on a dead level. As it had no "fall" the sand would not run out. But the hardest work of all was to dip and pour water from the dipper on the gravel in the sieve with one hand and rock the cradle with the other. There was a constant tendency on the part of the hand and arm employed in pouring to go through the motion of rocking, and *vice versa*. The hand and arm that rocked were more inclined to go through the motion of pouring. I seemed cut up in two individuals, between whom existed a troublesome and perplexing difference of opinion as to their respective duties and functions. Such a conflict, to all intents and purposes, of two different minds inside of and acting on one body, shook it up fearfully and tore it all to pieces. I was as a house divided against itself and could not stand. However, at last the physical and mental elements thus warring with each other inside of me made up their differences, and the left hand rocked the cradle peacefully while the right hand poured harmoniously, and the result was about $1.50 per day. Soon after I found my first mining partner. He wandered to the Bar, a melancholy-looking man, with three dogs accompanying, and was always in a chronic state of red bandana and nose-wiping. He and I joined forces and went up the river to "crevice" among the rocks near the Split Rock claim. He had all the skill, all the experience, and all the dogs, and I all the general ignorance and incapacity. I deemed it a great advantage to have thus secured a real "old miner" for a partner, and felt that such a man must turn up gold.

We built ourselves a rude brush house on a shelf of the rocky ledge in a canyon whose sides sloped at an angle of forty-five degrees. Even this shelf was not level. It pitched toward the river, and there was so little of it that during the night's repose our legs stuck out of the house-entrance. We were obliged to "chock" all our supply of provisions in their respective packages to prevent them from rolling out of our wigwams over the brink and into the Tuolumne. If a potato got loose it ran like a "thing possessed" over the rocks and down into the muddy, raging current. We were obliged to peg ourselves at night while sleeping to prevent a like catastrophe. It was a permanent and laborious existence at an angle of forty-five. To stand erect for any length of time was very tiresome. More frequently, like Nebuchadnezzar, we lived on all fours. "Crevicing" did not prove very profitable. By day the bare rocks become heated by the sun to a blistering capacity. With pick and sledge and crowbar and bent bits of hoop-iron we pried and pounded and scraped, and scraped and pounded and pried all the hot day long, or else were doubled up in all sorts of back-aching, back-breaking, body-tiring positions, drawing up at arm's-length from some deeper "pothole" or crevice spoonful after spoonful of yellow mould. It did hold considerable gold, and heavy gold too. But it took so long to get the mould. This was in the latter part of September. The termination of the dry season was reached. The first rain came. It came at night. It drizzled through our brush house. It sent tiny streams down the rocky mountain-sides, and some of these streams found their way under us. We had lain and endured the rain from above dripping on our faces and wetting our clothes. In those times one's day suit served for a nightgown. But when the aqueous enemy undermined our position we had to turn out.

It blew a gale. How the wind howled and tore up the canyon! We tried to kindle a fire. Match after match was blown out. Finally a blaze was attained. Then the rains descended heavier than ever and put it out. The chief misery was, we could not at night find our way out of the canyon to any place of shelter. Nor could we walk at all to keep warm. There was "standing room only." All about us were the steeply inclined rocks, molded into every irregularity of shape. We were obliged all through the night to "stand and take it" as it came, shivering in our thin summer clothing. With daylight we made our way to the camp of the Split Rockers. They gave us some gin. It was common gin—very common gin—but the comfortable and soothing remembrance of that gin after such a night exists for me even unto this day. I wore a black cloth cap. The rain had washed out the dye, and this dye had coursed over my brow and cheeks in tiny rivulets of jet. I noticed that I seemed to be more than a usual object of interest to those about me, and wondered, until a friend advised me to consult a mirror. I did so, and found my face marked like a railroad route map. Such was my inauguration in mining at Hawkins' Bar. What glorious old times they were! What independence! What freedom from the trammels and conventionalities of fashion! Who cared or commented if we did turn up the bottoms of our pantaloons, or wear, for coolness' sake, our flannel shirts outside the trousers? Who then was so much better than anybody else, when any man might strike it rich to-morrow? Who would beg for work or truckle and fawn and curry favor of an employer for the mere sake of retaining a situation and help that same man to make money, when he could shoulder pick, shovel, and rocker, go down to the river's edge and make his two or three dollars per day? Though even at that time this reputed three dollars was oftener one dollar and a half.

Even then reports of the paying capacities of claims were as apt to be watered as are stocks nowadays.

CHAPTER XII.

SWETT'S BAR.

I THINK and hope that these attempts of mine to portray the history of the camps on one California gold-bearing river will touch a responsive chord in the hearts of some old Californian, for the life and incident of the bars I describe reflect, in certain respects, the life, history, and incident of hundreds and thousands of places settled in "'49," and perhaps abandoned by "'60," which have now no name or place on the later maps of the State. Your genuine old miner likes to revisit the camp where first he dug for gold, in thought if not in person. It was no common affection they entertained for these places. If the "boys" moved away to other diggings, they had always to make a yearly pilgrimage back, so long as the camp lasted. So, yearly from Vallecito, thirty miles distant, used Jake Yager to revisit Swett's, and he tramped the whole distance, too. What was it that so drew them back? Perhaps the memory of the new and exciting life they experienced from "'49" say till "'58" or "'60," with its "ups and downs," its glittering surprises in the shape of "strikes," its comradeship so soon developed among men who, meeting as strangers, so soon found out each other's better qualities, its freedom from the restraints of older communities, its honesty and plainness in the expression of opinion, engendered by such freedom; all these thought over and over again during absence brought about that strong desire to see the old Bar again, the scene of so much experience and private history. Then the visitor always met a hearty welcome. He was an old "residenter." Cabin-owners contended for the pleasure of entertaining him. No wives or families were in the way. Conviviality was uninterrupted.

If a black bottle could be produced it could be worshipped undisturbed until long past midnight. And such was always produced on the return of the old acquaintance. When the "boys" at last tumbled into their bunks and smoked a night-cap pipe abed, there was no wife in special charge of husband to molest or make them afraid or disturb their internal peace by reason of her near presence. Those were the golden seasons of masculine domestic tranquillity on the banks of the Tuolumne. Woman never disturbed the Bar proper with her presence. It was always a masculine Bar, at least on the right bank of the river. On the left, at a later date, on a flat, where I enjoyed the privilege of digging for next to nothing for two years, there did live for a time three foreign households glorified by woman's presence. But this was after the palmy days of Swett's Bar proper right bank. I have heard that Swett's Bar was named after John Swett, once Superintendent of Public Instruction in California. If so, he never there left any relics or reminders of himself—not even a grammar. Swett's lies equidistant from Hawkins' and Indian Bars. When last I passed through it the floods had washed out every trace of man's presence on one side of the river, leaving there an enormous heap of logs and brush-wood. The Bar proper had been smoothed down by the flood, every hole or boulder heap, or heap of "headings" or "tailings," or the deep pits dug and laboriouly kept free of water by machinery, or heavily rock-freighted crib of logs, the work of miners in the river's bed, had been planed away. The pebbles and boulders had all been rearranged, the sands were smooth, white, and glistening as though "fresh from the Creator's hands;" and none save those conversant with the river's history could have guessed that every foot of the bank adjoining the river had been turned over and over again in the search for gold.

We elected one member of the Legislature from Swett's. When he left the Bar he distributed his cabin, blankets, and household effects among the remaining miners. He confidently thought never to need these articles again. That was as great a miscalculation as when a Swett's Bar or any other bar miner would resolve and swear violently that never again would he "strike a pick" in the river. We came to regard such an oath with a superstitious credulity that he certainly would strike such pick again, for never did such a case occur in my recollection but that the mad resolver was back next season, ignoring his vow and striking his pick on some claim generally poorer than the one he worked the season previous. So at the end of four months, after cumbering the law books of the State of California with statutes, whose very existence was forgotten eight months after their passage, our Swett's Bar legislator was seen one evening coming down the hill, bearing in one hand two whiskey bottles tied together by one string— one being empty and the other full. "Silver and gold have I none," said he, as he came to my cabin door, "but what I have give I unto thee," which he did. Next day came his trunk. The principal accession to the legislative wardrobe were three new shirts and a blue coat with brass buttons. That, the session I think of 1859, was known as the "Legislature of ten thousand drinks." Our law-maker said it had been the "Star Winter" of his existence, and he never expected to see such another. Three days after his arrival at the Bar he borrowed a pair of blankets, "cabined" with a chum and contentedly resumed his pick and shovel. Did Cincinattus do more when he buckled once more to the plough? But our Swett's Bar Cincinattus was never hunted for to save his country. There were too many other country savers on hand, even in our immediate locality.

Generally speaking, Swett's was divided in two portions. There was the old bar on the right bank of the river, settled in "'49," and there was the flat on the other side, whose golden store was not discovered until 1859. Attempts were made to give this flat a distinct name. Various settlers and miners craved the immortality which they supposed might thus be conferred. For a time it was called "Frazier's Flat," from a diabolical Scotchman of that name who lived there. Only one of these names would stick, and finally everybody settled down on the old appellation, "Swett's." I do not believe that John Swett, if he did confer his name on this Bar, ever realized the local fame and reputation of his name. When first we struck the diggings at Swett's left bank, we had great expectations. It was a later discovery, a "back river channel." Consequent on the discovery of pay ground 1,000 feet back of the river, and the definite fixing of the boundary lines between the various claimants, there ensued the usual series of disputes, rows, bad blood, assaults, and threatened shootings. Nobody was shot. Not even a mining law-suit came of it. A local capitalist threw a flume across the river and brought to bear on the flat the upland muddy water, which came down from Columbia diggings, twenty-five miles away, through Wood's Creek. That flume was being talked of, being planned, being hoped for and very gradually being erected, during the years of "'59" and "'60," while the rest of the nation was agitated by "Bleeding Kansas," "John Brown," "Squatter Sovereignty," "The Douglas Party," "The Little Giant" and all that foreboding series of watchword and motto which preceded "The War." But the Swett's Bar mind, the Swett's Bar hope, the Swett's Bar expedition, was concentrated principally on a wire cable, two uprights on either side of the river, and some 400 feet of rough wooden flume thereby supported, all of which was to bring us water to wash out the expected gold. At last the suspension flume was finished. We had water. We commenced washing. The dirt did not pay as we expected. We averaged week in and week out about three dollars per day, and one dollar of this went for water money.

After the suspension flume was finished and water was on the Flat our claim cleaned up for the first week's work about fifty dollars a piece. We used quicksilver plentifully in the sluices; and the amalgam was taken to my cabin in a gold-pan and put on the hot coals to drive off the mercury, which it did, and salivated the four of us besides. The sublimated mineral covered walls, tables and chairs with a fine, frost-like coating, and on rubbing one's finger over any surface a little globule of quicksilver would roll up before it. Then we went to Chinese Camp and gave the doctor about half our individual week's dividends to get the mercury out of us. Three weeks of sore mouths and loosened teeth followed this intelligent exposure. It was through such experiences as these that we became in California practical mineralogists. However, it's an easy way of taking "blue mass." The claim from which great gains had been expected eventually settled down to an average of two dollars and a half to three dollars per day. Break-downs of the flume, failure of water from up country, very stormy weather, building and repairing reservoirs, cutting tail races through rock—all caused numerous delays, and every such delay lessened the average per diem. It was necessary to build reservoirs, to store the water for washing, and these reservoirs broke with the ease and facility of a Bowery savings bank.

CHAPTER XIII.

ONE DAY'S DIGGING.

WE got out of our blankets heavily. Legs and back were apt to be a little stiff in the morning. Or if not stiff, they lacked action. Working all the day previous, possibly in the water, or with it splashing all about, tugging at heavy boulders, shouldering wet sluices, to say nothing of the regular pick-and-shovel exercise, would make itself felt even when the limbs and blood were younger than now. Dressing was a short job. A pair of damp overalls, a pair of socks, a pair of shoes, or possibly the heavy rubber mining boots. Flannel shirts we slept in. A face-swabbing with cold water in the tin basin outside and a "lick and a promise" for the hair with the comb. That was about all for week days. Vanity of apparel there was little for the working miner. Who was there to dress for? Woman? The nearest was half a mile, fifty years of age, and married. Then breakfast. The fire kindled in the contrary little stove. Possibly it was necessary to attack with a axe that dried old stump near by and hack off a few chips to cook with. The miner's wood-pile was generally small. He got in fuel on rainy days, or at the odd intervals to be spared from work. You put on the worn tin teapot, lowered the gauze-covered meat safe from the tree, cut a steak from the chunk of bull mahogany within called beef, slung a dab of lard in the frying-pan, put therein the meat and let it sizzle. Two or three boiled potatoes might be sliced, fried more or less brown in the gravy, and this, with bread and tea, formed the breakfast. The bread was the bread of your own laborious baking, the loaf of an irregular shape, the crust very hard and thick, the color often "pied," being black where it had burned, brown where it had baked, and of a pallid whiteness where it had not baked at all. Within the loaf might be close, heavy, and in color either a creamy or a canary yellow, in proportion to the improper amount of yeast powder used.

The table is a broad shelf against the wall. There is no table-cloth. You did not always wash up after breakfast, for the dishes, as they stood, were all in place for dinner. Some fastidious miners washed their dishes after each meal; most of us did not. It was too much to expect of hard-worked humanity. The cabin door is open while you eat and from it you look forth on the claim. There lies the bank of red earth as you left it yesterday after the "cave." There is the reservoir full of coffee-colored ditch water which had run in during the night after being used for washing in a dozen claims "up country." Then you draw on those damp, clammy rubber boots, either to the knee or hip high, the outside splashed with the dried reddish mud, and smelling disagreeably of rubber as you pulled them on and smelling worse as you became heated and perspiring. In these you waddle to the claim. I forgot. Breakfast over, one of the most important acts of the day was next on the programme. That was the filling, lighting, and smoking of your pipe. Nothing could hurry you through this performance. The filling was cut in slivers with a careful and solemn consideration; the weed was carefully bestowed in the bowl; the match was applied with a deliberation savoring of a religious act; the first puff rose in the air as incense to the early morn, and smoking thus you waddled in your big boots to the claim. There you met your three partners, all likewise smoking. There they stand on the bank, looking into the ground-sluice. There is no "good morning" or other greeting: if anything, grunts. There lay the tools—shovels, picks, crowbar, and sluice-fork—helplessly about, as left last evening. A little muddy water trickles through the line of sluices. One of us goes to the reservoir, a few hundred yards off, and turns on the water. Another goes to the tail of the sluices with the sluice-fork. Then is heard the clicking of the pick and the grating of the shovel against the red dirt; down comes the muddy water over the bank and the day's work has fairly commenced.

We stand in a row, allowing sufficient room between each for swinging the pick. We are undermining the bank, the water running at our feet and between us and the bottom of the bank. Each chunk of red dirt dislodged by the pick falls into the running water, and if it be hard and will not readily dissolve it must be broken up by pick or shovel to keep the stream clear and unimpeded. The large boulders are picked out by hand and thrown behind us—not in disordered fashion, either. Room in the cut is scarce and must be economized, so the ever-accumulating bowlder pile is "faced up" with a neat wall, laid without mortar, but with some care and skill. The bed-rock is under our feet. We are undermining the bank and keeping the stream turned in as much as possible to the part undermined. The gravel for a foot or six inches is pretty hard and the stones here are harder and closer packed than those nearer the surface. There the gravel is lighter. Many of the stones are light and rotten; a blow with the pick dashes them to pieces. This streak just above the ledge and for a few inches in the crevices of the ledge is our "pay streak" where ages on ages ago some stream ran, depositing, as all streams do, the heavier gravel on the bottom and the lighter above. Occasionally the pick strikes a firmly embedded boulder hard and square on its point, in such a way as to send the vibration like a shock along the iron, up the handle and into one's arm and "crazy-bone." Our bank of dirt is about eight feet in height. A few inches of the top is a dark mould, below that is three or four feet of "hard-pan," below the "hard-pan" light sandy gravel and rotten boulders, and near the ledge is the pay streak. This order of formation has varied as we have worked up and into the bank. At first, near the river's edge, there was only mould on a very light alluvial sand. This was readily washed off and paid four dollars or five dollars per day. A little farther back we struck the edge of the red gravel streak. This for a time paid better. Farther still came the deposit of light sandy gravel, and lastly came in the accursed "hard-pan."

Our claim, on being first prospected, was reported to pay three cents to the pan from the top down. We believed it at first, not having learned that "three cents to the pan from the top down" means the biggest kind of luck. If you get an average of half a cent a pan from the top down, and the dirt would wash easily, we should make money. It was hard even for an "honest miner" to give as the result of a prospect anything less than "three cents to the pan." But "hard-pan" is our foe. "Hard-pan" is the essence of brickbats. Its consistency is about that of chalk. It seems the finest kind of sand cemented and pressed together. It can be carved into any form with a knife. It takes as much time to work off a square foot of hard-pan as ten square feet of soft gravel. When, after half a day's labor, we succeed in getting down a cave, it goes into the ground-sluice in a few great lumps, which must be battered to pieces with our picks before the water will slowly dissolve them into mud. And it doesn't hold a "color" of gold. The work in the ground-sluice goes on hour after hour. Pick and shovel and scrape, scrape and shovel and pick, the water meantime tumbling and roaring over the bank and making it difficult for us to hear each others' voices. The sun climbs higher and gets hotter. The water pail is frequently visited. The backs of the gray shirts are wet with perspiration. In an easy, companionable claim, where the partners are all good fellows and on good terms and not too insane in the matter of getting an enormous quantity of dirt through the sluices each day, there may be more or less brief suspensions from the work, when all hands lean on their shovels and talk politics, or horses, or last night's poker game, or have a short service of tobacco smoke, with the usual solemn preliminaries of cutting the plug and filling pipes. But if the majority of the "company" are a mean, crabbed, close-fisted lot, the misery goes on without cessation.

A queerly assorted group are we thus laboring together. Jack Gwin's impelling hope and life's idea is to earn enough to pay his passage home to Philadelphia and buy him a suit of clothes. A decent suit he has not owned these five years. He would be the terror and distress of his relatives if ever he got back, for with him five dollars in his pocket over expenses and sobriety are an impossibility. McFadden dreams of a cabin, a cow, some geese and goats, a horse and a wife, and is in a fair way of realizing them all. He saves most of his earnings, gets drunk wisely only on holidays, pays his debts regularly, hates the English, lives in that little black, brownish cabin up yonder, does all his cooking in two tin pots, sleeps in one pair of ancient blankets and a most disreputable bed quilt, and three dollars will cover the cost of all his domestic fittings and utensils. Bill Furnea, a French Canadian, has drifted here into this hole in the foothills very much as he drifted into the world—without aim or object in life save present enjoyment. He is a good worker and works because he was brought up to it and can't help it. He is a good boatman, a good logger, a skilled woodcutter, a devotee of poker and generally a successful one, an entertaining scamp, full of wit and originality, quick to take in the peculiarities and eccentricities of others, something of a dandy, as far as dandyism can be indulged in this out-of-the-way place, and a born scamp, glib of tongue, unreliable, and socially the best man of the crowd.

It is near eleven o'clock. There stands in a cool corner of the claim and carefully shielded from any stray flying pebble, a black bottle. It is nearly full of whiskey—very common corn whiskey. It is most welcome at this hour. Poison it may be, but a draught from the tin cup brightens up and makes all things new. The sunshine is more cheerful. All Nature smiles. The picks descend with increased force and a host of new day-dreams start into being. It revives hope. It quenches despair. It gilds the monotony of our lives. It was ever thus, and possibly ever shall be, world without end. It is high noon. The sun is over our heads and the shadows are at their shortest length. One of our number trudges wearily up to the reservoir to shut off the water. So soon as its flow lessens we trudge off in wet overalls or heavy rubbers to our respective cabins. We are now ground-sluicing at or about the year 1860, when miners generally had abandoned "cabining" in squads and each man kept house by himself. Cause—general incompatibility of temper, temperament, disposition, and habit. The sober miner found it disagreeable to live permanently with the spreeing miner, and the miner nice in his domestic economy and particular about his food soon became tired of a companion who never aired his blankets and didn't care whether his bread was light or heavy, sweet or sour. Trudging to our cabins, we pick up the dried twigs in our path. These are to kindle the dinner fire. Dinner is very much like breakfast, beef or bacon, bread, tea, dried-apple sauce. The boots are kicked off and thumped into a corner. The temperature is up to that notch that induces perspiration without any exertion at all and the ugly little stove makes it hotter still. We sit down to the noon meal in a melting condition and rise from it in the same state. Dinner is eaten, the "nooning" is over, back again to the claim, turn on the water, pick, shovel, scrape, pry, toss back boulders and prop up sluices slipped from their supports. Between two and three o'clock a snowy-white cloud rises over a distant peak to the eastward. It seems like a great bank of snow against the blue sky and the longer we look at it the farther we seem to peer into its translucent, clear-white depths. It rises over that peak at almost the same hour every afternoon and is almost of the same shape. It is the condensed vapor of the snow melting on the higher Sierra summits eighty-six miles distant. It is imposing in its silent imperceptible rising, its wonderful whiteness, its majesty, its distance. It seems a fit bed of snowy splendor for fairies or some sort of ethereal beings to bask and revel in. It seems to be looking down half in scorn half in pity at us four weary, miserable worms of the dust, feebly pecking at a bit of mother earth, muddy, wet, and feebly squirming in and about this bank of dirt.

At four o'clock there are longer pauses in our labors. There is more leaning on shovels and more frequent glances at our timepiece, the sun, as he sinks in the western heavens. The shadow of the hill opposite creeps slowly down its side. It is a cool, welcome shadow. The strongest worker secretly welcomes it. Though he be a "horse of a man," his muscles also feel the effects of the long day's labor. It is more his strong will than his body which keeps him swinging the pick. We are in duty bound to work till six o'clock. Everybody works till six o'clock. Everybody is more or less tired at four o'clock, but it is not the capacity of the body for labor that fixes the time. It is custom, stupid custom. The gauge is the limit of physical strength, not for the weakest, but the strongest. The great, brawny-armed, big-boned Hercules of our company doesn't feel it much. He may walk three miles after supper to the Bar store, play cards and drink whiskey till nine o'clock and then walk back again and be up fresh for work next morning by 5:30 o'clock. This is 1860. In 1870 he showed it, however, and in the marks of age was ten years ahead of his time. You can't keep up this sort of thing—digging, tugging, lifting, wet to the skin day after day, summer and winter, with no interval of rest, but a steady drag twelve months of the year—without paying for it. There's dissipation in the use of muscle as well as in the use of whiskey. Every old miner knows it now and feels it. Don't you? How does the muscle of forty-five years in 1882 compare with that of twenty-five in 1862? Of course, man must live by the sweat of his brow, or the sweat of his brain, but many of you sweat too long in those days, and I hear you all saying, "That's so!" Start anew the fire in the little stove; thump the wet boots in the corner; drag yourself down to the spring a few hundred yards distant for a pail of fresh water; hack a few more chips from the dried stump; mix some flour, water, and yeast powder for the day's baking; set down a minute on your flour-barrel chair and look on your earthly possessions. The worn and scarred trunk you brought years ago from the States; it holds your best suit of a forgotten fashion, two or three white shirts, a bundle of letters from home, a few photographs, a Bible, not worn out with use, a quartz crystal, a few gold "specimens," a tarantula's nest, the tail of a rattlesnake and six vests. Do you remember how vests would accumulate in the mines? Pants, coat, everything else would wear out—vests never.

CHAPTER XIV.

THE MINER'S RAINY DAY.

NO work on the claim to-day. It rains too hard. It is the winter rain of California—a warm, steady, continuous drizzle. The red earth is soft and soppy. It mires to the ankles. The dark green of the chaparral on the hill sides seems to-day almost black. The hue of the river by my cabin door is yellower than ever. The water-mark is three feet higher than last night and it creeps upward every hour. Over the mountain crags yonder white sheets of foam are tumbling where none has been seen before for many months. This is an enforced day of rest. I have finished my breakfast and sit down for a few minutes in a keen enjoyment of idleness. There is a ceaseless patter of raindrops on the cabin roof. The river roars louder than ever over the riffle close by. That roar is the first sound I hear in the morning and the last at night. It has roared thus for me these three years. In one sense of times' duration they seem as three hundred years; in another, they seem not much over three months. It is three months when I think only of the date of my arrival on Frazier's flat. It is three hundred years as I attempt to recall the daily round of experience and thought since I came here. Outwardly it has been what many would consider a monotonous experience. Weeks have been so much alike that they leave no distinguishing marks in my memory. A big freshet or two, a mining lawsuit, an election, a few weeks when the claim "came down rich," a fight at the bar store, a bigger spree than usual, a visit from county candidates travelling for votes, a giving out of ditch water, a break in the reservoir, a man drowned in the river—these are the great events on Frazier's flat.

I wonder how many years more I shall spend here. I wonder if I must live and die here. I am no nearer fortune than three years ago, not so near by three years. I seem more and more chained down here by force of habit. I seem fit for little else but to dig. I long to see something of the great world beyond this lone foothill nook. Yet without money I feel less and less capable of going out and "getting on" in that world. And as for saving money—well, we call this a "three-dollar claim," which means an average daily profit, when all expenses are paid, of two dollars more or less. These thought are making it as gloomy within as the weather is without. I must get out of this. My gray flannel working shirt needs mending. The right sleeve is ripped from wrist to elbow. It has been so ripped for about six weeks. I have rolled that wet sleeve up to the elbow about a hundred times a day, and at every tenth stroke of the pick it has unrolled again and flapped in my face. I sew up the sleeve with a very large needle and a very coarse thread doubled. This is a good time to clean up a little. I will be domestic to-day. I will bake a fresh batch of bread and make a pie. It shall be a mince pie. We are ten miles from the nearest baker's mince pie. It shall be made of salt beef previously soaked to freshness, dried apples, molasses and vinegar in lieu of cider. The crust I roll out with a junk bottle on a smooth, flat board. I bake it on a shallow tin plate. It will be, when done, a thin, wafery pie; but it will be a pie—the shadow of a pie at least—such as I used to eat at home; only a shadow.

Rain, rain, rain. The wind is up and about too, tearing around among the trees and shaking the cloth roof of my cabin. Here and there little trickles of water are coming through and running down the logs. Mine is a log cabin of the roughest make. Four logs piled atop of each other form the sides. A mud chimney at one end; a door at the other. The logs are very dry and very rotten and abound in those insects that delight in rotten wood. I have found scorpions under the bark and occasionally an earwig promenades over the table. I open the door and look out on the river. It is rising. Wrecks are coming down—boards, logs, lumber and an occasional sluice and pieces of fluming. There is an eddy around the turn of the hill above, where much of this drift runs in. I repair thither and make a few hauls. I secure a half-dozen good boards, some pieces of joist, some driftwood for fuel, and pile it up on the bank out of the swelling water's reach. "Halloa!" That cry is from a couple of men on the other side of the river, plodding down the trail in oilskins. I know them. Two of the "boys" from Poverty Bar. They are going to Price's store two miles below—store, grogshop, boarding-house, polling booth at election, ferry, etc. Being a rainy day they are going there to get drunk. That is not their avowed purpose on setting out, but it's as near a certainty as anything can be in this world.

I return to my cabin. The pie has baked. It is browner than I intended it should be. On one side it is almost black. It is ornamented about the rim with a row of scollops made by pressure of the thumb. Now I put in the bread, previously mixed and kneaded. I am not a good breadmaker. It is always bread too much baked, or too little, or too sour, or too yellow, or too heavy. But I don't care. I bake only for myself and I am unfortunately too easily pleased and probably too lazy to take that care and elaborate preparation necessary for good bread. I never measure accurately the proportions of flour, water, and yeast powder necessary for good bread. I throw them together at random. It's a "hit or miss"—generally miss. It's too much trouble to bother about these small details. A particular friend of mine who stayed with me a few days reproved me for the poor quality of my bread and the general slovenliness apparent about my cooking utensils.

"You have no pride," said he.

I owned up. What was the use of pride about a tin kettle. This friend was my backer. He had set me up on this claim and put me, after a fashion, on my feet. He had come to see how I was getting along. While on this visit a man of some standing from a camp up the river came along looking for a stray cow. My friend asked him to dinner—one of my dinners—graced by about the worst baking of bread I ever accomplished. My friend did not realize what he was about when he asked the future Lieutenant-Governor of the State of California to that dinner. But when he sat down to my board and when they tried to eat my bread, he sorrowed in secret and gave me some good and forcible advice afterward relative to culinary and domestic matters. In these matters he was a very particular man. During his stay he inaugurated a reign of neatness and for me one of terror and discomfort. He put his whole mind on cooking and covered the stove with dishes. He was an animated bill of fare. He scoured all the tinware brightly. I was quite surprised at the new, fresh look of things, and in secret thought seriously of reform, and hoped he wouldn't stay long.

But the man didn't enjoy eating his elaborately prepared meals so much as I did. He worked too hard getting them up. He exhausted too much of his force in planning, worrying, and cooking. He worked his mind in too many channels at once. He lacked repose. There's where I had the best of him. I was reposeful, and if you please so to term it, lazy. He is dead—I am alive. There's the result of different mental conditions. It is noon. I have no clock to tell the hours, but we acquire a faculty of feeling when noon arrives. The rain has ceased temporarily, but it will soon recommence, for which I am glad, as it will prevent work on the claim during the afternoon. Having eaten dinner, finishing with a piece of my mince pie, it occurs to me that this is a good time to write home. It's hard work writing home. I put it off for weeks and months. It lays a load on my mind. I receive at times letters from people complaining of my neglect. I know I ought to write, but what is there to write? Nothing but the same old story "Hope soon to do well." I have written in this strain for the last six years until I am tired and sick of it. It is of no use telling any more about the country. All that has been told. If my people only knew how much I suffered in this endeavor to be dutiful, perhaps they would not insist on my writing more than the line, "I am still alive; yours truly." Thousands more of letters from California wanderers would have been received by anxious relatives had they been content with this. But you were expected to write. Bricks without straw.

It is a hard thing to realize, and few will realize it, that no matter how close the tie of relationship, in reality there can be a wider and wider drifting apart. Interests are not the same; associations are not the same;

location, surrounding, environment are not the same. Through some or all of these influences you are growing into another man; another woman. You would hardly recognize yourself could you see your own identity and individuality as it was ten years ago; you believe differently, you are another individual. What is that cry from the old home so far away? It is the longing for some expression from the being of 1850 and not from the one of 1860, who, did he stand under the shadow of that roof and sit at that well-remembered table, would still after a few days show the change, proving in himself or herself the lack of something which once existed, and so prove a disappointment. The ink in my cabin is thick, the pen a bad one and my mind seems in this epistolary effort thicker and rustier than ink or pen. "Dear ——" and then a big blot, and then a long pause and the patter of the rain and the roar of the river. I write about a page and a half, feeling as if every stroke of the pen were encumbered with a ball and chain. I accomplish half a dozen more blots and I finish in a wretched state of mind and in a prickly heat. It is a barren, pithless, sapless effort. I will go out and get a breath of fresh air and rain. It is four o'clock. Still it rains. The heavens are dark and already the first shades of the winter's night are coming on. I revisit my haul of lumber from the river. It is gone. The river has not reached the spot where I placed it. It is the work of those thieving Chinamen on Chamber's Bar, half a mile above. There is no use in going after them. My lumber is deposited and hidden amid the piles they have to-day dragged out of the river.

I spend about an hour getting in fuel. I have a woodyard on the hillside yonder. Nature has kindly felled and seasoned there a few scrub oaks for my use. I drag down a few branches. The land here is free—very free. No fences, no boundary lines, no gates, no proprietors. It's a pretty flat when the sun shines. A dark background of mountain, in front a river, with its curving and varied outline of tule and bank up and down stream, and close about the oaks are so scattered as to give one the impression of a park and an old mansion hidden somewhere in the background. What a luxury would be this spot to thousands in crowded cities who haven't even the range of a back yard nor the shadow of a tree! Yet I am discontented and would get away to these crowded cities. The early darkness has come. I light my candle. My candelabra is of glass—dark olive-green—a bottle. I did use a big potato with a hole therein scooped. But the esthetic nature requires constant change and I adopted a bottle. I spread the evening repast. I sit down alone. From the window I see lights glimmering in the few other neighboring cabins.

McSkimmins drops in after tea. I know all that McSkimmins will say, for I have often heard it before; but McSkimmins is better than nobody—or rather better than one's own thoughts, unrefreshed and unrelieved by mixture with any other minds' thought. McSkimmins goes. I take refuse in the effort to repair my best and only pair of broadcloth pantaloons. I brought these with me from the States. They show decided signs of wear. I am putting in a patch. It is a job I take hold of at intervals. There is about it a mystery and a complication I can't fathom. I can't get the patch to fit, or, rather, to set. There is more in the tailor's art than I imagined. Every time I have put them on I find a difference and a seeming division of action and sentiment between the new cloth I have sewed inside and the old cloth outside. They won't hold together. The stitches rip apart and everything goes by the run. I seem to fail in making the new cloth accommodate itself to the varying proportions of this part of the garment. And so the dreary night wears on. Rain, rain, rain; roar, roar, roar. Is this living?

CHAPTER XV.

THE MINER'S SUNDAY.

THIS is the Sunday sun that streams through the cabin window and through the chinks of the cabin wall.

It is the same sunshine as that of the week day. Yet as the miner wakes and realizes it is Sunday it has a different appearance and conveys a different impression from that of the weekday sun. Everything seems more quiet, more restful, and even more staid and serious. There belongs to it and to the landscape as he looks out a flavor of far-away Eastern Sabbath bells and Sunday morning's hush and longer family prayer than usual and Sunday-school. But there is not a church bell within ten miles and there never will be one heard on this flat. There is not the least approach to church society or religious organization or observance. There is not, so far as known, so much as a man in the least religiously inclined. We are a hard lot. No work on the claim to-day. The pick and shovel will rest where thrown Saturday afternoon and only a trickle of yellowish water from the reservoir will seep through the long line of sluices instead of yesterday's muddy surge rushing through—sand, gravel and grating pebble and boulder.

But there is work of another sort to be done and a great deal of it. After breakfast shaving. That small mirror of most imperfect glass, whose reflection distorts the features, screwing up one side of the face and enlarging the other in an unnatural fashion, is suitably adjusted. A smell of soap pervades the air. He lathers and shaves and relathers and reshaves with a tedious and painful precision, the while making faces at himself in the glass as he brings one portion of his countenance after another more directly under the sweep of the razor. In some cases he comes off with a few scratches or leaves a hirsute oasis here and there of uncut bristle. Black pantaloons, a white shirt, a felt or straw hat, a linen duster and the Sunday boots. This is his dandy outfit. In his pocket is a buckskin purse, once yellow, now faded to a dull gray, holding gold dust, a few ounces more or less, perhaps five, perhaps ten. It is the company dust and is to be sold and turned into bright, yellow gold pieces. And why all this preparation? "To go to camp." Camp is three miles away over the mountain yonder. A group of ramshackle cabins, alternating with saloons, three grocery stores, a hotel, an express office and a Justice of the Peace, all in a hot gulch, with hillsides long ago swept of trees, scarred with cuts and streaked with patches of dry yellowish ledge. "Camp" to him has all the importance and interest of a great metropolis. It is the centre of news. The stage passes through it on the way to a larger camp. Two boss gamblers reside there. There is a faro game on occasions, a billiard table with a mountainous sort of bed, where the balls roll as they please and after an eccentric fashion of their own.

The camp is for him the first nerve-centre of civilization and the only outlet to the great world which he has left. You, fresh from the great city, regard this dilapidated place as an out-of-the-way corner; but to him, living on his remote flat, with but two cabins in sight for as many miles, camp is a place of importance. The news is fresh here; the city papers are here; the political candidates speak here; the one-horse show comes here and all the minor lawsuits untried here. Camp is reached after a long, hot walk. He suffers in his store clothes from the heat. In his working every-day flannels he would not so much mind it, but the restraint and chokiness of starched linen are fatiguing. It is laborious even to be "dressed up" on a hot day. Of this he is not aware. He has not yet so far analyzed into the depth and causes of sensations, yet it is a labor in tropical weather to wear and bear good clothes—clothes which cannot safely be perspired in; clothes which one can't "lop down" in; clothes which require care in the keeping, as well as dignity and uprightness; I mean physical uprightness. He never so much suffered from the heat on a week day as on Sundays and the cause was mainly the difference between clothes which demanded consideration and respect and those which did not.

He repairs first to the Magnolia. He has long in imagination seen it from afar. How cool is the big barroom. The landlord keeps the floor well wet down. That Magnolia floor is one of the few places where water, unmixed with other fluid, is useful and grateful. How comforting and soothing is the first drink. A long drink in a long tumbler, with plenty of ice, soda water and whiskey. If heaven be anywhere as a material locality it is in that first cool drink after a three-mile July tramp over the kiln-dried hills and herbage of the California foothills. The Magnolia is the social heart-centre of camp. There he finds the doctor. The doctor drinks with him. The doctor drinks with everybody. There, too, is the Justice of the Peace. The Justice drinks with him. The Justice holds his Court at the Magnolia. The proprietor of the Magnolia is the camp constable and between drinks during trials calls *viva voce* the witnesses in the case. The Judge drinks with him. The Judge generally drinks. The principal camp gambler is at the Magnolia. He takes a light drink. He is a wise man and knows the advantage and profit of keeping a cool head. The regular camp drunkard sits in the rear in one of the arm-chairs back of the billiard table. He looks so humble, so respectful—and so dry, that our miner's heart moves to pity and he "asks him up." He complies, but not with undue haste. This treats of the era between 1865 and 1870. The camp drunkard had not then so "lost his grip" as to be unmindful of a certain slowness, deliberation and dignity befitting a gentleman. But when he does arrive at the bar he takes a "four-fingered" drink.

They stand in a row at the bar. The barkeeper is mixing the "long" and the short drinks. Each man waits, says nothing and eyes every motion of the bartender. The silence is impressive. All is ready. Each glass is grasped and raised, and then from each to each, and more than all, from all to the drink donor, there is a nod, that incantatory phrase is uttered, "Well, here's luck," and the poison is down. As it rasps, they call "Ahem!" with varied degrees of modulation. But this is a careful and prudent miner and he now repairs to the store. There his dust is weighed, sold, and the week's provision ordered. His combined partners' "divvys" are put aside in a lump and safely stored. Now the weight is off his mind. He returns to the attractions of camp.

These are not numerous. There is the Magnolia, the Bella Union, the Court Exchange, the post and express office. There are the "boys." He learns the news of the county or district. The Mount Vernon is paying four dollars per day. Long Shortman has gone on another spree and hasn't done any work for the last ten days. Jimmy McNeil has sent for his wife's sister. She is unmarried. Sullivan has had another row with his wife and she has complained to the authorities. Sam Gedney is going to run for County Clerk on the Democratic ticket. Bob Delmame lost $200 at the game the other night. A San Francisco company have bought the Crazy gulch quartz lead and will put a ten-stamp mill on it. The schoolmaster was drunk last Friday night. Ford shot at McGillis the other night, but did not hit him. There is scandal and talk concerning the Frenchwoman who keeps the peanut stand and the Justice of the Peace. The Wiley girls, two sisters who have recently moved into camp, are making a sensation, and their small parlor at times won't hold the crowd of semi-bald and unconsciously middle-aged miners and others who are calling on them with possible matrimony in prospective. They may pass along the street about the middle of the afternoon and such "ragging out" was never seen before in this camp. The curious have investigated the tracks made by their little gaiters in the red dust of the upper road and report them the smallest feet ever seen in this section. Billy Devins of the Blue-jay claim is thought to have the best show with the eldest, and Goldberry of the lively stable with the youngest. No. He won't let his best horse and buggy to anybody now and takes her out riding three times a week. But they're snappy and uncertain, and nobody can count on them for a certainty. So runs the week's news, which he picks up with sundry drinks.

He enjoys the luxury of a hotel dinner—a dinner he is not obliged to prepare with his own hands—a decidedly plain dinner in metropolitan estimation, but to him, commencing with soup and ending with pie, a sumptuous repast. It is moonlight and he takes his way back by the old trail home. Old not in years, but in association. It is but the track of twenty years or so, yet for him how old is it in thought. How many, many times he has travelled over it.

That poker game is going on in one corner of the Magnolia. The "hard case" from over the hill is trying to beat it. He has been so trying every Sunday night in that same saloon and in that same corner for the last twenty years. He has grown old in trying. It has kept him poor, yet he thinks he can play poker. He is encouraged in this impression by a considerate few. He works for them. They "scoop him in" regularly. He will go home to-morrow morning, and during the week wash out a couple of ounces more for the benefit of "Scotty" and "Texas." It is 11 o'clock and time to go home. That three-mile walk is before him; he has taken as many drinks as is prudent, possibly one or two more. The camp saloon revelries are beginning to quiet down. Most of the prominent drunks have fallen in the cause. The chronic drunk of the camp is talking at the bar. But he will thus talk all night; he never stops talking—or drinking. He has been here more or less drunk ever since 1852. He is phenomenal and not a standard for ordinary intemperates. Almost every camp has known such a drunkard. Some are alive yet. They are of the immortal few not born to die. It would be madness to compete with such.

So he sets out on his lonely walk. Of how much has he thought while plodding over it. Here the same big buckeye brushes against his face as it did in the "spring of '50," when he was twenty years younger and had a sweetheart in the "States," whose memory was fresh and warm. It has all died out since. The letters became less and less, the years more and more, and then all came to a dead standstill and he received the village paper, and there, appropriately below the column of deaths, he read of her marriage, whereat he went to camp and plunged wildly into all the concert saloon could give and made things howl and boldly challenged the chronic poker game and won. The trail turns suddenly. It has run over the rocks by the river, its trail at times for many feet almost illegible, a vague smoothly-worn streak over ledge and loose boulders, polished and strewn with new white sand and pebbles by some unusually high freshet. But here the shelving bank suddenly ceases. It becomes a precipice. Up the hard-worn path in the red earth he climbs forty, fifty, sixty feet. It is closely hedged with chemisal. Now he emerges near the brow of the high rocky bluff. In all its moonlit glory surges, bubbles, and roars the river below. Its yellow muddiness of the day is now changed to a dark shade of brown, with tremulous silver bars. Night and the moon are the artists.

CHAPTER XVI.

THE COW FEVER.

ABOUT this time (1861) a cow fever began to rage throughout the State. It got hold of people, and impressed them with a burning idea that the road to fortune was a cow path, and that fortunes lay in keeping cattle. The cow fever reached the seclusion of Swett's Bar. We invested all our spare cash in cows and waited for results. Cattle were spoken of as a sure card for fortune. Keep cattle. Buy improved breeds. Raise them. "Cross" them. Feed them for nothing on the native grass. Buy cows. Cows give milk. People can live on milk. Milk then to us was a luxury. It paid no milkman to travel up and down the rough and rocky ledges of the Tuolumne ringing his bell at miners' cabins half a mile apart. Indeed he could not so travel without carrying his milk *à la* panier on a donkey's back, and by the time it had reached its place of destination it would have been agitated to butter. So all of us miners went in for cows. Improved cows. We bought each an improved cow. We hauled this cow by ropes across the raging, eddying, furious river to our side. Frequently she arrived more dead than alive. Then came a season of hope and expectation as to fortunes through cows. We arose at five in the morning, built the fire for breakfast, went out and sought our cows, generally feeding or reposing a mile or more from our cabins, caught these cows, milked them, returned to the cabin, finished the cooking of either a burned or cold breakfast, went forth and labored in the claim till noon, came home, cooked dinner, went forth again, at 1 P.M., labored till six, went back to the cabins, chopped wood for fuel, travelled 500 feet or yards to the spring for water, returned, mixed our bread, put it in the oven, went out and milked the cow, then bent over the hot stove for an hour until bread was baked, and then, heated, flushed, perspiring, exhausted from the day's labor, and with nerves quivering by reason of such exhaustion, we arranged the miner's table, sat down to the meal, and wondered why we had so little appetite.

Keeping cows proved laborious work for miners. When, in addition to kindling the fire in the morning, cooking your own breakfast, coming home at night wet and tired after working all day in the ground-sluice, then hacking away at some old stump to get wood enough to cook the supper, travelling may be an eighth of a mile to the nearest spring for a pail of water, and bending and bothering with meat-frying and bread-making, you add, chasing night and morn, milk pail in hand, some contrary cow all over the flat in order to milk her, you pile too heavy a load on any man's back.

Because, in the matter of housekeeping, we had ceased the co-operative system. We dwelt all apart, each a hermit in his own cabin. We were diverse in habit, and could not get along with each other's peculiarities. The neat man couldn't abide the slovenly man; the economical man couldn't sit patiently by and see his partner cut potato parings a quarter of an inch in thickness; the nervous man was exhausted by his partner's whistling or snoring, and all these and numberless other opposing peculiarities at last caused each man hermit-like, to retire into his own cell.

We had other trouble with our cows, for they were ravenous after salt. We neglected to "salt them." Result: If any article containing the least incrustation of salt was left outside our cabins, the entire herd would gather about it at night, lick it, fight for its possession and keep up a steady grunting, stamping, lowing, and bellowing. They would eat clothing left out over night on the clothes-line to dry. In such manner and for such reason also would they eat through the cotton walls of our houses. Once, when away for three days attending a county convention at Sonora, on returning to my lone cabin, I found it a scene of ruin and desolation. A cow had eaten through the cloth wall on one side, and eaten her way out at the other, and had stopped long enough inside to eat up all my flour, rice and vegetables. Once, when moving my household effects from one cabin to another, on a wheelbarrow, I left it near the middle of the flat for a few minutes. On returning I saw a cow making off with my best coat. She held it in her mouth by one sleeve. On seeing me she started off on a run, still thus holding the sleeve in her mouth and making violent efforts to eject it. The coat-sleeve was a ruin when I did get it. She had chewed it for salt's sake to the likeness of a fish net. Keeping cows did not make our fortunes at Swett's. Then everybody said: "Keep hogs. They will feed on acorns and increase very rapidly. In a few years the plains and hills will groan under the burden of your pork." So I bought hogs. I bought a sow and seven pigs. They gave me much to think of. Before I had owned them a week complaints concerning them came from neighboring miners, who owned no hogs. These pigs of mine broke through the cloth walls of the cabins and would consume the miner's entire weekly stock of provisions in a few minutes. Then they would go outside and root from out the hot coals—his "Dutch oven," wherein his bread was baking while he labored afar in his claim, and this bread when cooled they would also devour. I had, on buying these animals, engaged that they should "find themselves."

There was no reasoning with the suffering miners in this matter. I argued that my pigs had a right to run at large, and that they should make their houses more secure. The miners argued that right or not right, they would shoot my pigs even if found near their cabins. If that was not sufficient, they might shoot me. Their positiveness in this matter was of an intense and violent character. There was no such thing as discussion with them on legal or equitable grounds. I think now that I and the pigs had law and right on our side, but the miners were in the majority and had might. Nor was this all. These pigs, seemingly recognizing my ownership, came home at night to sleep. They slept in a pile just outside my cabin door, and as the night air wafted down from the higher Sierra summits became cooler, the pigs on the outside of the pile became uncomfortable. Being uncomfortable they tried to get inside the pile. This the warm pigs inside resisted. The resistance was accompanied with squealing and grunting, which lasted all night long and disturbed my sleep. This pig pile consisted of a rind of cold and uncomfortable pigs and a core of warm and comfortable pigs, and there was a continual effort on the part of the cold porcine rind to usurp the places of the warm and comfortable porcine core. They gave me no rest, for when, with the warm morning sun, this uproar ceased, there came the season of complaint and threat from my plundered neighbors. Finally a cold storm chilled half of these pigs to death. I sold the remainder as quickly as possible to a ranchman who better understood the hog business.

During the receding of the waters after one of the annual spring freshets, I saw several hundred dollars in gold dust washed out near the base of a pine tree on the river's bank, between Hawkins' and Swett's Bar, where probably it had years before been buried by some unknown miner. That is, I saw it after it had been washed out and found by another more fortunate miner. In all probability there are many thousands of dollars in dust so dug by hard-working hands and so buried in California, there to remain until the Last Day perhaps longer. Where's the utility of resurrecting the "Root of all Evil" on the Last Day, just at the time when people in heaven or elsewhere are presumed to be able to get along without it? Yet it is a mysterious Providence that impels any poor fellow to dig his pile bury it for safekeeping, and then go off and die in some out-of-the-way place without being able to leave any will and testament as to the exact hole where his savings lay. Regarding buried treasure, there is a hill near Jamestown concerning which, years ago, there hovered a legend that it held somewhere thousands of dollars in dust, buried in the early days by a lone miner, who was, for his money's sake, murdered in his cabin. They said that by the roots of many trees on that hillside it had been unsuccessfully dug for. Anyway, the miner left a memory and a hope behind him. That's more than many do. If you want to leave a lasting recollection of yourself behind drop a hint from time to time ere you depart for "The Bright and Shining Shore" that you have interred $10,000 somewhere in a quarter section of land, you will then long be remembered and your money dug for.

CHAPTER XVII.

RED MOUNTAIN BAR.

THE California mining camp was ephemeral. Often it was founded, built up, flourished, decayed, and had weeds and herbage growing over its site and hiding all of man's work inside of ten years. Yet to one witnessing these changes it seemed the life of a whole generation. Of such settlements, Red Mountain Bar was one. Red Mountain lay three miles above Swett's Bar, "up river." I lived "off and on" at the "Bar" in its dying days. I saw it decay gently and peacefully. I saw the grass, trees, and herbage gradually creep in and resume their sway all over its site as they had done ere man's interruption.

I lived there when the few "boys" left used daily, after the close of an unsuccessful river season, to sit in a row on a log by the river's edge, and there, surveying their broken dam, would chant curses on their luck. The Bar store was then still in existence. Thompson was its proprietor. The stock on hand had dwindled down to whiskey. The bar and one filled bottle alone survived. On rainy nights, when the few miners left would gather about the stove Thompson would take down his fiddle, and fiddle and sing, "What can't be cured must be endured," or, "The King into his garden came; the spices smelt about the same"—a quotation of unknown authorship. Of neighbors, living in their cabins strung along the banks for half a mile above the store, there was Keen Fann, an aged mercantile and mining Chinaman, with a colony about him of lesser and facially indistinguishable countrymen of varying numbers. Second, "Old Harry," an aged negro, a skilled performer on the bugle and a singer, who offered at times to favor us with what he termed a "little ditto." He was the Ethiopic king of a knot of Kanakas gathered about him. Third, "Bloody Bill," so-called from his frequent use of the sanguinary adjective, and, as may be guessed, an Englishman. Fourth, an old Scotchman, one of the Bar's oldest inhabitants, who would come to the store with the little bit of gold dust, gathered after a hard day's "crevicing" complaining that gold was getting as scarce as "the grace of God in the Heelands of Scotland." Fifth, McFarlane, a white-bearded old fellow, another pioneer, who after a yearly venture into some strange and distant locality to "change his luck," was certain eventually to drift back again to the Bar, which he regarded as home. Down the river, nestled high up in a steep and picturesque gulch, stood the buckeye-embowered cabin of old Jonathan Brown, the ditch tender, a great reader of weekly "story papers," who lived like a boy in the literature of the

Western Frontier Penny Awful, and who, coming to the store and perching himself on the counter, would sometimes break out in remarks about how "Them thar Indians got the better of 'em at last," to the astonishment of the "boys," who imagined at first that he referred to Indians in the locality, suggesting possibilities of a repetition of the great Oak Flat uprising of 1850.

At the "top of the hill," a mile and a half away, stood the "Yankee Ranch," kept by a bustling, uneasy, and rather uncomfortable man from Massachusetts, aided by his good-natured, easy-going son-in-law. One rainy winter's day the "boys" congregated about Thompson's store became seized with a whim for the manufacture of little pasteboard men turning grindstones, which, fastened to the stove, were impelled to action by the ascending current of hot air. So they smoked their pipes, and wrought all day until the area of stovepipe became thickly covered with little pasteboard men busily turning pasteboard grindstones. Then, George M. G., the son-in-law of the Yankee Ranch, came down the hill to borrow an axe. George was of that temperament and inclination to be of all things charmed with a warm stove on a cold, rainy day, a knot of good fellows about it, a frequent pipe of tobacco, maybe an occasional punch and the pleasing manufacture of hot-air-driven little pasteboard men turning pasteboard grindstones. He forgot his axe—sat down and began with the rest the manufacture of pasteboard men and grindstones. And he kept on till a late hour of the night, and stayed at the Bar all night and all the next day and that next night, until the stovepipe was covered to its very top with little men, all working away for dear life turning grindstones; and on the second day of his stay the exasperated father-in-law suddenly appeared and delivered himself in impatient invective with regard to such conduct on the part of a son-in-law sent forty-eight hours previously to borrow an axe. Such was the circle oft gathered on the long, rainy winter's eve about the Thompson store stove. All smoked. Keen Fann frequently dropped in. He stood respectfully, as a heathen should in such a Christian assemblage, on its outer edge, or humbly appropriated some unoccupied keg, and for the rest—grinned. From his little piggy eyes to his double chin Keen's face was a permanently settled grin.

Keen Fann had learned about twenty words of English and would learn no more. In his estimation, these twenty words, variously used, after a sort of grammatical kaleidoscopic fashion, seemed adequate to convey everything required. One of his presumed English expressions long puzzled the boys. Asking the price of articles at the store he would say: "Too muchee pollyfoot." At last the riddle was correctly guessed. He meant: "Too much profit."

For protection Keen Fann built his house opposite the store. The Mexicans were then attacking and robbing isolated bands of Chinamen. At one bar a few miles below, then deserted by the whites, the Chinese had inclosed their camp with a high stockade of logs. Yet one night they were attacked. The Mexicans besieged their fortress for hours, peppering them from the hillside with revolvers, and at last they broke through the Mongolian works and bore off all their dust and a dozen or more revolvers. Keen Fann's castle was in dimensions not more than 12x15 feet, and in height two stories. Within it was partitioned off into rooms not much larger than dry-goods boxes. The hallways were just wide enough to squeeze through, and very dark. It was intensely labyrinthian, and Keen was always making it more so by devising new additions. No white man ever did know exactly where the structure began or ended. Keen was a merchant, dealing principally in gin, fish, and opium. His store was involved in this curious dwelling, all of his own construction. In the store was a counter. Behind it there was just room for Keen to sit down, and in front there was just room enough for the customer to turn around. When Keen was the merchant he looked imposing in an immense pair of Chinese spectacles. When he shook his rocker in the bank he took off these spectacles. He was a large consumer of his own gin. I once asked him the amount of his weekly allowance. "Me tink," said he, "one gallun, hap (half)." From the upper story of the castle protruded a huge spear-head. It was made by the local blacksmith, and intended as a menace to the Mexican bandits. As they grew bolder and more threatening, Keen sent down to San Francisco and purchased a lot of old pawn-shop revolvers. These being received, military preparation and drill went on for several weeks by Keen and his forces. He practised at target-shooting, aimed at the mark with both eyes shut, and for those in its immediate vicinity with a most ominous and threatening waver of the arm holding the weapon. It was prophesied that Keen would kill somebody with that pistol. None ever expected that he would kill the proper person. Yet he did. One night an alarm was given. Keen's castle was attacked. The "boys," hearing the disturbance, grabbed their rifles and pistols, and sallied from the store. The robbers, finding themselves in a hornets' nest, ran. By the uncertain light of a waning moon the Bar was seen covered with Chinamen gabbling and wildly gesticulating. Over the river two men were swimming. Keen, from the bank, pointed his revolver at one, shut his eyes and fired. One of the men crawled out of the water and tumbled in a heap among the boulders. The "boys" crossed, and found there a strange white man, with Keen's bullet through his backbone.

I experienced about the narrowest escape of my life in a boat during a freshet on the Tuolumne crossing. I counted myself a good river boatman, and had just ferried over a Swett's Bar miner. He had come to purchase a gallon of the native juice of the grape, which was then grown, pressed and sold at Red Mountain Bar. When he crossed with me he was loaded with it. Some of it was outside of him in a demijohn and some of it was inside. Indeed it was inside of us both. I set him across all right. On returning, by taking advantage of a certain eddy, one could be rushed up stream counter to the current coming down for a quarter of a mile, and at a very rapid rate. It was very exciting thus to be carried in an opposite direction, within ten feet of the great billowy swell coming down. It was a sort of sliding down hill without the trouble of drawing one's sled up again. So I went up and down the stream. The Red Mountain wine meantime was working. Night came on, a glorious moon arose over the mountain tops, and I kept sliding up and down the Tuolumne. I became more daring and careless. So that suddenly in the very fury of the mid-stream billows I slipped off the stern sheets at a sudden dip of the boat and fell into the river. I was heavily clad in flannels and mining boots. Of my stay under water I recollect only the thought, "You're in for it this time. This is no common baptism." The next I knew I was clinging to a rock half a mile below the scene of the submergence. I had been swept under water through the Willow Bar, the walls of whose rocky channel, chiselled by the current of centuries, were narrower at the top than on the river-bed, and through which the waters swept in a succession of boils and whirlpools. Wet and dripping, I tramped to the nearest cabin, a mile and a half distant, and stayed there that night. Red Mountain Bar, on seeing the mishap, gave me up for lost—all but one man, who was negative on that point for the reason, as he alleged, that I was not destined to make the final exit by water. I reappeared the next morning at the Bar. When I told the boys that I had been swept through the Willow Bar they instituted comparisons of similarity in the matter of veracity betwixt myself and Ananias of old. It was the current impressions that no man could pass through the Willow Bar alive.

Chinese Camp, five miles distant, stood as the metropolis for Red Mountain Bar. It contained but a few hundred people. Yet, in our estimation at that time it bore the same relative importance that New York does to some agricultural village a hundred miles way. Chinese Camp meant restaurants, where we could revel in the luxury of eating a meal we were not obliged to prepare ourselves, a luxury none can fully appreciate save those who have served for years as their own cooks. Chinese Camp meant saloons, palatial as compared with the Bar groggery; it meant a daily mail and communication with the great world without; it meant hotels, where strange faces might be seen daily; it meant, perhaps, above all, the nightly fandango. When living for months and years in such out-of-the-way nooks and corners as Red Mountain Bar, and as were thousands of now forgotten and nameless flats, gulches, and bars in California, cut off from all regular communication with the world, where the occasional passage of some stranger is an event, the limited stir and bustle of such a place as Chinese

Camp assumed an increased importance and interest. Chinese Camp Justice presided at our lawsuits. Chinese Camp was the Mecca to which all hands resorted for the grand blow-out at the close of the river mining season. With all their hard work what independent times were those after all! True, claims were uncertain as to yield; hopes of making fortunes had been given over. But so long as $1.50 or $2 pickings remained on the banks men were comparatively their own masters. There was none of the inexorable demand of business consequent on situation and employment in the great city, where, sick or well, the toilers must hie with machine-like regularity at the early morning hour to their posts of labor. If the Red Mountaineer didn't "feel like work" in the morning he didn't work. If he preferred to commence digging and washing at ten in the morning instead of seven, who should prevent him? If, after the morning labor, he desired a *siesta* till two in the afternoon, it was his to take.

Of what Nature could give there was much at the Bar to make pleasant man's stay on earth, save a great deal of cash. We enjoyed a mild climate—no long, hard winters to provide against; a soil that would raise almost any vegetable, a necessity or luxury, with very little labor; grapes or figs, apples or potatoes; land to be had for the asking; water for irrigation accessible on every hand; plenty of pasture room; no crowding. A quarter of a section of such soil and climate, within forty miles of New York City, would be worth millions. Contrast such a land with the bleak hills about Boston, where half the year is spent in a struggle to provide for the other half. Yet we were all anxious to get away. Our heaven was not at Red Mountain. Fortunes could not be digged there. We spent time and strength in a scramble for a few ounces of yellow metal, while in the spring time the vales and hillsides covered with flowers argued in vain that they had the greatest rewards for our picks and shovels. But none listened. We grovelled in the mud and stones of the oft-worked bank. Yearly it responded less and less to our labors. One by one the "old-timers" left. The boarding-house of Dutch Bill at the farther end of the Bar long stood empty, and the meek-eyed and subtle Chinaman stole from its sides board after board; the sides skinned off, they took joist after joist from the framework. None ever saw them so doing. Thus silently and mysteriously, like a melting snowbank, the great, ramshackle boarding house disappeared, until naught was left save the chimney. And that also vanished brick by brick. All of which material entered into the composition and construction of that irregularly built, smoke-tanned Conglomerate of Chinese huts clustered near the Keen Fann castle.

"Old Grizzly" McFarlane went away. So did Bloody Bill. So the Bar's population dwindled. Fewer travellers, dot-like, were seen climbing the steep trail o'er Red Mountain. Miller, the Chinese Camp news-agent, who, with mailbags well filled with the New York papers, had for years cantered from Red Mountain to Morgan's Bar, emptying his sack as he went at the rate of fifty and twenty-five cents per sheet, paid the Bar his last visit and closed out the newspaper business there forever. Then the County Supervisors abolished it as an election precinct, and its name no longer figured in the returns. No more after the vote was polled and the result known did the active and ambitious partisan mount his horse and gallop over the mountain to Sonora, the county seat, twenty miles away, to deliver the official count, signed, sealed and attested by the local Red Mountain Election Inspectors. Finally the Bar dwindled to Thompson, Keen Fann and his Mongolian band. Then Thompson left. Keen Fann grieved at losing his friend and protector. He came on the eve of departure to the dismantled store. Tears were in his eyes. He presented Thompson with a basket of tea and a silver half-dollar, and bade him farewell in incoherent and intranslatable words of lamenting polyglot English.

CHAPTER XVIII.

MY CALIFORNIA SCHOOL.

I WAS not confident of my ability to teach even a "common school" when the situation was offered me in a little Tuolumne County mining camp. I said so to my old friend, Pete H., who had secured me the position. "Well," said he, after a reflective pause, "do you retain a clear recollection of the twenty-six letters of the alphabet? For if you do, you are equal to any educational demand this camp will make on you."

It was a reckless "camp." No phase of life was viewed or treated seriously. They did walk their horses to the grave slowly at a funeral, but how they did race back!

It was legally necessary, however, that I should be examined as to my ability by the school trustees. These were Dr. D., Bill K., a saloon-keeper, and Tom J., a miner. I met them in the Justice's office. The doctor was an important appearing man, rotund, pompous, well-dressed, and spectacled. He glared at me with an expression betwixt sadness and severity. I saw he was to be the chief inquisitor. I expected from him a searching examination, and trembled. It was years since I had seen a school-book. I knew that in geography I was rusty and in mathematics musty.

Before the doctor lay one thin book. It turned out to be a spelling book. The doctor opened it, glared on me leisurely, and finally said: "Spell cat." I did so. "Spell hat." I spelled. "Rat," said the doctor, with a look of explosive fierceness and in a tone an octave higher. I spelled, and then remarked: "But, doctor, you surely must know that I can spell words of one syllable?" "I don't," he shouted, and propounded "mat" for me to spell, with an increase of energy in his voice, and so went on until I had so spelled long enough to amuse him and the other two trustee triflers. Then he shut the book, saying: "Young man, you'll do for our camp. I wouldn't teach that school for $5,000 a year; and there are two boys you'll have for scholars that I advise you to kill, if possible, the first week. Let's all go over and take a drink."

My school house was the church, built and paid for partly by the gamblers and partly by the good people of Jimtown "for the use of all sects" on Sundays, and for educational purposes on week days.

I was shut up in that little church six hours a day with sixty children and youths, ranging from four to eighteen years of age. In summer it was a fiercely hot little church. The mercury was always near 90 by noon, and sometimes over 100, and you could at times hear the shingles split and crack on the roof of the cathedral. A few years of interior California summers' suns will turn unpainted boards and shingles almost as black as charcoal.

The majority of my pupils' parents being from New England and North America, they brought and carried into effect all their North American ideas of education. The California summer heat is, I think, unfit for educational purposes. It is too hot to herd sixty restless children together six hours a day. They proved this in several cases. Some fell sick suddenly. Some fainted. But this made no difference. The school went on in all its misery. I sent a fainting child home one day, and the father returned with it an hour afterward. He was fierce, and said he wanted his child kept in school when he sent it to school.

This was in California's early days. My scholars were the children of the Argonauts, and in some cases had come out with them. There was then no regular system of text-books. Publishers had not commenced making fortunes by getting out a new school-book system every three years.

My scholars came, bringing a great variety of school-books. They brought "Pike's Arithmetic," which had come over the plains, and "Smith's Geography," which had sailed around Cape Horn. Seldom were two alike. But the greatest variety lay in grammars. There was a regular museum of English grammars, whose authors fought each other with different rules and called the various parts of speech by different names. I accounted for the great variety of grammars on the supposition that it is or was the ambition of a large proportion of schoolmasters to write a work on grammar before they died and say: "I have left another grammar to bless and confuse posterity."

Besides bringing grammars, most of the boys brought dogs. Dogs of many breeds and sizes hovered around the school-house. They wanted frequently to come in, and did often come in, to sneak under the seats and lay themselves at their masters' feet. I had frequently to kick or order them out, and I noticed that whenever a dog was chased out he would take the longest road to get out and under as many seats as possible, in order to receive as many kicks as possible from the youthful owners of the other dogs.

I could not so organize a battalion of ten different grammars as to act in concert on my grammar class of twenty pupils. So I put them all on the retired list and tried to teach this so-called "science" orally. I chalked the rules on the blackboard, as well as the names of the different parts of speech. I made my scholars commit these to memory, standing, although I will not argue that memory takes any stronger grip on a thing while the pupil stands. At last I taught a few with good memories to "parse." I worked hard with that grammar class, and was very proud of their proficiency until I found that after months of this drilling they neither spoke nor wrote any better English than before. However, I lost nothing by this experience, for it helped me to the conviction I have held to ever since, that the entire grammar system and method does very little to make one habitually use correct language, and that a taste for reading and constant association with correct English-speaking people does a great deal. As for spending time in "parsing," I think it would be better to use that force in learning the boy to shoe horses and the girl to make bread, or let the girl shoe the horses if she wants to and the boy make the bread.

The labor of teaching the alphabet to ten infants, calling them up once an hour "to say their letters," is, in my estimation, greater than that of swinging a pick in the surface gold "diggings." I have tried both, and infinitely prefer the pick. It is not so much work when you are employed with them as when you are occupied with the other pupils. Then these poor little alphabetical cherubs can do nothing but squirm on their low benches, catch flies, pinch each other, make and project spit-balls and hold up their hands for another drink of water. I could not let them out of doors to play in the sand, where they should have been, because the North American parent would have considered himself as defrauded of a part of his infant's schooling were they not imprisoned the whole six hours.

Neither can you set a child to studying A or M or any other letter. There is not an idea in A or B. During the two years of my administration I wrought with one child who never could get successfully beyond F. Her parents questioned my ability as a teacher. Some days she would repeat the whole alphabet correctly. I would go home with a load off my mind. The next day her mind would relapse into an alphabetical blank after F. She grew to be an eyesore to me. The sight of her at last made me sick.

I held public examinations every six months, and was careful to do all the examining myself. An interloper among the audience I invited did me great damage on one of these memorized performances by asking a simple arithmetical question of the show-off geographical boy. The urchin was brilliant in dealing with boundary lines, capes, and islands, but his head was one that mathematics could not readily be injected into. On the other hand, my specimen grammarian was as likely to describe an island as a body of land surrounded—by land as by water. I had no heart to find fault with this poor barefooted urchin who, when in class, was always trying to stand on one leg like a crane, and sending his right big toe on exploring scratching expeditions up his left trouser. He had been born and brought up in an inland country, where no body of water was to be seen save an occasional fleeting mud puddle; and what earthly conception could he form of the ocean and its islands?

But the parents who attended these exhibitions of stuffed memories were struck at the proficiency of the progeny, and retired with the impression that their children knew a great deal because they had parroted off so much that was all Greek to them; and after I had been in this occupation a year I would sit in my empty theological school-house when they had gone and try and convict myself as a profound humbug, and one, too, compelled, in order to get a living, to encourage and foster a system which had so much humbug in it.

The California schools were not then "graded." They were conducted on the "go-as-you-please" plan, sometimes going as the teachers pleased, sometimes as the parents pleased, sometimes as the pupils pleased. The parents of the youthful brains I was trying to develop into future statesmen and presidents wanted me to teach many things. One father wished his son taught Latin. It is bringing extremes pretty near each other to teach Latin and A B C's. But I "taught" the young man Latin as I was "taught" many things at school. I started him committing to memory the Latin declensions and conjugations, and then heard him "say his lesson." If he got anything out of it I didn't know what it was, except tough work. He never reached any translations of the classics, for several reasons.

Another father was annoyed because I exercised his son mathematically in what, in those days, were called "vulgar fractions." "I don't want," said he, "my son to have anything to do with fractions, anyway. They're no use in bizness. Ennything over half a cent we call a cent on the books, and ennything under it we don't call nothin'. But I want Thomas to be well grounded in 'tare and tret.'"

So I grounded Thomas in 'tare and tret.' He grew up, took to evil ways, and was hung by a vigilance committee somewhere in Southern California. A boy who stammered very badly was sent me. I was expected to cure him. Five or six of my pupils were Mexicans, and spoke very little English.

One of my hardest trials was a great stout boy, so full of vitality that he could not remain quiet at his desk. I could not blame him. He had force enough inside of him to run a steam engine. It would have vent in some direction. But it would not expend itself in "learning lessons." He would work his books into a mass of dog's ears. His writing book was ever in mourning with ink stains. His face was generally inky. His inkstand was generally upset. He would hold a pen as he would a pitchfork. He seemed also to give out his vitality when he came to school and infect all the others with it. He was not a regular scholar. He was sent only when it was an "off day" on his father's "ranch." In the scholastic sense he learned nothing.

But that boy at the age of fifteen would drive his father's two-horse wagon, loaded with fruit and vegetables, 150 miles from California to Nevada over the rough mountain roads of the Sierras, sell the produce to the silver miners of Aurora and adjacent camps, and return safely home. He was obliged in places to camp out at night, cook for himself, look out for his stock, repair harness or wagon and keep an eye out for skulking Indians, who, if not "hostile," were not saints. When it came to using the hand and the head together he had in him "go," "gumption" and executive ability, and none of my "teaching" put it where it was in him, either. He may have grown up "unpolished," but he is one of the kind who are at this moment hiring polished and scholarly men to do work for them on very small wages.

I do not despise "polish" and "culture" but is there not an education now necessary which shall give the child some clearer idea of the manner in which it must cope with the world in a few years? The land to-day is full of "culture" at ten dollars a week. Culture gives polish to the blade. But it is not the process which makes the hard, well-tempered steel.

The "smartest" boy in my school gave me even more trouble than the son of the rancher. He could commit to memory as much in ten minutes as the others could in an hour, and the balance of the time he was working off the Satanism with which he was filled. His memory was an omnivorous maw. It would take in anything and everything with the smallest amount of application. It would have required two-thirds of my time to feed this voracious and mischievous little monster with books for his memory to devour.

But he was not the boy to drive a team through a wild country and dispose of the load in Nevada, though he could on such a trip have committed to memory several hundred words per day on any subject, whether he understood it or not.

My young lady pupils also gave me a great deal of trouble. They were very independent, and for this reason: Girls, even of fifteen, were very scarce then in the mines. So were women of any marriageable age. There were ten men to one woman. The result was that anything humanly feminine was very valuable, much sought after and made much of by men of all ages. My girls of fifteen, as to life and association, were grown-up women. Young miners and middle-aged, semi-baldheaded miners, who did not realize how many of their years had slipped away since they came out from the "States," took these girls to balls and whirled them by night over the dusty roads of Tuolumne County in dusty buggies.

It was difficult for one lone man, and he only a schoolmaster, to enforce discipline with these prematurely matured children, who had an average of two chances a month to marry, and who felt like any other woman their power and influence with the other sex. Half of them did have a prospective husband in some brawny pick-slinger, who never went abroad without a battery of portable small artillery slung at his waist, and who was half-jealous, half-envious of the schoolmaster for what he considered the privilege of being in the same room with his future wife six hours a day.

One needs to live in a country where there is a dearth of women to realize these situations. When my school was dismissed at four o'clock P.M., all the unemployed chivalry of "Jimtown" massed on the street corner at the Bella Union saloon to see this coveted bevy of California rosebuds pass on their way home. The Bella Union, by the way, was only a few yards from the church. Extremes got very close together in these mining camps. But the frequenters of the Bella Union, who gambled all night on the arid green baize of the monte table, had more than half paid for that church, and, I infer, wanted it in sight so that no other persuasion should run off with it. I was glad when these girls got married and entered another school of life, where I knew within a year's time they were likely to have a master.

I was once "barred out" at the close of a summer term. This was a fashion imported from the extreme southwestern part of what some call "Our Beloved Union." Returning from dinner I found the doors and windows of the university closed against me. I parleyed at one of the windows a few feet from the ground. I was met by a delegation of the two biggest boys. They informed me I could get in by coming out with a disbursement of $2.50, to treat the school to nuts, candies, and cakes. I did not accede, smashed the window and went in. Most of the undergraduates went suddenly out. I clinched with the biggest boy. The other, like a coward, ran away. The two together could easily have mastered me. Order was restored. The mutiny did not hang well together. It was not a good "combine." The Northern-bred scholars did not quite understand this move, and did not really enter heartily into it. Their backing had been forced by the two big boys, and therefore had not good stuff in it.

The big boy had a cut face. So had I. His still bigger brother met me a few days after and wanted to pick a quarrel with me about the affair. A quarrel with his class always lay within easy approach of knife or pistol. Besides, I was a Yankee. He was a Texan. And this was in 1862, when the two sections in California were neighbors, but not very warm friends, and about equal in numbers.

I was discreet with this gentleman, if not valorous, and think under the same circumstances now I should take the same course. I do not believe in taking great risks with a ruffian because he abuses you.

My successor, poor fellow, did not get off as easily as I did. He corrected the son of another gentleman from the South. The gentleman called at the school-house the next day, asked him to the door and cracked his skull with the butt of his revolver. The risks then of imparting knowledge to the young were great. School teaching now in the mines is, I imagine, a tame affair compared with that past, so full of golden dreams and leaden realities.

If I could have taken that portion of my scholars who were beyond the A, B, C business to a shady grove of live oaks near by and talked to them for an hour or two a day, devoting each day to some special subject, at the same time encouraging questions from them, I believe I could have woke up more that was sleeping in their minds in a week than I did in a month by the cut-and-dried system I was obliged to follow. I would have taken them out of sight of the school-house, the desks and all thereunto appertaining, which to most children suggests a species of imprisonment. I think that amount of time and effort is enough in one day for both teacher and pupil. It would not be trifling work if one's heart was in it, short as the time employed may seem, because a teacher must teach himself to teach. Knowing a thing is not always being able to make it plain to others. The gifted dunderhead who tried to teach me to play whist commenced by saying: "Now that's a heart, and hearts is trumps, you know," and went on with the game, deeming he had made things clear enough for anybody.

Would not one topic to talk about be enough for one day? Take the motive power of steam the first day, the cause of rain the second, the flight of birds and their structure for flying the third, the making of soil and its removal from mountain to plain the fourth, a talk on coal or some other kind of mining the fifth, and so on. Would not subjects continually suggest themselves to the interested teacher? And if you do get one idea or suggestion per day in the scholar's mind, is not that a good day's work? How many of us wise, grown-up people can retire at night saying, "I have learned a new thing to-day?"

But I am theorizing. I have placed myself in the ranks of those disagreeable, meddlesome people who are never satisfied with present methods. So I will say that I do not imagine that my suggestions will revolutionize our educational system, based rather heavily on the idea that youth is the time, and the only time, to learn everything, and also to learn a great many things at a time. In after years, when we settle down to our work, we try, as a rule, to learn but one thing at a time. How would a man stagger along if it was required of him five days out of seven to learn a bit of painting, then of horseshoeing, then of printing, and top off with a slice of elocution? It seems to me like an overcrowding of the upper intellectual story.

CHAPTER XIX.

"JIMTOWN."

ON those hot July and August afternoons, when the air simmered all along the heated earth, and I was trying to keep awake in my seminary on the hill, and wrestling with the mercury at 100 deg. and my sixty polyglot pupils, the grown up "boys" would be tilted back in their chairs under the portico and against the cool brick wall of the Bella Union. They did not work, but they spun yarns. How half the boys lived was a mystery—as much a mystery, I do believe, to themselves as any one else. Some owned quartz claims, some horses, and all ran regularly for office. They belonged to the stamp of men who worked and mined in earlier times, but come what might, they had resolved to work in that way no longer. And when such resolve is accompanied by determination and an active, planning, inventive brain, the man gets along somehow. It is speculation that makes fortunes, and plan, calculation, and forethought for speculation, require leisure of body. A hard-working, ten-hour-per-day digging, delving miner works all his brains out through his fingers' ends. He has none left to speculate with. When I was mining at Swett's Bar, there came one day to my cabin a long, lean, lank man looking for a lost cow. The cow and the man belonged near Jacksonville, twelve miles up the Tuolumne. I dined that man principally off some bread of my own making, and I had the name then of making the best bread of any one in the house, where I lived alone. After dinner the man sat himself down on one boulder and I on another, and I asked him if he had a good claim. That roused him to wrath. He had, it seems, just reached the last point of his disgust for hard work and mining. Said he: "Don't talk to me of a good claim; don't. It sounds like speaking of a good guillotine, or a beautiful halter, or an elegant rack you're about to be stretched on." He had gone through his probation of hard work with his hands and had just resolved to let them rest and give his head a chance to speculate. So he did. I don't know that he ever met the cow again, but eight or nine years after I met him in the Legislature of California. He sat in the biggest chair there, and was Lieutenant-Governor of the State.

In 1860 the certain class of men of whom I speak were in a transition state. They had left off working with their hands and they were waiting for something to turn up on which to commence working with their heads. While thus waiting they became boys and played. The climate and surroundings were eminently favorable to this languid, loafing condition of existence, no long, sharp winters forcing people to bestir themselves and provide against its severities; little style to keep up; few families to maintain; no disgrace for a man to cook his own victuals; houses dropping to pieces; little new paint anywhere to make one's eyes smart; gates dropping from their hinges; few municipal improvements, with accompanying heavy taxes, and that bright summer sun for months and months shining over all and tempting everybody to be permanently tired and seek the shade. The boys forgot their years; they dreamed away their days; they gossiped all the cool night; they shook off dignity; they played; they built waterwheels in the ditch running by the Bella Union door; they instituted ridiculous fictions and converted them into realities; they instituted a company for the importation of smoke in pound packages into Jamestown; Muldoon was President and the "Doctor" Secretary. It was brought by a steamer up Wood's Creek; the steamer was wrecked on a dam a mile below town; the company met day after day in old Nielsen's saloon to consult; the smoke was finally taken to Jamestown and sold; the proceeds were stored in sacks at the express office; there was an embezzlement consequent on the settlement; the money, all in ten-cent pieces, was finally deposited in the big wooden mortar over Baker's drug store; this the "Doctor" was accused of embezzling, having time after time climbed up the mortar and abstracted the funds dime after dime and spent them for whiskey. Then came a lawsuit. Two mule teams freighted with lawyers for the plaintiff and defendant were coming from Stockton, and the Pound Package Smoke Company met day after day in preparation for the great trial. This fiction lasted about four months, and amused everybody except Captain James S——, an ex-Sheriff of the county, who, being a little deaf, and catching from time to time words of great financial import regarding the Pound Package Jamestown Smoke Company, as they dropped from Muldoon's and the "Doctor's" mouths, and being thereby time after time misled into a temporary belief that this fiction was a reality, and so often becoming irritated at finding himself ridiculously mistaken, burst out upon these two worthies one day with all the wrath becoming the dignity of a Virginia gentleman, and denounced them profanely and otherwise for their frivolity and puerility.

Another specimen thinker and speculator of that era was Carroll. He, too, had forever thrown aside pick and shovel, and when I met him he was a confirmed "tilter-back" under the Bella Union portico. Carroll was the theorist of Jamestown. He broached new ones daily; he talked them to everybody in Jamestown, and after making clean work of that hamlet would go up to Sonora and talk there, and lastly published them in the *Union Democrat*. Said Carroll one Monday morning to the Presbyterian domine: "Mr. H——, I heard your sermon yesterday on 'Heaven.' You argue, I think, that heaven is really a place. I think it ought to be a place, too. I've been thinking about it all night. I'm satisfied not only that it is a place, but that I've got at the locality, or at least have approximated to it. I've reasoned this out on purely scientific data, and here they are. We have an atmosphere, and they say it is from thirty-three to forty-five miles high. Angels only live in heaven, and angels have wings. If angels have wings, it's proof that they must have an atmosphere to fly in. Now, the only atmosphere we are sure of is that around the earth. Therefore, putting all these facts and conclusions together, I've proved to myself that heaven must be from thirty-three to forty-five miles from the ground we stand on."

On commencing my pedagogical career, I rented a room of Carroll. He owned at that time a quantity of real estate in Jamestown, some of which, including the premises I occupied, was falling rapidly and literally on his hands. The house I lived in was propped up several feet from the ground. The neighbors' chickens fed under this house from the crumbs swept through the cracks in the floor. It was an easy house to sweep clean. Rumor said that during my landlord's occupancy of these rooms many chickens had strangely disappeared, and that pistol shots had been heard from the interior of the house. The floor cracks did show powder marks, and there was an unaccountable quantity of feathers blowing about the yard. In a conversation with my landlord he admitted that his boomerang could beat a six-shooter in fetching a chicken. Then he showed me his boomerang, which was of accidental construction, being the only remaining leg and round of an oaken arm-chair. Properly shied, he said, it would kill a chicken at twenty yards. French Joe, who kept the grocery next to Keefe's saloon, and it was in Jimtown a current report that Carroll and Joe had once invited the Catholic priest, Father A———, from Sonora to dinner; that the backbone of this dinner was a duck; that at or about this time Mrs. Hale, five doors down the street, had missed one of her flock of ducks; that on the morning of the dinner in question a strong savor of parboiling duck permeated all that part of Jamestown lying between Joe's and Mrs. Hale's; that Mrs. Hale smelt it; that putting two and two—cause and effect and her own suspicions—together, she armed herself with her bun-tormentor fork and going from her back yard to the little outdoor kitchen in Joe's back yard found a pot over a fire and her presumed duck parboiling in it; and that, transfixing this duck on her tormentor, she bore it home, and the priest got no duck for dinner.

Carroll's mortal aversion was the hog. His favorite occupation for ten days in the early spring was gardening, and his front fence was illy secured against hogs, for Carroll, though a man of much speculative enterprise, was not one whose hands always seconded the work of his head. There was not a completed thing on his premises, including a well which he had dug to the depth of twelve feet and which he had then abandoned forever. The hogs would break through his fence and root up his roses, and the well caving in about the edges became a yawning gulf in his garden, and during the rainy season it partly filled up with water, and a hog fell in one night and, to Carroll's joy, was drowned.

Men did their best in the dead of a rainy night to get the poor animal out, but a hog is not a being possessed of any capacity for seconding or furthering human attempts at his own rescue. So he drowned, and was found the morning after a grand New Year's ball at the Bella Union Hall hanging by Joyce's clothes-line over the middle of the street between the Bella Union and the Magnolia. The next night they put him secretly in the cart of a fish-peddler who had come up with salmon from the lower San Joaquin, and this man unwittingly hauled the hog out of town.

About four weeks after this transaction, coming home one dark, rainy night, I heard a great splashing in the well, and called out to Carroll that he had probably caught another hog. He came out with a lantern and both of us peering over the brink of the cavity saw, not as we expected, a hog, but a man, a friend of Carroll's, up to his chest in the water. He was a miner from Campo Seco, who, on visiting Jimtown on one of his three months periodical sprees, had called on Carroll, and on leaving had mistaken the route to the gate and walked into the well. We fished him out with much difficulty, and on gaining the brink he came near precipitating us and himself into the unfinished chasm through the unsteadiness of his perpendicular. As we turned to leave, looking down the well by the lantern's flash I saw what appeared to be another man half floating on the surface. There was a coat and at the end of it a hat, and I remarked, "Carroll, there is another man down your well." The rescued miner looked down also, and chattered as he shivered with cold, "Why, s-s-so there is!" We were really horrified until we discovered the supposed corpse to be only Lewellyn's coat with his hat floating at the end of it, which he had taken off in his endeavor to clamber out.

Carroll, unfortunately, allowed his mind to wander and stray overmuch in the maze of theological mysteries and its (to him) apparent contradictions. He instituted a private and personal quarrel between himself and his Creator, and for years he obtruded his quarrel into all manner of places and assemblages. He arrived at last at that point where many do under similar circumstances—a belief in total annihilation after death, and this serving to make him more miserable than ever, his only relief was to convert others to the same opinion and make them as wretched as himself. Occasionally he succeeded. He came to me one day and on his face was the grin of a fiend. "I've got Cummings," said he. "Cummings thought this morning he was a good Methodist, but I've been laboring with him for weeks. I've convinced him of the falsity of it all. I knocked his last plank of faith from under him to-day. He hasn't now a straw to cling to, and he's as miserable as I am."

"But with Mullins," he remarked afterward, "I've slipped up on him. I wrought three weeks with Mullins; took him through the Bible, step by step—unconverted him steadily as we went along—got him down to the last leaf in the last chapter of the last book of Revelations, and there, fool like, I let up on him to go home to supper. And do you know when I tackled him next morning, to close out Mullins' faith in the religion of his fathers, I found Mullins, in my absence, had got scared. He'd galloped in belief way back to Genesis, and now, I've got all that job to do over again."

There was a great deal of life in those little mining camps in Tuolumne County like Jamestown. They might not have the population of a single block in New York City, but there was a far greater average of mental activity, quickness, and intelligence to the man, at least so far as getting the spice out of life was concerned.

The social life of a great city may be much more monotonous through that solitude imposed by great numbers living together. Everybody at these camps knew us, and we knew everybody, and were pretty sure of meeting everybody we knew. In the town one is not sure of meeting an acquaintance socially, save by appointment. There are few loafing or lounging resorts; people meet in a hurry and part in a hurry. Here in New York I cross night and morning on a ferry with five hundred people, and of these 495 do not speak or know each other.

Four hundred of these people will sit and stare at each other for half an hour, and all the time wish they could talk with some one. And many of these people are so meeting, so crossing, so staring, and so longing to talk year in and year out. There is no doctor's shop where the impromptu symposium meets daily in the back room, as ours did at Doc Lampson's in Montezuma, or Baker's in Jamestown, or Dr. Walker's in Sonora. There's no reception every evening at the Camp grocery as there used to be at "Bill Brown's" in Montezuma. There's no lawyer's office, when he feels privileged to drop in as we did at Judge Preston's in Jamestown, or Judge Quint's in Sonora. There's no printing office and editorial room all in one on the ground floor whereinto the "Camp Senate," lawyer, Judge, doctor, merchant and other citizens may daily repair in the summer's twilight, tilted back in the old hacked arm chairs on the front portico, and discuss the situation as we used to with A. N. Francisco of the *Union Democrat* in Sonora, and as I presume the relics of antiquity and "'49" do at that same office to-day. These are a few of the features which made "Camp" attractive. These furnished the social anticipations which lightened our footsteps over those miles of mountain, gulch, and flat. Miles are nothing, distance is nothing, houses a mile apart and "Camps" five miles apart are nothing when people you know and like live in those camps and houses at the end of those miles. An evening at the Bella Union saloon in "Jimtown" was a circus. Because men of individuality, character, and originality met there. They had something to say. Many of them had little to do, and, perhaps, for that very reason their minds the quicker took note of so many of those little peculiarities of human nature, which when told, or hinted, or suggested prove the sauce piquant to conversation.

When Brown, the lawyer, was studying French and read his Telemaque aloud by his open office window in such a stentorian voice as to be heard over a third of the "camp," and with never a Frenchman at hand to correct his pronunciation, which he manufactured to suit himself as he went along, it was a part of the Bella Union circus to hear "Yank" imitate him. When old Broche, the long, thin, bald-headed French baker, who never would learn one word of English, put on his swallow-tailed Sunday coat, which he had brought over from La Belle France, and lifted up those coat tails when he tripped over the mud-puddles as a lady would her skirts, it was a part of the Bella Union circus to see "Scotty" mimic him. When John S——, the Virginian, impressively and loudly swore that a Jack-rabbit he had killed that day leaped twenty-five feet in the air on being shot, and would then look around the room as if he longed to find somebody who dared dispute his assertion, while his elder brother, always at his elbow in supporting distance, also glared into the eyes of the company, as though he also longed to fight the somebody who should dare discredit "Brother John's" "whopper," it was a part of the circus to see the "boys" wink at each other when they had a chance. When one heard and saw so many of every other man's peculiarities, oddities, and mannerisms, save his own, set off and illustrated while the man was absent, and knew also that his own, under like circumstances, had been or would be brought out on exhibition, it made him feel that it was somewhat dangerous to feel safe on the slim and slippery ice of self-satisfaction and self-conceit. People in great cities haven't so much time to make their own fun and amusement, as did the residents of so many of those lazy, lounging, tumbling-down, ramshackle "camps" of the era of "1863" or thereabouts.

People in the city have more of their fun manufactured for them at the theatres of high and low degree. Yet it was wonderful how in "camp" they managed to dig so many choice bits and specimens out of the vein of varied human nature which lay so near them. Whenever I visited "Jimtown" my old friend Dixon would take me into his private corner to tell me "the last" concerning a character who was working hard on an unabridged copy of Webster's Dictionary in the endeavor to make amends for a woeful lack of grammatical knowledge, the result of a neglected education. "He's running now on two words," Dixon would say, "and these are 'perseverance' and 'assiduity.' We hear them forty times a day, for he lugs them in at every possible opportunity, and, indeed, at times when there is no opportunity. He came to business the other morning a little unwell, and alluded to his stomach as being 'in a chaotic state.' And, sir, he can spell the word 'particularly' with six i's. How he does it I can't tell; but he can."

CHAPTER XX.

THE ROMANCE OF AH SAM AND HI SING.

THE culminating events of the following tale occurred in "Jimtown" during my pedagogical career, and I was an indefatigable assistant in the details as below stated.

Ah Sam loved Miss Hi Sing. Ah Sam was by profession a cook in a California miners' boarding house and trading post combined, at a little mining camp on the Tuolumne River. Following minutely the culinary teachings of his employer, having no conception of cooking, save as a mere mechanical operation—dead to the pernicious mental and physical effect which his ill-dressed dishes might have on the minds and stomachs of those he served—Ah Sam, while dreaming of Hi Sing, fried tough beef still tougher in hot lard, poisoned flour with saleratus, and boiled potatoes to the last extreme of soddenness, all of which culinary outrages promoted indigestion among those who ate; and this indigestion fomented a general irritability of temper—from whence Swett's Camp became noted for its frequent sanguinary moods, its battles by midnight in street and bar-room, with knife and six-shooter, and, above all, for its burying ground, of which the inhabitants truthfully boasted that not an inmate had died a natural death.

Hi Sing was the handmaid of old Ching Loo. Her face was broad, her nose flat, her girth extensive, her gait a waddle, her attire a blue sacque reaching from neck to knee, blue trousers, brass rings on wrist and ankle, and wooden shoes, whose clattering heels betrayed their owner's presence, even as the shaken tail of the angry rattlesnake doth his unpleasant proximity. She had no education, no manners, no accomplishments, no beauty, no grace, no religion, no morality; and for this and more Ah Sam loved her. Hi Sing was virtually a slave, having several years previously, with many other fair and fragile sisters, been imported to California by Ching Loo; and not until meeting Ah Sam did she learn that it was her right and privilege in this land of occasional laws and universal liberty to set up for herself, become her own mistress and marry and unmarry whenever opportunity offered.

But Ching Loo had noticed, with a suspicious eye, the growing intimacy between Ah Sam and Hi Sing; and arguing therefrom results unprofitable to himself, he contrived one night to have the damsel packed off to another town, which happened at that time to be my place of residence; and it is for this reason that the woof of my existence temporarily crossed that of Ah Sam and Hi Sing.

Ah Sam following up his love, and discovering in me an old friend, who had endured and survived a whole winter of his cookery at Swett's Bar, told me his troubles; and I, resolving to repay evil with good, communicated the distressed Mongolian's story to my chosen and particular companion, a lean and cadaverous attorney, with whom fees had ceased to be angels' visits, and who was then oscillating and hovering between two plans—one to run for the next State Legislature; the other to migrate to Central America, and found a new republic. Attorney, Spoke on hearing Ah Sam's case, offered to find the maid, rescue her from her captors, and marry her to him permanently and forever in consideration of thirty American dollars; to which terms the Mongolian assenting, Spoke and myself, buckling on our arms and armor, proceeded to beat up the filthy purlieus of "Chinatown;" and about midnight we found the passive Hi Sing hidden away in a hen-coop, whither she had been conveyed by the confederates of Ching Loo.

We bore Hi Sing—who was considerably alarmed, neither understanding our language nor our purpose—to Spoke's office, and then it being necessary to secure the services of a magistrate in uniting the couple, I departed to seek the Justice of the Peace, who was still awake—for Justice rarely slept in camp at that hour, but was commonly engaged at the Bella Union playing poker, whilst Spoke sought after the groom, Ah Sam, whom he found in a Chinese den stupidly drunk from smoking opium, having taken such means to wear the edge off his suspense while we were rescuing his affianced. Not only was he stupidly but perversely drunk; but he declared in imperfect English that he had concluded not to marry that night, to which observation Attorney Spoke, becoming profane, jerked him from the cot whereon he lay, and grasping him about the neck with a strangulating hold, bore him into the street and toward his office, intimating loudly that this business had been proceeded with too far to be receded from, and that the marriage must be consummated that night with or without the consent of the principals. Ah Sam resigned himself to matrimony. The office was reached, the door opened and out in the darkness bolted the bride, for she knew not what these preparations meant, or whether she had fallen among friends or enemies. After a lively chase we cornered and caught her; and having thus at last brought this refractory couple together we placed them in position, and the Justice commenced the ceremony by asking Hi Sing if she took that man for her lawful wedded husband, which interrogatory being Chaldaic to her, she replied only by an unmeaning and unspeculative stare. Spoke, who seemed destined to be the soul and mainspring of this whole affair, now threw light on the Mongolian intellect by bringing into play his stock of Chinese English, and translating to her the language of the Justice thus: "You like 'um he, pretty good?" Upon which her face brightened, and she nodded assent. Then turning to the groom, he called in a tone fierce and threatening, "You like 'um she?" and Ah Sam—who was now only a passive object in the hands of Spoke, forced and galvanized into matrimony—dared not do otherwise than give in his adhesion, upon which the Justice pronounced them man and wife; whereupon two Virginians present with their violins (all Virginians fiddle and shoot well) struck up the "Arkansas Traveller;" and the audience—which was now large, every bar-room in Jamestown having emptied itself to witness our Chinese wedding—inspired by one common impulse, arose and marched seven times about the couple. Ah Sam was now informed that he was married "American fashion," and that he was free to depart with his wedded encumbrance. But Ah Sam, whose intoxication had broken out in full acquiescence with these proceedings, now insisted on making a midnight tour of all the saloons in camp, and treating everybody to the deathly whiskey vended by them, to which the crowd—who never objected to the driving of this sort of nails in their own coffins—assented, and the result of it was (Ah Sam spending his money very freely) that when daylight peeped over the eastern hills the Bella Union saloon was still in full blast; and while the Justice of the Peace was winning Spoke's thirty hard-earned dollars in one corner, and the two Virginians still kept the "Arkansas Traveller" going on their violins in another, Stephen Scott (afterward elected to Congress) was weeping profusely over the bar, and on being interrogated as to the cause of his sadness by General Wyatt, ex-member of the State Senate, Scott replied that he could never hear played the air of "Home, Sweet Home" without shedding tears.

Ah Sam departed with his bride in the morning, and never were a man's prospects brighter for a happy honeymoon until the succeeding night, when he was waylaid by a band of disguised white men in the temporary service and pay of old Ching Loo; and he and Hi Sing were forced so far apart that they never saw each other again.

Ah Sam returned to the attorney, apparently deeming that some help might be obtained in that quarter; but Spoke intimated that he could no longer assist him, since it was every man's special and particular mission to keep his own wife after being married; although he added, for Ah Sam's comfort, that this was not such an easy matter for the Americans themselves, especially in California.

Upon this Ah Sam apparently determined to be satisfied with his brief and turbulent career in matrimony; and betaking himself again to Swett's Bar cooked in such a villainous fashion and desperate vigor, finding thereby a balm for an aching heart, that in a twelvemonth several stalwart miners gave up their ghosts through indigestion, and the little graveyard on the red hill thereby lost forever its distinctive character of affording a final resting place only to those who had died violent deaths.

CHAPTER XXI.

ON A JURY.

YEAR after year, and term after term, the great case of Table Mountain Tunnel vs. New York Tunnel, used to be called in the Court held at Sonora, Tuolumne County. The opposing claims were on opposite sides of the great mountain wall, which here described a semicircle. When these two claims were taken up, it was supposed the pay streak followed the Mountain's course; but it had here taken a freak to shoot straight across a flat formed by the curve. Into this ground, at first deemed worthless, both parties were tunnelling. The farther they tunnelled, the richer grew the pay streak. Every foot was worth a fortune. Both claimed it. The law was called upon to settle the difficulty. The law was glad, for it had then many children in the county who needed fees. Our lawyers ran their tunnels into both of these rich claims, nor did they stop boring until they had exhausted the cream of that pay streak. Year after year, Table Mountain vs. New York Tunnel Company was tried, judgment rendered first for one side and then for the other, then appealed to the Supreme Court, sent back, and tried over, until, at last, it had become so encumbered with legal barnacles, parasites, and cobwebs, that none other than the lawyers knew or pretended to know aught of the rights of the matter. Meantime, the two rival companies kept hard at work, day and night. Every ounce over the necessary expense of working their claims and feeding and clothing their bodies, went to maintain lawyers. The case became one of the institutions of the county. It outlived several judges and attorneys. It grew plethoric with affidavits and other documentary evidence. Men died, and with their last breath left some word still further to confuse the great Table Mountain vs. New York Tunnel case. The county town throve during this yearly trial. Each side brought a small army of witnesses, who could swear and fill up any and every gap in their respective chains of evidence. It involved the history, also, of all the mining laws made since "'49." Eventually, jurors competent to try this case became very scarce. Nearly every one had "sat on it," or had read or heard or formed an opinion concerning it, or said they had. The Sheriff and his deputies ransacked the hills and gulches of Tuolumne for new Table Mountain vs. New York Tunnel jurors. At last, buried in an out-of-the-way gulch, they found me. I was presented with a paper commanding my appearance at the county town, with various pains and penalties affixed, in case of refusal. I obeyed. I had never before formed the twelfth of a jury. In my own estimation, I rated only as the twenty-fourth. We were sworn in: sworn to try the case to the best of our ability; it was ridiculous that I should swear to this, for internally I owned I had no ability at all as a juror. We were put in twelve arm-chairs. The great case was called. The lawyers, as usual, on either side, opened by declaring their intentions to prove themselves all right and their opponents all wrong. I did not know which was the plaintiff, which the defendant. Twenty-four witnesses on one side swore to something, to anything, to everything; thirty-six on the other swore it all down again. They thus swore against each other for two days and a half. The Court was noted for being an eternal sitter. He sat fourteen hours per day. The trial lasted five days. Opposing counsel, rival claimants, even witnesses, all had maps, long, brilliant, parti-colored maps of their claims, which they unrolled and held before us and swung defiantly at each other. The sixty witnesses testified from 1849 up to 1864. After days of such testimony, as to ancient boundary lines and ancient mining laws, the lawyers on either side, still more to mystify the case, caucused the matter over and concluded to throw out about half of such testimony as being irrelevant. But they could not throw it out of our memories. The "summing up" lasted two days more. By this time, I was a mere idiot in the matter. I had, at the start, endeavored to keep some track of the evidence, but they managed to snatch every clue away as fast as one got hold of it. We were "charged" by the judge and sent to the jury room. I felt like both a fool and a criminal. I knew I had not the shadow of an opinion or a conclusion in the matter. However, I found myself not alone. We were out all night. There was a stormy time between the three or four jurymen who knew or pretended to know something of the matter. The rest of us watched the controversy, and, of course, sided with the majority. And, at last, a verdict was agreed upon. It has made so little impression on my mind that I forget now whom it favored. It did not matter. Both claims were then paying well, and this was a sure indication that the case would go to the Supreme Court. It did. This was in 1860. I think it made these yearly trips up to 1867. Then some of the more obstinate and combative members of either claim died, and the remainder concluded to keep some of the gold they were digging instead of paying it out to fee lawyers. The Table Mountain vs. New York Tunnel case stopped. All the lawyers, save two or three, emigrated to San Francisco or went to Congress. I gained but one thing from my experience in the matter—an opinion. It may or may not be right. It is that juries in most cases are humbugs.

CHAPTER XXII.

SOME CULINARY REMINISCENCES.

I LIVED once with an unbalanced cook. Culinarily he was not self-poised. He lacked judgment. He was always taking too large cooking contracts. He was for a time my partner. He was a lover of good living and willing to work hard for it over a cook stove. He would for a single Sunday's dinner plan more dishes than his mind could eventually grasp or his hands handle. And when he had exhausted the whole of the limited gastronomical repertoire within our reach he would be suddenly inspired with a troublesome propensity to add hash to the programme. In cooking, as I have said, he lost his balance. His imagination pictured more possibilities than his body had strength to carry out. So busied in getting up a varied meal, he would in a few minutes' leisure attempt to shave himself or sew on shirt or pantaloon buttons. This put too many irons in the fire. A man who attempts to shave while a pot is boiling over or a roast requiring careful watching is in the oven, will neither shave nor cook well. He will be apt to leave lather where it is not desirable, as he sometimes did. Trousers-buttons are not good in soup. I do not like to see a wet shaving brush near a roast ready to go into the oven. The æsthetic taste repudiates these hints at combination. Then sometimes, in the very crisis of a meal, he became flurried. He rushed about in haste overmuch, with a big spoon in one hand and a giant fork in the other, looking for missing stove-covers and pot-lids, seldom found until the next day, and then in strange places. Nothing is well done which is done in a hurry, especially cooking. Some argue that men and women put their magnetic and sympathetic influences in the food they prepare. If a man kneading bread be in a bad temper he puts bad temper in the bread, and that bad temper goes into the person who eats it. Or if he be dyspeptic he kneads dyspepsia in his dough. It is awful to think what we may be eating. I think the unbalanced cook puts flurries in his stews, for I felt sometimes as if trying to digest a whirlwind after eating this man's dinners. He ruled the house. I was his assistant. I was his victim. I was the slave of the spit, and the peon of the frying-pan. When his energies culminated and settled on hash, when already the stove-top was full of dishes in preparation, I was selected as the proper person to chop the necessary ingredients. We had neither chopping-knife nor tray. The mining stores then did not contain such luxuries. This to him made no difference. He was a man who rose superior to obstacles, circumstances, and chopping trays. He said that hash could be chopped with a hatchet on a flat board.

He planned; I executed. He theorized and invented; I put his inventions in practice. But never successfully could I chop a mass of beef and boiled potatoes with a hatchet on a flat board. The ingredients during the operation would expand and fall over the edge of the board. Or the finer particles would violently fly off at each cut of the hatchet, and lodge on the beds or other unseemly places.

I do not favor a dinner of many courses, especially if it falls to my lot to prepare these courses. Few cooks enjoy their own dinners. For two reasons: First—They eat them in anticipation. This nullifies the flavor of the reality. Second—The labor of preparation fatigues the body and takes the keen edge from the appetite. You are heated, flushed, exhausted, and the nerves in a twitter. The expected relish palls and proves a myth. Ladies who cook will corroborate my testimony on this point. It is a great, merciful and useful vent for a woman that a man can come forward able and willing to sympathize with her in regard to this and other trials of domestic life. Having kept my own house for years I know whereof I speak. Two hours' work about a hot stove exhausts more than four hours' work out of doors. Americans in Europe are shocked or pretend to be at sight of women doing men's work in the fields. They are much better off than the American woman, five-sixths of whose life is spent in the kitchen. The outdoor woman shows some blood through the tan on her cheeks. The American kitchen housewife is sallow and bleached out. I have in Vienna seen women mixing mortar and carrying bricks to the sixth story of an unfinished house, and laying bricks, too. These women were bare-legged to the knee, and their arms and legs were muscular. They mixed their mortar with an energy suggestive of fearful consequences to an ordinary man of sedentary occupations. They could with ease have taken such a man and mixed him with their mortar. Coarse, were they? Yes, of course they were. But if I am to choose between a coarse woman, physically speaking, and one hot-housed and enervated to that extent that she cannot walk half a mile in the open air, but requires to be hauled, I choose the coarse-grained fibre.

I once lived near a literary cook. It was to him by a sort of natural heritage that fell the keeping of the Hawkins Bar Library, purchased by the "boys" way back in the A.D. eighteen hundred and fifties. The library occupied two sides of a very small cabin, and the man who kept it lived on or near the other two sides. There, during nights and rainy days, he read and ate. His table, a mere flap or shelf projecting from the wall, was two-thirds covered with books and papers, and the other third with a never-cleared-off array of table furniture, to wit: A tin plate, knife, fork, tin cup, yeast-powder can, pepper-box, ditto full of sugar, ditto full of salt, a butter-plate, a bottle of vinegar and another of molasses, and may be, on occasions, one of whiskey. On every book and paper were more or less of the imprint of greasy fingers, or streaks of molasses. The plate, owing to the almost entire absence of the cleansing process, was even imbedded in a brownish, unctuous deposit, the congealed oleaginous overflow of months of meals. There he devoured beef and lard, bacon and beans and encyclopedias, Humboldt's "Cosmos" and dried apples, novels and physical nourishment at one and the same time. He went long since where the weary cease from troubling, and the wicked, let us hope, are at rest. Years ago, passing through the deserted Bar, I peeped in at Morgan's cabin. A young oak almost barred the door, part of the roof was gone, the books and shelves had vanished; naught remained but the old miner's stove and a few battered cooking utensils. I had some thought at the time of camping for the night on the Bar, but this desolate cabin and its associations of former days contrasted with the loneliness and solitude of the present proved too much for me. I feared the possible ghost of the dead librarian, and left for a populated camp. Poor fellow! While living, dyspepsia and he were in close embrace. A long course of combined reading and eating ruined his digestion. One thing at a time; what a man does he wants to do with all his might.

Eggs in the early days were great luxuries. Eggs then filled the place of oysters. A dish of ham and eggs was one of the brilliant anticipations of the miner resident in some lonesome gulch when footing it to the nearest large camp. A few enterprising and luxurious miners kept hens and raised chickens. The coons, coyotes, and foxes were inclined to "raise" those chickens too. There was one character on Hawkins Bar whose coop was large and well stocked. Eggs were regularly on his breakfast-table, and he was the envy of many. Generous in disposition, oft he made holiday presents of eggs to his friends. Such a gift was equivalent to that of a turkey in older communities. One foe to this gentleman's peace and the security of his chickens alone existed. That foe was whiskey. For whenever elevated and cheered by the cup which does inebriate, he would in the excess of his royal nature call his friends about him, even after midnight, and slay and eat his tenderest chickens. Almost so certain as Kip got on a spree there came a feast and consequent midnight depletion of his chicken-coop—a depletion that was mourned over in vain when soberer and wiser counsels prevailed. The pioneer beefsteaks of California were in most cases cut from bulls which had fought bull-fights all the way up from Mexico. Firm in fibre as they were, they were generally made firmer still by being fried in lard. The meat was brought to the table in a dish covered with the dripping in which it had hardened. To a certain extent the ferocity and combativeness of human nature peculiar to the days of "'49" were owing to obstacles thrown in the way of easy digestion by bull beef fried to leather in lard. Bad bread and bull beef did it. The powers of the human system were taxed to the uttermost to assimilate these articles. The assimilation of the raw material into bone, blood, nerve, muscle, sinew and brain was necessarily imperfect. Bad whiskey was then called upon for relief. This completed the ruin. Of course men would murder each other with such warring elements inside of them.

The ideas of our pioneer cooks and housekeepers regarding quantities, kinds, and qualities of provisions necessary to be procured for longer or shorter periods, were at first vague. There was an Argonaut who resided at Truetts' Bar, and, in the fall of 1850, warned by the dollar a pound for flour experience of the past winter, he resolved to lay in a few months' provisions. He was a lucky miner. Were there now existing on that bar any pioneers who lived there in '49, they would tell you how he kept a barrel of whiskey in his tent on free tap. Such men are scarce and win name and fame. Said he to the Bar trader when the November clouds began to signal the coming rains, "I want to lay in three months' provisions." "Well, make out your order," said the storekeeper. This troubled G——. At length he gave it verbally thus: "I guess I'll have two sacks of flour, a side of bacon, ten pounds of sugar, two pounds of coffee, a pound of tea, and—and—a barrel of whiskey."

My own experience taught me some things unconsidered before. Once, while housekeeping, I bought an entire sack of rice. I had no idea then of the elastic and durable properties of rice. A sack looked small. The rice surprised me by its elasticity when put on to boil. Rice swells amazingly. My first pot swelled up, forced off the lid and oozed over. Then I shoveled rice by the big spoonful into everything empty which I could find in the cabin. Still it swelled and oozed. Even the washbasin was full of half-boiled rice. Still it kept on. I saw then that I had put in too much—far too much. The next time I tried half the quantity. That swelled, boiled up, boiled over and also oozed. I never saw such a remarkable grain. The third time I put far less to cook. Even then it arose and filled the pot. The seeds looked minute and harmless enough before being soaked. At last I became disgusted with rice. I looked at the sack. There was the merest excavation made in it by the quantity taken out. This alarmed me. With my gradually decreasing appetite for rice, I reflected and calculated that it would take seven years on that Bar ere I could eat all the rice in that sack. I saw it in imagination all boiled at once and filling the entire cabin. This determined my resolution. I shouldered the sack, carried it back to the store and said: "See here! I want you to exchange this cereal for something that won't swell so in the cooking. I want to exchange it for something which I can eat up in a reasonable length of time."

The storekeeper was a kind and obliging man. He took it back. But the reputation, the sting of buying an entire sack of rice remained. The "boys" had "spotted" the transaction. The merchant had told them of it. I was reminded of that sack of rice years afterward.

CHAPTER XXIII.

THE COPPER FEVER.

IN 1862-63 a copper fever raged in California. A rich vein had been found in Stanislaus County. A "city" sprung up around it and was called Copperopolis. The city came and went inside of ten years. When first I visited Copperopolis, it contained 3,000 people. When I last saw the place, one hundred would cover its entire population.

But the copper fever raged in the beginning. Gold was temporarily thrown in the shade. Miners became speedily learned in surface copper indications. The talk far and wide was of copper "carbonates," oxides, "sulphurets," "gosson." Great was the demand for scientific works on copper. From many a miner's cabin was heard the clink of mortar and pestle pounding copper rock, preparatory to testing it. The pulverized rock placed in a solution of diluted nitric acid, a knife blade plunged therein and coming out coated with a precipitation of copper was exhibited triumphantly as a prognosticator of coming fortune from the newly found lead. The fever flew from one remote camp to another. A green verdigris stain on the rocks would set the neighborhood copper crazy. On the strength of that one "surface indication" claims would be staked out for miles, companies formed, shafts in flinty rock sunk and cities planned. Nitric acid came in great demand. It was upset. It yellowed our fingers, and burned holes in our clothes. But we loved it for what it might prove to us. A swarm of men learned in copper soon came from San Francisco. They told all about it, where the leads should commence, in what direction they should run, how they should "dip," what would be the character of the ore, and what it would yield. We, common miners, bowed to their superior knowledge. We worshipped them. We followed them. We watched their faces as they surveyed the ground wherein had been found a bit of sulphuret or a green stained ledge, to get at the secret of their superior right under ground. It took many months, even years for the knowledge slowly to filter through our brains that of these men nine-tenths had no practical knowledge of copper or any other mining. The normal calling of one of the most learned of them all, I found out afterward to be that of a music teacher. Old S——, the local geologist of Sonora, who had that peculiar universal genius for tinkering at anything and everything from a broken wheelbarrow to a clock and whose shop was a museum of stones, bones and minerals collected from the vicinity, "classified," and named, some correctly and some possibly otherwise, took immediately on himself the mantle of a copper prophet, and saw the whole land resting on a basis of rich copper ore. He advised in season and out of season, in his shop and in the street, that all men, and especially young men, betake themselves to copper mining. It was, he said, a sure thing. It needed only pluck, patience, and perseverance. "Sink," he said, "sink for copper. Sink shafts wherever indications are found. Sink deep. Don't be discouraged if the vein does not appear at twenty, thirty, sixty or an hundred feet."

And they did sink. For several years they sunk shafts all over our county and in many another counties. In remote gulches and cañons they sunk and blasted and lived on pork and beans week in and week out and remained all day underground, till the darkness bleached their faces. They sunk and sunk and saw seldom the faces of others of their kind, and no womankind at all. They lived coarsely, dressed coarsely, and no matter what they might have been, felt coarsely and in accordance, acted coarsely. They sunk time and money and years and even health and strength, and in nineteen cases out of twenty found nothing but barren rock or rock bearing just enough mineral not to pay.

I took the copper fever with the rest. In a few weeks I became an "expert" in copper. I found two veins on my former gold claim at Swett's Bar. I found veins everywhere. I really did imagine that I knew a great deal about copper-mining, and being an honest enthusiast was all the more dangerous. The banks of the Tuolumne became at last too limited as my field for copper exploration and discovery. I left for the more thickly populated portion of the county, where there being more people, there was liable to be more copper, and where the Halsey Claim was located. The "Halsey" was having its day then as the King claim of the county. It had really produced a few sacks of ore, which was more than any other Tuolumne copper claim had done, and on the strength of this, its value was for a few months pushed far up into high and airy realms of finance.

I told some of my acquaintances in Sonora that I could find the "continuation" of the Halsey lead. They "staked" me with a few dollars, in consideration of which I was to make them shareholders in whatever I might find. Then I went forth into the chapparal to "prospect." The Halsey claim lay about a mile east of Table Mountain near Montezuma, a mining camp then far in its decline. Table Mountain is one of the geological curiosities, if not wonders of Tuolumne and California. As a well-defined wall it is forty miles long. Through Tuolumne it is a veritable wall, from 250 to 600 feet in height, flat as a floor on the top. That top has an average width of 300 yards. The "table" is composed of what we miners call "lava." It is a honey-combed, metallic-looking rock, which on being struck with a sledge emits a sulphurous smell. The sides to the ungeological eye seem of a different kind of rock. But parts of the sides are not of rock at all—they are of gravel. On the eastern slope you may see from the old Sonora stage road two parallel lines, perhaps 200 feet apart, running along the mountain side. Mile after mile do these marks run, as level and exact as if laid there by the surveyor. Climb up to them and you find these lines enlarged to a sort of shelf or wave-washed and indented bank of hard cement, like gravel. You may crawl under and sit in the shade of an overhanging roof of gravel, apparently in some former age scooped out by the action of waves. Not only on the Table Mountain sides do you find these lines, but where Table Mountain merges into the plains about Knight's Ferry will you see these same water marks running around the many low conical hills.

A geological supposition. That's what water seems to have done outside of Table Mountain. Were I a geologist I should say that here had been a lake—maybe a great lake—which at some other time had suddenly from the first mark been drained down to the level of the second, and from that had drained off altogether. Perhaps there was a rise in the Sierra Nevada, and everything rising with it, the lake went up too suddenly on one side and so the waters went down on the other. Inside of Table Mountain there is an old river bed, smoothly washed by the currents of perhaps as many if not more centuries than any river now on earth has seen, and this forms a layer or core of gold-bearing gravel. In some places it has paid richly: in more places it has not paid at all.

I said to myself: "This Halsey lead, like all the leads of this section, runs northeast and southwest." (N. B.—Three years afterward we found there were no leads at all in that section.) "The Halsey lead must run under Table Mountain and come out somewhere on the other side." So I took the bearings of the Halsey lead, or what I then supposed were the bearings, for there wasn't any lead anyway, with a compass. I aimed my compass at a point on the ledge of the flat summit of Table Mountain. I hit it. Then I climbed up over the two water shelves or banks to that point. This was on the honey-combed lava crags. From these crags one could see afar north and south. South, over Tuolumne into Mariposa the eye following the great white quartz outcrop of the Mother or Mariposa lead. North was Bear Mountain, the Stanislaus River and Stanislaus County. This view always reminded me of the place where one very great and very bad historical personage of the past as well as the present showed another still greater and much better Being all the kingdoms of the earth. For the earth wasn't all laid out, pre-empted and fenced in those days, and its kingdoms were small. Then I ran my lines over the flat top of Table Mountain, southeast and northwest. So they said ran all the copper leads, commencing at Copperopolis. So then we believed, while tossing with the copper fever. Certainly they ran somewhere, and ran fast too, for we never caught any paying copper vein in Tuolumne County, at least any that paid—except to sell.

I aimed my compass down the other side of the mountain. There, when the perpendicular lava rock stopped pitching straight up and down, sometimes fifty, sometimes two hundred feet, was a dense growth of chaparral—the kind of chaparral we called "chemisal." I got into the chemisal. Here the compass was of no more use than would be a certificate of Copperhead copper stock to pay a board bill. It was a furry, prickly, blinding, bewildering, blundering, irritating growth, which sent a pang through a man's heart and a pricker into his skin at every step. At last, crawling down it on all-fours, for I could not walk, dirty, dusty, thirsty, and perspiring, I lit on a rock, an outcrop of ledge. It was gray and moss grown. It hid and guarded faithfully the treasure it concealed. Like Moses, I struck the rock with my little hatchet. The broken piece revealed underneath a rotten, sandy-like, spongy formation of crumbling, bluish, greenish hue. It was copper! I had struck it! I rained down more blows! Red oxides, green carbonates, gray and blue sulphurets! I had found the Copperhead lead! I was rich. I got upon that rock and danced! Not a graceful, but an enthusiastic *pas seul*. I deemed my fortune made. I was at last out of the wilderness! But I wasn't.

CHAPTER XXIV.

RISE AND FALL OF COPPERHEAD CITY.

I TRUDGED back nine miles to Sonora, my pockets full of "specimens" from the newly discovered claim, my head a cyclone of copper-hued air castles. I saw the "boys." I was mysterious. I beckoned them to retired spots. I showed them the ores. I told them of the find. They were wild with excitement. They were half crazed with delight. And in ten minutes some of them went just as far into the domains of unrest and unhappiness for fear some one might find and jump the claim ere I got back to guard it. The Copperhead Company was organized that night. The "Enthusiast," a man who lived in the very top loft of copper insanity, was sent down with me to superintend the sinking of the shaft. The secret was soon out. Shares in the vein were eagerly coveted. I sold a few feet for $500 and deemed I had conferred a great favor on the buyer in letting it go so cheaply. I lived up, way up, in tens of thousands and hundreds of thousands of dollars. The "company" in Sonora met almost every night to push things while the Enthusiast and myself blasted and burrowed in the rock. By day they exhausted their spare cash in horse hire, riding down to the claim in hope of being on hand when the next blast should reveal a bed of ore, immense in breadth and unfathomable in depth.

My Company was made up chiefly of lawyers, doctors, politicians, and editors. They never realized how much they were indebted to me. For four months I made them feel rich,—and if a man feels rich, what more should he want? For a millionaire can do no more than feel rich.

Feeling certain that the Copperhead was a very rich claim, and that other rich claims would be developed from the "extensions," and that a bustling town would be the result, I pre-empted a section of the land which I deemed most valuable, on which it was intended that "Copperhead City" should be built. This "city" I partly laid out. I think this was the third city I had laid out in California. There is a sepulchral and post-mortem suggestion in the term "laid out" which is peculiarly applicable to all the "cities" which I attempted to found, and which "cities" invariably foundered. Actuated, also, at that time, by those business principles so largely prevalent in most Christian communities, I "claimed" the only spring of good drinking water in the neighborhood of my "city." My intent in this was in time to realize a profit from the indirect sale of this water to such of the future "city's" population as might want water—not to sell it by the glass or gallon, of course; but if there was to be a "city" it would need water-works. The water-works would necessarily lie on my land. I would not be guilty of the inhumanity of selling water to parch-tongued people, but I proposed that the "city" should buy of me the ground out of which came the water.

But one house was ever erected in Copperhead City proper, and that had but one room. But three men ever lived in it. Yet the city was thickly populated. It was located in a regular jungle, so far as a jungle is ever attained in California, and seemed the head-centre and trysting-place of all the rattlesnakes, coons, skunks, owls, and foxes on the west side of Table Mountain. When the winter wore off and the warm California spring wore on and merged into the summer heat of May, and the pools made by the winter rains dried up, I think all the rattlesnakes and copperheads for miles around went for my pre-empted spring of pure water. The "city," I mean the house, was located within a few feet of the spring. Returning thither at noon for dinner, I have started half a dozen snakes from the purlieus and suburbs of that spring. Snakes get dry like human beings. Snakes love water. Snakes, poor things, can't get anything else to drink, and must fill up on water. These were sociable snakes. When startled at our approach they would not run away from our society. No. They preferred to remain in the "city," and so, in many instances they ran under the house. It is not pleasant at night to feel that you are sleeping over a veteran rattler four feet long, with a crown of glory on his tail in the shape of fourteen or fifteen rattles. You won't crawl under your house to evict such a rattlesnake, either. Skunks inhabited our "city," also. Skunks know their power—their peculiar power.

The evening gloaming seems the favorite time for the skunk to go abroad. He or she loves the twilight. There must be a vein of sentiment in these far-smelling creatures. I have in the early evening travelled up the only street our "city" ever laid out—a trail—and ahead of me on that trail I have seen a skunk. I was willing he should precede me. In the matter of rankness I was perfectly willing to fall a long way behind him. Now, if you have studied skunks you will know that it is far safer to remain in the skunk's rear than to get ahead of him, because when he attacks with his favorite aromatic means of offensive defence he projects himself forward (as it were). I have then, in my city, had a skunk keep the trail about fifty feet ahead of me at a pace which indicated little alarm at my presence, and, do my best, I could not frighten the animal, nor could I get ahead of him or her. If I ran he ran; if I walked he concurred in rapidity of pace. I dared not approach too near the animal. I would rather break in upon the "sacred divinity" which, they say, "doth hedge a king" than transgress the proper bounds to be observed with reference to a skunk. Let a king do his best, and he cannot punish an intruder as can a skunk.

The skunk is really a pretty creature. Its tail droops over its back, like the plumes of the Knight of Navarre. It is an object which can really be admired visually at a distance. Do not be allured by him to too near approach. "Beware! he's fooling thee!"

At last it dawned upon the collective mind of the Copperhead Company that their Superintendent, the Enthusiast, was digging too much and getting down too little. They accepted his resignation. It mattered little to him, for by this time his mind was overwhelmed by another stupendous mining scheme, to which the Copperhead was barely a priming. He had the happy talent of living in these golden visions which, to him, were perfect realities. He held the philosophy that the idea, the hope, the anticipation of a thing is sometimes more "the thing" than the thing itself. The Enthusiast's rich mines lay principally in his head, but his belief in them gave him as much pleasure as if they really existed. It was like marrying, sometimes. The long-sought-for, longed-for, wished-for wife, or husband, turns out, as a reality, a very different being from what he or she was deemed while in process of being longed and sought for. The long-longed-for may have been estimated an angel. The angel, after wedlock, may prove to have been a myth. The reality may be a devil, or within a few shades or degrees of a devil.

So the shaft was sunk, as they said, properly and scientifically, by the new Superintendent. The rock got harder as we went down, the ore less, the vein narrower, the quantity of water greater, the progress slower, the weekly expenses first doubled and then trebled, the stock became less coveted, and as to reputed value, reached that fatal dead level which really means that it is on its downward descent. The shareholders' faces became longer and longer at their weekly Sunday afternoon meetings in the Sonora Court-house.

The Copperhead Claim and Copperhead City subsided quietly. The shareholders became tired of mining for coin to pay assessments out of their own pockets. They came at last to doubt the ever-glowing hopeful assertion of the Enthusiast that from indications he knew the "ore was forming." The inevitable came. Copperhead City was deserted by its human inhabitants. The skunk, the snake, the squirrel, the woodpecker, and the buzzard came again into full possession, and I bitterly regretted that I had not sold more at ten dollars a foot when I found the stock a drug at ten cents.

CHAPTER XXV.

PROSPECTING.

THE failure of the Copperhead Claim and the collapse of Copperhead City did not discourage me. The flame only burned the brighter to go forth and unearth the veins of mineral wealth which imagination showed me lying far and near in this land still of such recent settlement.

This was in 1863-64. The great silver leads of Nevada had but recently been discovered. The silver excitement was at its height. People were thinking that barely the threshold of the mineral richness of the Pacific slope had been reached and that untold treasure underground awaited the prospector's exploration north, south, and east, so far as he could go.

Fired with this all-pervading thought I projected one of the grandest of my failures. I organized the "Mulford Mining, Prospecting, and Land Company," whose intent was to take up and hold all the mineral veins I found and secure all desirable locations I might come upon for farms, town sites, and other purposes.

"Holding" a mineral vein, or whatever I might imagine to be a mineral vein, could be done after the proper notices were put up, by performing on such veins one day's work a month, and such "day's work" was supposed to be done by turning up a few shovelfuls of dirt on the property.

My Company consisted of thirty members, who lived at varying distances apart, within and without the county of Tuolumne. For my services as general prospector, discoverer, and holder of all properties accumulated (by myself) I was to receive from each member three dollars per month.

I fixed this princely stipend myself, being then ever in fear that I should overcharge others for services rendered.

By dint of great exertion, I succeeded in getting one-third of the members together one hot summer afternoon in a Montezuma grocery. I unfolded then the Company's Constitution and By-Laws, written by myself at great length on several sheets of foolscap pasted together. I read the document. It provided for the Company a President, Secretary, Treasurer, and Board of Directors. It set forth their duties and my duties as "General

Prospector." I was particularly stringent and rigid regarding myself and my responsibilities to the Company.

The fragment of the new Company present assented to everything, paid in their first installment of three dollars, and bade me go forth and "strike something rich" as quickly as possible.

I went forth at first afoot with the few dollars paid me. I subsisted in a hap-hazard—indeed I must say beggarly fashion, stopping with mining friends and dependent to great extent on their hospitality, while I "held" the few claims I had already found and found others in their neighborhood.

At last I found a man who subscribed the use of a horse for the summer in consideration of being enrolled as a shareholder. On similar terms I gained a saddle, a shot-gun, a dog, and some provisions. This put the "Company" on a more stable footing, for I was now no longer dependent on house or hospitality, and could stop wherever night overtook me, and wood, water, and grass were at hand.

My horse I think was the slowest of his kind in the Great West, and my gun kicked so vigorously when discharged that I frequently sustained more injury than the game aimed at.

My field of operations extended over 150 miles of country, from the foot hills of the Sierras to their summits and beyond in the Territory of Nevada. Land, wood, water, grass, and game, if found, were free in every direction. The country was not fenced in, the meaning of "trespassing" on land was unknown—in fact it was then really a free country—a term also not altogether understood in the older States, where if you build a camp-fire in a wood lot you run some risk from the farmer who owns it, and his bulldog.

Sometimes, I would be a week or ten days without seeing a human face. A roof rarely covered me. I would camp one day near a mountain summit looking over fifty or sixty miles of territory and the next at its base with a view bounded by a wall of rock a few hundred yards distant. Sometimes I was very lonesome and uneasy at night in these mountain solitudes. I longed generally about sundown for some one to talk to. Anything human would answer such purpose then. In the bright clear morning the lonesome feeling was all gone. There was companionship then in the trees, the clouds, the mountain peaks, far and near, yet there were times when the veriest clod was better than all of these. Sometimes nothing but another human tongue will answer our needs, though it be a very poor one.

The first evening I spent alone in the forest, I left my dog "Put" to guard the camp. He wanted to follow me. I drove him back. He went back like a good dog and ate up most of my bacon which I had not hung high enough on the tree. By this experience I learned to hang my bacon higher. Wisdom must always be paid for.

I journeyed in the primeval forests of the Sierras. The primeval forest is dismal and inconvenient to travel through with fallen and rotten tree trunks interlacing each other in every direction. I have travelled half a day and found myself farther than ever from the place I wanted to reach. I have made at eve a comfortable camp under a great tree and when all arrangements were completed scrabbled out of it precipitately and packed my baggage elsewhere on looking up and seeing directly above me a huge dead limb hanging by a mere splinter, ready to fall at any moment and impale me. I think I know just how Damocles felt in that sword and hair business. Wolves sometimes frightened me at night exceedingly with their howlings. Bands of then unwarlike Indians also scared me. They were Utes fishing in the Walker River. Five years previous they had been hostile. Once I stumbled on one of their camps on the river bank. Before I could sneak off unseen one of them came up to me, announcing himself as the chief. He wanted to know who I was, where I came from, and where I was going. I answered all the questions this potentate asked me, acceded to his request for some "hoggadi" (tobacco), and when I found myself half a mile distant from His Majesty with a whole skin and all of my worldly goods intact, believed more firmly than ever in a kind and protecting Providence. I don't suppose I stood in any real danger, but a lone man in a lone country with an average of one white settler to every five square miles of territory won't naturally feel as easy in such circumstances as at his own breakfast table.

I learned never to pass a spot having wood, water, and grass after four o'clock in the afternoon, but make my camp for the night there. I learned on staking my horse out, not to give him pasture too near my camp-fire, for more than once in changing his base for a better mouthful of grass, has he dragged the lariat over my temporary possessions, upsetting coffee-pot and frying-pan and knocking the whole camp endways. I learned to camp away from the main road or trail leading over the mountains to Nevada, for it was beset by hungry, ragged men who had started afoot for the silver mines with barely a cent in their pockets, trusting to luck to get through, and who stumbling on my camp must be fed. You can't sit and eat in your own out-door kitchen and see your fellow-beings eye you in hunger. But they ate me at times out of house and home, and the provision laid in for a week would not last three days with such guests. An old Frenchman so found me one day at dinner. He was starved. I kept my fresh meat in a bag. I handed him the bag and told him to broil for himself over the coals. Then I hauled off in the bush a little while to look at some rock. When I returned the bag was empty; two pounds of beef were inside the Frenchman and he didn't seem at all abashed or uneasy. These experiences taught me that charity and sympathy for others must be kept under some government or our own meal bags, bread bags, and stomachs may go empty.

Grizzlies were common in those mountain solitudes, but I never saw one nor the track of one, nor even thought of them near as much as I would now, if poking about in the chaparral as I did then. I was camped near a sheep herder one evening, when, seeing my fire about a quarter of a mile from his cabin, he came to me and said, "Young man, this isn't a good place to stop in over night. You're right in the track of the grizzlies. They've killed twenty-six of my sheep inside of three weeks. You'd better sleep in my barn." I did so.

I learned never to broil a steak on a green pitch-pine branch till I got accustomed to the flavor of the turpentine which the heat would distil and the meat absorb.

I learned that when you have nothing for breakfast and must kill the only robin in sight or go without him, that robin will be ten times shyer and harder to coax within gunshot than when you don't hunger for him.

I was not strong physically, and indeed far from being a well man. It was only the strong desire of finding a fortune in a mineral vein, that gave me strength at all. Once I was sick for three days, camped near a mountain top, and though it was June, every day brought a snow squall. A prospector from Silver City stumbled on my camp one day and declared he would not stay in such a place for all the silver in Nevada. The wind blew from a different quarter about every hour, and no matter where I built my fire, managed matters so as always to drive the smoke in my face. It converted me for a time into a belief of the total depravity of inanimate things.

I pre-empted in the name of the Company some of the grandest scenery in the world—valleys seldom trodden by man, with clear mountain streams flowing through them—lakes, still unnamed, reflecting the mountain walls surrounding them a thousand or more feet in height, and beautiful miniature mountain parks. In pre-empting them their commercial value entered little into my calculations. Sentiment and the picturesque, did. Claimants stronger than I, had firmer possession of these gems of the Sierras. The chief was snow, under which they were buried to the depth of ten or fifteen feet, seven months at least out of the twelve.

When once a month I came out of the mountains and put in an appearance among my shareholders, my horse burdened with blankets, provisions, tools, the frying-pan and tin coffee-pot atop of the heap, I was generally greeted with the remark, "Well, struck anything yet?" When I told my patrons of the land sites I had gained for them so advantageous for summer pasturages, they did not seem to catch my enthusiasm. They wanted gold, bright yellow gold or silver, very rich and extending deep in the ground, more than they did these Occidental Vales of Cashmere, or Californian Lakes of Como. They were sordid and sensible. I was romantic and ragged. They were after what paid. I was after what pleased.

The monthly three-dollar assessment from each shareholder came harder and harder. I dreaded to ask for it. Besides, two-thirds of my company were scattered over so much country that the time and expense of collecting ate up the amount received, a contingency I had not foreseen when I fixed my tax rate.

At last the end came. The man who subscribed the use of his horse, wanted him back. I gave him up. This dismounted the Company. Operations could not be carried on afoot over a territory larger than the State of Connecticut. I had indeed found several mineral veins, but they were in that numerous catalogue of "needing capital to develop them." The General Prospector also needed capital to buy a whole suit of clothes.

I was obliged to suspend operations. When I stopped the Company stopped. Indeed I did not find out till then, that I was virtually the whole "Company."

CHAPTER XXVI.

HIGH LIFE.

THE "Company" died its peaceful death where I brought up when the horse was demanded of me in Eureka Valley, some 8,000 feet above the sea level, at Dave Hays' mountain ranch and tavern on the Sonora and Mono road. This was a new road built by the counties of Stanislaus, Tuolumne and Mono to rival the Placerville route, then crowded with teams carrying merchandise to Virginia City. The Mono road cost three years of labor, and was a fine piece of work. It ran along steep mountain sides, was walled in many places fifteen or twenty feet in height for hundreds of yards, crossed creeks and rivers on a number of substantial bridges, and proved, like many another enterprise undertaken in California, a failure. In Eureka Valley I spent the winter of 1864-65. I had the company of two men, Dave Hays and Jack Welch, both good mountaineers, good hunters, good miners, ranchmen, hotel-keepers, good men and true at anything they chose to turn their hands to. Both are deserving of a fair share of immortal fame. Hays had most of his toes frozen off at the second joint a winter or two afterward, as he had become over-confident and thought he could risk anything in the mountains. He was belated one winter night crossing the "Mountain Brow," distant some forty miles east of Eureka Valley. Over the "Brow" swept the coldest of winds, and Hays betook himself for shelter to a sort of cave, and when he emerged in the morning he was as good as toeless. In point of weather the Sierra summits are fearfully deceitful. You may cross and find it as fair as an October day in New England. In two hours a storm may come up, the air be filled with fine minute particles of snow blown from the surrounding peaks, and these striking against you like millions on millions of fine needle-points will carry the heat from your body much faster than the body can generate it. I was once nearly frozen to death in one of these snow-driving gales when less than three miles from our house. Hays built the house we lived in and it would have been a credit to any architect. It was fifty feet in length by eighteen in width, and made of logs, squared and dovetailed at the ends. It was intended for a "road house." Hays was landlord, cook, chambermaid, and barkeeper. I have known him to cook a supper for a dozen guests and when they were bestowed in their blankets, there being no flour for breakfast, he would jump on horseback and ride to Niagara creek, twelve miles distant, supply himself and ride back to cook the breakfast.

When the winter set in at Eureka Valley, and it set in very early, it commenced snowing. It never really stopped snowing until the next spring. There were intervals of more or less hours when it did not snow, but there was always snow in the air; always somewhere in the heavens that grayish-whitey look of the snow cloud; always that peculiar chill and smell, too, which betoken snow. It snowed when we went to bed; it was snowing when we got up; it snowed all day, or at intervals during the day; it was ever monotonously busy, busy; sometimes big flakes, sometimes little flakes coming down, down, down; coming deliberately straight down, or driving furiously in our faces, or crossing and recrossing in zigzag lines. The snow heavens seemed but a few feet above the mountain-tops; they looked heavy and full of snow, and gave one a crushing sensation. We seemed just between two great bodies of snow, one above our heads, one lying on the ground.

Our house, whose ridge-pole was full eighteen feet from the ground, began gradually to disappear. At intervals of three or four days it was necessary to shovel the snow from the roof, which would otherwise have been crushed in. This added to the accumulation about us. Snow covered up the windows and mounted to the eaves. The path to the spring was through a cut high above our heads. That to the barn was through another similar. Snow all about us lay at an average depth of eight feet. Only the sloping roof of the house was visible, and so much in color did it assimilate with the surrounding rocks, pines, and snow that one unacquainted with the locality might have passed within a few feet of it without recognizing it as a human residence.

December, January, February, and March passed, and we heard nothing from the great world outside of and below us. We arose in the morning, cooked, ate our breakfast, got out fencing stuff till dinner time, going and returning from our work on snowshoes, and digging in the snow a pit large enough to work in. We ate our noon beans, returned to work, skated back to the house by half-past two to get in firewood for the night, and at half-past three or four the dark winter's day was over, and we had fifteen hours to live through before getting the next day's meagre allowance of light, for Eureka Valley is a narrow cleft in the mountains not over a quarter of a mile in width, and lined on either side by ridges 1,500 to 2,000 feet in height. The sun merely looked in at the eastern end about nine A.M., said "good day," and was off again. We rolled in sufficient firewood every night to supply any civilized family for a week. Two-thirds of the caloric generated went up our chimney. It did not have far to go, either. The chimney was very wide and very low. At night a person unacquainted with the country might have tumbled into the house through that chimney. The winds of heaven did tumble into it frequently, scattering ashes and sometimes cinders throughout the domicil. Sometimes they thus assailed us while getting breakfast. We consumed ashes plentifully in our breakfasts; we drank small charcoal in our coffee; we found it in the bread. On cold mornings the flapjacks would cool on one side ere they were baked on the other. A warm meal was enjoyed only by placing the tin coffee-cup on the hot coals after drinking, and a similar process was necessary with the other viands. The "other viands" were generally bread, bacon, beans, and beef. It was peculiar beef. It was beef fattened on oak leaves and bark. Perhaps some of you California ancients may recollect the two consecutive rainless summers of "'63" and "'64," when tens of thousands of cattle were driven from the totally dried-up plains into the mountains for feed.

During those years, at the Rock River ranch in Stanislaus County, where the plains meet the first hummocks of the Nevada foothills, I have seen that long, lean line of staggering, starving, dying kine stretching away as far as the eye could reach, and at every hundred yards lay a dead or dying animal. So they went for days, urged forward by the vaquero's lash and their own agony for something to eat. Even when they gained the grass of the mountains it was only to find it all eaten off and the ground trodden to a dry, red, powdery dust by the hungry legions which had preceded them. It was a dreadful sight, for those poor brutes are as human in their sufferings through deprivation of food and water, when at night they lay down and moaned on the parched red earth, as men, women, and children would be. Well, the strongest survived and a portion reached the country about Eureka Valley. They came in, fed well during the summer, and one-third at least never went out again. The vaqueros could not keep them together in that rough country. They wandered about, climbed miles of mountain-sides, found little plateaus or valleys hidden away here or there, where they feasted on the rich "bunch grass." They gained, by devious windings, high mountain-tops and little nooks quite hidden from their keepers' eyes and quite past finding out. The herdsmen could not collect or drive them all out in the fall. They were left behind. All went well with them until the first snows of winter. Then instinctively those cattle sought to make their way out of the mountain fastnesses. Instinctively, too, they travelled westward toward the plains. And at the same time the first fall of snow was covered with tracks of deer, bear and Indians, all going down to the warmer regions. But the cattle were too late. Their progress was slow. More and more snow came and they were stopped. Some thus impeded trod down the snow into a corral, round which they tramped and tramped until they froze to death. Some of these cattle were thus embayed along the track of the Sonora and Mono road, and the white man making his way out was obliged to turn aside, for the wide, sharp-horned beast "held the fort" and threatened impalement to all that entered. Others, finding the south and sunny sides of the mountains, lived there until February, browsing on the oak leaves and bark. These we killed occasionally and buried the meat in the snow about our house. But it was beef quite juiceless, tasteless, tough and stringy. It was literally starvation beef for those who ate it, and the soup we made from it was in color and consistency a thin and almost transparent fluid.

Foxes in abundance were about us, and they stayed all winter. They were of all shades of color from red to grayish black. Now a story was current in the mountains that black-fox skins commanded very high prices, say from $80 to $100 each, and that "silvery-grays" would bring $25 or $30. So we bought strychnine, powdered bits of beef therewith, scattered them judiciously about the valley, and were rewarded with twenty or thirty dead foxes by spring. It required many hours' labor to dress a skin properly, for the meat and fat must be carefully scraped away with a bit of glass, and if that happened to cut through the hide your skin is good for nothing. Certainly, at very moderate wages, each skin cost $7 or $8 in the labor required to trap, or poison it, if you please, and to cure and dress it afterward. When the gentle spring-time came and access was obtained to certain opulent San Francisco furriers, we were offered $1.50 for the choicest skins and 37-1/2 cents for the ordinary ones. Whereat the mountaineer got on his independence, refused to sell his hard-earned peltries at such beggarly prices, and kept them for his own use and adornment.

Then our dogs too would wander off, eat the strychnined fox bait, and become dead dogs. We had five when the winter commenced, which number in the spring was reduced to one—the most worthless of all, and the very one which we prayed might get poisoned. These dogs had plenty of oak-bark fattened beef at home. They were never stinted in this respect. What we could not eat—and the most of the beef we cooked we couldn't eat—we gave freely to our dogs. But that wouldn't content the dog. Like man, he had the hunting instinct in his nature. He wanted something new; something rich, rare, racy, with a spice of adventure in it; something he couldn't get at home. He wanted to find a bit of frozen beef in some far-off romantic spot a mile or two from the house and this on finding he would devour, under the impression that stolen waters are sweet, and poisoned beef eaten in secret is pleasant. And then he would lay himself down by the frozen brookside and gently breathe his life away; or come staggering, shaking, trembling home, under the action of the drug, and thus dashing in our domestic circle scatter us to the four corners of the big log house, thinking him a mad dog. I lost thus my own dog, "Put," named briefly after General Israel Putnam of the Revolution, a most intelligent animal of some hybrid species; a dog that while alone in the mountains I could leave to guard my camp, with a certainty that he would devour every eatable thing left within his reach ere my return, and meet me afterward wagging his tail and licking his chops, with that truthful, companionable expression in his eye, which said plainer than words: "I've done it again, but it was so good." I shall never own another dog like "Put," and I never want to. He would climb a tree as far as one could hang a bit of bacon upon it. He would in lonesome places keep me awake all night, growling and barking at imaginary beasts, and then fraternize with the coyotes and invite them home to breakfast. Near the Big Meadows, in Mono County, a disreputable female coyote came down from a mountain side and followed "Put," one morning as I journeyed by on my borrowed steed, howling, yelping, and filling the surrounding air with a viragoish clamor. I presume it was another case of abandonment.

It was a winter of deathly quiet in Eureka Valley. Enveloped in snow, it lay in a shroud. Occasionally a tempest would find its way into the gorge and rampage around for a while, roaring through the pines and dislodging the frozen lumps of snow in their branches, which whirled down, bang! bang! bang! like so many rocks on our housetop. Sometimes we heard the rumble of rocks or snowslides tumbling from the mountains. But usually a dead, awful quiet prevailed. It wore on one worse than any uproar. No sound from day to day of rumble or rattle of cart or wagon, no church bells, no milkman's bell, no gossip or chatter of inhabitants, no street for them to walk down or gossip in, none of the daily clamor of civilized life save what we made ourselves. It was a curious sensation to see one or both of my two companions at a distance from the house. They looked such insignificant specks in the whitened valley. And to meet the same man after four or five hours of absence and to know that he had nothing new to tell, that he hadn't been anywhere in a certain sense, since without neighbors' houses or neighboring villages there was "nowhere" to get that sort of bracing-up that one derives from any sort of companionship.

We were very cozy and comfortable during those long winter nights, seated in the red glare of our rudely-built, wide-mouthed fireplace. But sometimes, on a clear moonlight night, I have, for the sake of change, put on the snowshoes and glided a few hundred yards away from the house. In that intense and icy silence the beating of one's heart could be distinctly heard, and the crunching of the snow under foot sounded harsh and disagreeable. All about the myriads of tall pines in the valley and on the mountain-side were pointing straight to the heavens, and the crags in black shadow above and behind them maintained also the same stern, unyielding silence. The faintest whisper of a breeze would have been a relief. If you gained an elevation it was but to see and feel more miles on miles of snow, pines, peaks, and silence. Very grand, but a trifle awful; it seemed as if everything must have stopped. In such isolation it was difficult to realize that miles away were crowded, babbling, bustling, rallying, roaring cities, full of men and women, all absorbed and intent on such miserably trifling things as boots and shoes, pantaloons and breakfasts, suppers, beds, corsets, and cucumbers. We were outside of creation. We had stepped off. We seemed in the dread, dreary outer regions of space, where the sun had not warmed things into life. It was an awful sort of church and a cold one. It might not make a sceptic devotional; it would certainly cause him to wonder where he came from or where he was going to. A half-hour of this cold, silent Sierran winter morning was quite enough of the sublime. It sent one back to the fireside with an increased thankfulness for such comforts as coffee, tobacco, and warm blankets.

CHAPTER XXVII.

LEAVING HIGH LIFE.

NEAR the end of March I resolved to leave Eureka Valley. Sonora, Tuolumne County, was fifty-six miles distant. That was my goal. Thirty miles of the way lay over deep snow, and was to be travelled over on snowshoes. The Norwegian snowshoe is a long wooden skate or runner, turned up at the forward end, greased on the lower side, with a strap in the middle to hold the foot. The Indian snowshoe is a flat network, fastened to a frame, in shape something like an enlarged tennis racket. It is like locomotion shod with a couple of market-baskets. The principal use of the pole, carried in the hands with the Norwegian shoe, is to serve as a brake and helm while going downhill. Some put it under the arm and others straddle it while making a descent. The arm position is the most dignified. The legs must be kept straddled at a ridiculous distance apart, and the first few days' practice seems to split a person nearly in two. If, with the Indian snowshoe, you tumble down on a hillside it is almost impossible to get up again, and the unfortunate must remain in a recumbent position very much like that assumed by the heathen when they go down on all fours before their god, until some one unstraps his shoes. I preferred the Norwegian shoe. The first pair I ever used I made one evening about dusk. I was going toward Eureka Valley from Sonora, and had met the first fallen snow. From a mere crisp it grew deeper and deeper. I found a pile of "shakes"—long, rough shingles used in the mountains—and made my shoes from two of them. They were not more than a quarter the proper length. They kept me busy the rest of the night picking myself up. I think I must have fallen down some four hundred times. When we came to a down grade they went of their own accord and ran away with me. Sometimes but one shoe would slip off and glide down a bank, sometimes two, sometimes all of us went together, balance-pole included, and a bag I had lashed to my back would swing over my head and bang me in the face. It was a lively night's entertainment for only one man in the heart of the wilderness. There was no monotony about it; nothing tedious or depressing. Just as fast as I recovered from one fall and started I got the next. I swore a good deal. There was not anything else to be said. One couldn't argue with—things. It was the only recreation afforded by that phase of the trip. To have kept one's temper and remained expletiveless would have been to burst. I avoided the superior and more expensive epithets as much as possible and confined myself to second-rate strong language. But when I started for my final trip out of the mountains, I had become a tolerable snowshoe amateur. A pack was lashed to my back. It held a blanket, some meat, bread, coffee, sugar, one fox skin and my worldly wardrobe. The morning light had not dawned when I started.

After a couple of miles' advance my feet felt like lumps of ice. I examined my boots. The leather was frozen hard and stiff. The pain was too great for endurance. I made my way back to the house, found Hays and Welch at breakfast, removed my boots and stockings, and saw three waxy-looking toes, the right big one included. They were frozen. The heat of the fire produced additional twinges, like boring with red-hot knitting-needles. I wrapped some thicknesses of flannel around both boots, put them on again, and made another start. Eureka Valley soon disappeared behind me. I never saw it again, and probably never shall. But its picture is indelibly graven on my memory. We lived in the gem of the locality. All the landscape gardening skill in the world could produce nothing to equal it. A clear crystal stream ran by the door. The grove was a natural park, level as a floor, with pines all about, 150 feet high. We had a cascade and little miniature mountains of rock, with oak and pines springing from their crevices. No tame tree could be coaxed to grow as did these wild ones of the mountains. Some were independent of soil altogether, and flourished vigorously rooted in rocky fissures. We had the tiniest of meadows concealed behind these little mountains of our domain. Other grassy plateaus were perched sixty or eighty feet over our heads on the mountain. Nor was this all at once revealed. It required half a day to get over all the labyrinth of meadow, mount, and dale within half a mile of our house. All this was set in a gigantic frame—the dark green, thickly-wooded mountain-sides running up 2,000 feet above our heads, while to the eastward through the narrow gorge rose bare peaks twenty and thirty miles away, from whose tops, on sunshiny, breezy mornings, the snow could be seen driving in immense vapor-like clouds and tinged a roseate hue. People who visit the Yosemite have seen but one of the thousand pictures set in the Sierras.

It was my calculation to get to Hulse's empty log-house, twelve miles distant, and camp there that night; but my progress was very slow. The road for miles ran along a steep mountain-side. It was buried many feet in snow. It was all a sheet of snow inclined at an angle most difficult to travel. In places acres of snow had slipped in a body from above, covering the ordinary level five or six feet in depth. These accumulations, while coming down, would have brushed a human being away with the facility with which a cart-load of sand dumped on your cellar-door would overwhelm a fly. I saw whole groves of pines whose trunks had been cut off by these slips ten or twelve feet from the roots. I felt small and insignificant, and speculated whether, after all, I was of any more importance than a fly or any other bug in the sum total of things generally. I thought of how much more importance a man was in a newspaper office than in the solitude of these mountains. Then the sun hurried toward the west and the cold blue and brassy tints of the winter's eve merged together. The route along the "River Hill" side became steeper and steeper, the snow more hummocky from successive slides and the way more disorganized. It was very slippery. The snow had an ice finish on the surface like a hard coating of enamel. I took off the snowshoes and bore them and the balancing-pole on my shoulders, picking my way laboriously, step by step. Below me extended a very long, smooth, steep slide, like a white Mansard roof, several hundred feet in height. Finally I was obliged to stamp an indentation in the enamelled surface at every step, with my heels, to secure footing. The slippery and regularly graded descent below broke off occasionally into precipices of fifty or sixty feet in height. A person slipping here would, of course, accomplish portions of the descent on mere empty air. The trouble was not so much in getting through the air as in bringing up after going through. A fall never hurts anybody. It's the sudden stoppage when you're through. I expected momentarily to slip. The sun was rapidly going down and I felt a tendency to follow suit. At the point where I did slip the view was magnificent. Over full thirty miles of peak and pine the setting sun was shedding. I saw these peaks disappear like a flash. The grand curtain of Nature was not rung down at the call of night. It was I who fell before the curtain. I went down perhaps three hundred feet of the incline, generally in a sitting position. My long Norwegian snowshoes, jerked from my grasp, sailed down ahead of me, one diverging a little to the right, the other to the left, and the balancing pole scooting straight ahead. All of us went together with a beautiful uniformity and regularity of formation. The whole descent of 300 feet did not occupy more than six seconds, yet in that brief space of time my mind appeared to photograph on itself at least a dozen phases of the situation and as many past memories and future possibilities. I saw the stumps seeming to rush past me uphill, while I was really rushing past them downhill, and the reflection came to me that if I collided with even one of them the result would be worse for me than the stump. This did not comfort me. As each successive stump hurried up the mountain I said, by the unspoken operation of thought, "There goes another stump. A miss is as good as a mile. I may bring up in one piece yet, though, if I go off one of these precipices, I may make my last appearance on any stage in several pieces." I remember, also, the sensation caused by the seat of my outside pantaloons tearing out through the excessive friction. I had on two pairs of pantaloons when I started. I thought, also, during all these risks and lightning-like escapades of my far-away Eastern home, of the girls I had left behind years before, of the dear old cool stone door-steps on the sycamore-embowered Main street of our village, on which the girls used to sit on warm summer and Sunday nights. Yes, in this inappreciable space of time and under such extraordinary conditions I thought of this, and even wondered if the other fellow sat there now with his arm hidden in the darkness of the hall, where they kept no lamp in summer for fear of drawing mosquitoes, trying to reach round that girl. The human mind is certainly a wonderful piece of business. I think the more it is shocked, agitated, and stirred up at certain intervals the faster it works and the more it takes cognizance of. The man who month in and month out moves backward and forward in a groove of habit is apt to think the same old thoughts over and over again in the same old way. The man who is beaten and banged about from pillar to post and Dan to Beersheba, who is continually tumbling into new events and situations, is liable to think a great many new things and think of them in many new ways. From a mundane consideration of time on this slide I soon reached my destination. Regarding my own mental sensations, the trip seemed one of many minutes. It was not the bottom of the hill where I stopped. The bottom of that hill terminated in the Stanislaus River, and was preceded by a precipice 200 feet high. Had I gone off that my journey downward would have been accomplished on a basis of three of the four elements known to the ancients, namely, earth, air, and water, and from all accounts, and my own impressions of my deserts at that period, it might have ultimately terminated in fire. The snow was soft where I brought up. I stopped. "It is good for me to be here," I said; "here will I pass the night." I possessed a little mountain wisdom, and foresaw the impossibility and inutility of making the ascent that night. I had belted to my waist a sharp hatchet. Around me were many dead pine limbs, projecting from the snow. The mountain-side exposure was southern. About the roots of a great pine on the little plateau where I had brought up the snow had partly melted away. I enlarged the cavity, using the hatchet as pick and shovel. I made my home for the night in this cavity. Kindling a fire with my dead branches, I chopped directly into it the thick dry bark of the pine. This supply of fuel alone was plentiful and lasted me the entire night. I disclaim here all intent of posing in print as a hero, for on many occasions I am disgusted by my mental and physical cowardice. But on this particular night, and it was a very long one, I felt no fear; I spent it very pleasantly. I cooked and ate, and drank my coffee with a relish, born of mountain air and exercise. My coffee-pot was another peripatetic appurtenance belted to my waist. Culinarily, I was for myself a travelling boarding-house, being guest, landlord and chambermaid all in one. The fire blazed cheerfully, and the fully-seasoned oak branches soon made a bed of solid live coals. My snow hole at the tree's base slowly enlarged as it melted away. The hillside being inclined carried away all the moisture. After supper I sang. I felt that here I could sing in safety and without damage to other ears, because no one could hear me. Music hath charms to soothe, and all that, but it must not be savage music. Mine at that time was savage. It is now. If I feel a tendency to inflict any vocal misery on mankind, I go forth into solitude, and commit the outrage on inanimate defenseless objects which cannot strike back. After singing, I spoke all the pieces of my schoolboy days. I quoted Shakespeare, and really admired myself in Hamlet's soliloquy. I never heard a more satisfactory rendition. This was another piece of consideration for my fellow-beings. Others, less sensitive to the ill they may do, rush on the stage and torture audiences. After the dramatic performance I rehearsed my political speech. I was even coming from the mountains with full intent to stand, or rather run, for the Legislature from Tuolumne County, which I did, greatly to the misery of the party. The speech was impromptu. So the long night wore away. The day became overcast. The winds occasionally stirred and moaned through the lofty pines above me. Then they sank to soft mournful whispering music and ceased. The snapping of the fire sounded sharply in the solitude. From the river far below came a confused, murmuring, babbling sound like the clamor of some vast, distant multitude, and this seemed varied at times by cries weird and louder. Lumps of frozen snow fell from treetops far and near, and as they struck branch after branch sounded like the plunging of horses in the drifts. I dozed fitfully and awoke with the red coals staring me in the face and the startling realization that the elements were preparing for a heavy storm.

CHAPTER XXVIII.

THE LAST OF HIGH LIFE.

IN writing this experience I disdain all intent of making myself out a first-class sufferer or adventurer. Other men by hundreds on our frontiers have endured far more, suffered far more, passed through many more perils and combated them more courageously. Mine as compared to theirs is a mere priming, a rush-light candle to an electric lamp. Our mountains and lone valleys hold many a skeleton whose unburied, unrecorded bones are the only relics and proofs of a live, lingering death, preceded by hours of pain and misery. Mine was the merest foretaste of their hardships and sufferings, and it is my chief desire that this story shall help to a clearer realization of the perils, hardships, and sufferings of our unknown pioneers. I passed a very comfortable night at the foot of my snowslide, save sundry aches in my three frozen toes. I have passed very many nights far more uncomfortably when surrounded by all the so-called comforts of civilization, in insect-infested beds at slovenly taverns, in rooms stifling with the midsummer heat of New York; in cold, fireless chambers with damp beds. Some of our civilization doesn't civilize in the matter of comfort. Down there in my snow hole I was better off in regard to artificial heat than one-third the population of France, who, in their damp stone houses, shiver over a pot of coals from November till April, while thousands have not even this luxury. I had any amount of fuel about me, provisions for days, powder and shot, and if more snow came I had but to let it fall, build up the walls of my hole and protect me from the blasts. I knew of a man caught thus in a storm on the Summit, who made a hole for himself by kindling a fire on the snow, allowing it to melt, and going downward with it as it melted. When the storm ended his cavity was twice the size of a hogshead, and he emerged from it and came to our house in Eureka Valley. Snow rightly applied, will prove man's greatest protector from cold, providing it is deep enough. It is the intensely cold blast sweeping over hard, frozen ground, that kills both animal and vegetable life.

I looked up at dawn, after finishing my breakfast, or rather the remains of the banquet which had continued at intervals all night—for there is nothing like eating and drinking to keep up one's spirits and keep out the cold, and one strong cup of coffee under such conditions is worth a pint of whiskey, since it gives a renewal of vigor which doesn't flash up and then out like alcohol. I looked on the contract before me. I had that three hundred feet of steep icy incline to climb. There was no getting round it by gradual or zigzag upward approaches. The way to the right and left broke off in ugly precipices. A little exploration to find an easier route satisfied me and sent me back frightened to my camp. For crossing on what I deemed snows with a firm foundation underneath, I was startled to find my pole running through this surface in an empty void beneath. Then the entire area for twenty feet square suddenly settled down an inch or two with an ominous scrunch! which sent my heart seemingly up in my mouth and my hair up on its various ends. I was walking on a frail crust of snow which had formed over the deep gorges ploughed by the rains and torrents of ages down the mountain side. Some of these were fifteen or twenty feet deep, with rocky sides almost perpendicular, and such pits, blocked up at either end with snow, were regular man-traps. I hauled myself up to the place from whence I had slipped the previous evening. The job occupied the entire morning. There were the two snowshoes, the pole and my pack to manage, besides my own earthly organization. In places the descent was so steep that I was obliged to drag myself and cargo upward a foot at a time, and then chock my feet with a knife to prevent slipping back. The moral of which is, it is easier to go down than to go up, and easier to fall than to rise in many ways. It does seem singular that these coincidences should be so coincident between the world of materiality and that of morality. It was a very laborious task, and when about noon I reached the top, I was sick from exhaustion, and lay down for some minutes on the ledge of snow hardly wide enough to hold me. Then, with shaky knees, I picked my way very slowly over another dangerous mile around the mountain-side, where every step was furnished with extra accommodation for slipping, and in many spots where, had I slipped, I should have gone farther and fared much worse than on the evening before. I wished I was a goose, for a goose could in four minutes have accomplished a distance which took me all day. We pride ourselves on our powers and the ways and means we have devised for transporting our clumsy carcases, but after all, in point of locomotion, we are individually miserably inferior to a goose, and all our ingenuity and mind has not been able only to lift us from the inferior position wherein nature has in this respect placed us, as compared with a goose.

I arrived at Hulse's empty cabin about an hour before dark. The place looked melancholy, murderous, and cold. The locality was higher than ours in Eureka Valley, and not so well protected. Of the house little was visible save the ridgepole. Five feet of snow lay on the kitchen roof, which could easily be walked on. I gained entrance with some difficulty through the upper sash of a front window. The door was permanently barred for the winter by snow. I was no sooner in the house than the requirements of the situation drove me out again to collect fuel for the night. There was no rest for the wicked. It is only when man is entirely alone that he realizes how many things are necessary not only to his comfort but his very existence. A bear could have lain during the night in comfort at that house on a bed of straw. The assertion that "man wants but little here below" is not true, and should no longer pass uncontradicted. Here was I, at that time, a dweller in the wilderness with the foxes—a tramp, standing almost within the threshhold of beggary, owner neither of house nor lands, and a cipher "on change." Yet I couldn't get along without iron and steel, phosphorus and sulphur, or my matches, coffee from the tropics, sugar from the Indies, salt from somewhere, pepper from pepperland, grain ground to flour, chemicals to "raise it," tea from China, and utensils of tin to keep it in. It is good to be so alone once in one's life to realize how much man's present development is due to the numberless articles he brings from all the ends of the earth for his subsistence and comfort, and what an endless amount of labor is necessary to keep him up to his present standard of development.

My fuel was pine bark, stripped from the surrounding trees. It came off easily in great sheets, making an imposing-looking pile as heaped in the kitchen, and burned like shavings. The night passed in alternate cat naps and firing up. I would doze, to wake up shivering, finding the room dark and the fire nearly out. Throwing on more bark, the flames leaped up. I dozed again, to wake up in cold and darkness as before. It was a gloomier camp than the one of the night previous. An empty house always has a tomb-like atmosphere about it, and, when alone, I prefer a bivouac under the trees. With morning came a heavy snowstorm, or rather a continuation of the snow that had been falling all winter. I started out. The pine boughs along the road brushed my face, where, in summer, they would have been many feet over my head. The strap of one of my snowshoes tore out of the wood, and left me crippled as to further progress until I repaired it. The snow was soft, and to get off the shoes was to sink in it to the middle. I was literally afloat on a sea of snow, and to get overboard was to founder and flounder—another proof of man's miserable helplessness as compared with the goose. It began to occur to me that this storm was one of unusual severity. It blew violently, and the snow at times came in such whirls that I could not open my eyes for several seconds. If I had not in this story determined, in point of detail, to reduce everything to a rigid mathematical accuracy of statement, I might say that the snow blinded me for minutes, since seconds seem very long under these circumstances. Time seems to be a quality or a something, which, in point of length or shortness, is largely dependent on one's condition and sensations. A good time is always short—a bad time always long.

The aim on starting that morning was to reach Strawberry Flat, fourteen miles distant. There is no road over the Sierras without its Strawberry Flat, generally so called because no strawberries are ever found there. This Strawberry Flat, then, contained a population of four men, and was regarded by us in Eureka valley as a bustling place. In two hours I gave up all idea of reaching Strawberry Flat, and I concentrated my hopes on an empty house four miles below Hulse's. Given good weather and a crust on the snow, I could with tolerable ease have made the fourteen miles between Hulse's and Strawberry. But the wind was ahead, the snow constantly blinded me, and as it came much more horizontally as driven by the blast than perpendicularly, and being of a sleety nature, formed at intervals of every few minutes a slim film of ice on my face, which, as with my hand I swept it off, fell to the ground in broken ice casts of my ordinary countenance. The empty house was at last reached. It was past noon. The empty house was not there. Where it once stood was more empty than ever. The weight of the snow had crushed the shanty. A few timbers and splinters sticking out told the story. There was but one thing to do—return to Hulse's. To go forward was impossible, and so I fought my way back. It was a hard fight, for the wind and the snow at times seemed as if inspired by the demons of the air or some spirit cause or effect which is expressed by such term. They beat and buffeted and blinded me, so that twice I lost my way, blundered about in circles, and got back to Hulse's about three in the afternoon only through the wandering of sheer stupidity or the guidance of some special providence—perhaps both. Tired as I was it was necessary to go straightway to work and get in more pine bark for the night. There was no lack of business on this trip. I never had a moment to spare from morning till night. One's body is an imperious master, and, unsupported by civilization or the help of one's fellow-beings, it keeps one on the keen jump to supply it with food, fuel, and cover.

As I lay stretched in my blankets before the blaze that night I heard from time to time a sharp crack overhead. I gazed upward and made a most unpleasant discovery. It was another form of Damocles' sword over me. The rafters were bent like bows from the great pressure of the snow on the roof. The cracking was a notice that they might not stand the strain much longer. The roof might at any time tumble in with several tons of snow upon me. This weight was steadily increasing. I could not go out in the storm, nor could I remove the snow from the roof. The situation kept my mind busy while the body was at rest, and anxiety and suspense are about as wearing as toting in pine bark after snow-shoeing all day in a snowstorm. Hulse's was my home and anxious seat for two days. The sword of Damocles hung and cracked, but did not fall. I found Hulse's store of provision under the boards of the front room floor. The boards were weighted down by a great pile of shingles. It was this monument of shingles in the parlor which caused me to suspect the existence of the cache. Taking from the big box I found underneath a renewed supply of flour and pork, and breaking the face of Hulse's family clock, also packed therein, a matter never revealed until this present writing, I re-closed it, buried it, boarded it over and re-piled the shingles over it.

On the fourth morning of this excursion the storm was over, the sky clear, the heavens brightly blue, and the newly fallen snow had dressed the pines all in new suits. For the second time I bade Hulse's lone house a doubtful farewell, for after travelling all day I had before succeeded only in bringing up there at night, and knew not but that I might do so again. The newly fallen snow being very light and feathery, I made slow progress. A frozen crust grants the best track for snowshoes. As the sun got higher it melted this feathery top snow, fusing it into a close, sodden mass, which stuck and bunched on the bottoms of the shoe runners. This delayed me still more. Other troublesome obstacles were the little rivulets and brooks, which, cutting through the snow, left banks on either side six or seven feet in height. To climb these was difficult. The snow gave way, and one could only flounder through and up to the top. Besides, it was necessary to wade the creeks. This wet my feet and caused more snow to bunch and freeze on them. Night came, and with it an increase of cold, which, causing the snow to freeze to a crust on top, iced and smoothed the track anew for me. But with one additional facility for making progress, I lacked another. That was the strength and freshness with which I had started at morn.

My day had been one of most laborious progress, wading creeks, floundering through their soft snowbanks, and stopping every ten minutes to clean my shoes of damp snow. I had no other grease for their bottoms save a bit of pork, which I wore out upon them. Snowshoes won't run well unless frequently greased. Then there was no rest for my body. The supply of pines from about whose roots the snow had melted away had given out; to step off the shoes was to sink to the middle; to rest at all was to rest squatting; a few minutes' trial of this position under the most favorable circumstances will convince any reader of its back-aching tendencies. Man is a lying animal; I mean he must lie down to recuperate. My meals I cooked on the snow. The regular *menu* was coffee, bread, and pork. The base of the kitchen was a big piece of dry pine bark, always at hand. On this the fire was kindled. The evolution of coffee under these conditions was slow, because the water for making it had first to be melted from snow in the coffee-pot, and snow under these circumstances melts with an exasperating slowness. The quantity required to make a single pint of water is something remarkable. I think I was obliged to fill that vessel four or five times with snow to get the suitable quantity of water. Then it must be remembered that the water would not proceed to boil until all the snow was melted. "A watched pot never boils," but a watched pot of plain water is velocity itself when compared with a pot of snow and water watched by a tired and hungry being in the wilderness. Night found me twelve miles from

Strawberry Flat. About one in the morning I found another empty cabin. This was four miles from the desired haven. It was desolation inside and out—the windows gone, the door torn from its hinges, the inside a litter of snow and rubbish, and one dead cow in the kitchen. The cooking-stove remained. I cleared the grate of snow and attempted a fire. It wouldn't draw. Of course it wouldn't draw, for the stovepipe was full of snow. Then I kindled the fire on the top of the stove and gradually burned up a portion of the house. Like Sherman and Napoleon, I lived on the country invaded. The firelight cast its ruddy glow on the surrounding domestic desolation and the red dead cow, which, being frozen hard as a rock, served for a seat. I waited for the morn; but the morn would not come. I saw from the sashless windows the preliminary streaks of dawn ever so faintly lighting up the eastern horizon full forty times, and found they were only in my imagination, so covetous for the coming day. When the sun did rise he came up in the opposite direction.

Impatient of waiting longer, and converting myself to the false belief that the light was really coming in what turned out to be the west, I did battle in the dark with the last four miles of the journey. All went well until I reached a certain point in the road, which was now well defined through the trees. There every time I brought up in a clump of bushes and lost the track. Back, time after time, I went, seeking with careful calculation to make a fresh and truer start, only to bring up again in brambles and briers. When the light did come, I had, for two hundred yards, in this going and coming, beaten a path in the snow which looked as if travelled over for a week. Daylight showed what a ridiculously trifling turn had caused me thus to miss the route. The moral of which is that man's welfare is often wrecked on some trifling error. A failure to say, "Good morning" to an acquaintance, a long, gloomy countenance or putting one's knife in the mouth, or guzzling down soup or coffee with undue noise, has repelled one man from another, and such repulsion has sent our fortunes on the wrong track altogether. I was welcomed at the Strawberry House by six hounds, who, in the still faint light, made at me as they would at another beast, and the first few moments of my arrival on this outpost of civilization was occupied in energetic attempts to keep what was left of me from being eaten by the dogs. Indeed, the way of the transgressor is hard. I had never injured these dogs. However, the hospitality I experienced at Palmer's stood out in bold relief against the churlishness of their brute creation.

CHAPTER XXIX.

ON THE ROSTRUM.

ON reaching Sonora, Tuolumne County, with the frozen toes alluded to in the great slide down the mountain, I went to work and dug post-holes for a living. Inspired by the posts or the holes, I wrote what I called a lecture. This I learned by heart. Next I practised its delivery in the woods, behind barns, and sometimes at early morn in the empty Court-house—for the Temple of Justice in Sonora stood open night and day, and he that would might enter and sleep on the benches, or even in the bar itself, as many did in those days. Many weeks I drilled and disciplined this lecture, addressing it to rocks, trees, barns, and sometimes to unseen auditors wandering about, whose sudden appearance would cover me with confusion and send me blushing home. But I dreaded bringing it to an engagement with the enemy—the audience. The glories and triumphs of oratory I eagerly coveted, but the preliminary labor, the pangs and the terrible chances of speaking in public I dreaded and avoided as long as possible. But Destiny, despite all our backwardness, steadily pushes us on to the most painful experiences. I required yet feared the living audience. Rocks, trees, and barn doors will not do for a speaker the specific work of a few listening human beings. Listening ears sooner or later teach a man who would speak to multitudes to modulate his voice or increase it to a volume, or spend more time and strength in accentuating each syllable; and above all, to take things coolly and not get hurried. At last I concluded to risk myself on an experimental audience. I borrowed one for the occasion. Going into the main street of Sonora one evening, I collected half a dozen appreciative souls and said, "Follow me to the Court-house; I would have a few words with you." There was a County Clerk, his deputy, a popular physician and saloon-keeper, and an enterprising carpenter. They followed me wonderingly. Arrived at the Court-house I seated them, marched myself to the Judge's bench, stuck two candles in two bottles, lit them, and then informed the crowd that I had brought them hither to serve as an experimental audience to a lecture I proposed delivering. After which I plunged into the subject, and found that portion of the brain which with a speaker always acts independent of the rest wondering that I should be really talking to live auditors. There is a section of a man's faculties, during the operation of speaking in public, which will always go wandering around on its own hook, picking up all manner of unpleasant thoughts and impressions. Apparently it is ever on the watch to find something which shall annoy the other half. It seems to me that no one can become a very successful speaker or actor until this idle, vagrant part of the mind is put down altogether, total forgetfulness of all else save the work in hand be established, and self-consciousness abolished. However, I spoke half the piece to my borrowed audience, and then, feeling that I could really stand fire, told them they could go home. But Dr. ———, constituting himself spokesman, rose and declared that having served as hearers for half the lecture they thought they were entitled to the other half. Being thus encored, I gave them the other half. A great apprehension was now taken from my mind. I could speak to a crowd without forgetting my lines, and deemed myself already a lecturer if not an orator. I did not then realize how vast is the difference between mere speaking and the properly delivering of words and sentences to a multitude, be it large or small; how unfit are the tone, pitch, and manner of ordinary converse to public speaking; how a brake must be put on every word and syllable, to slow down its accentuation and make it audible in a hall; how great the necessity for deliberation in delivery; how the force and meaning of entire sentences may be lost by a gabbling, imperfect, and too rapid enunciation; how the trained speaker keeps perfect control of himself, not only as to his delivery, but the mood underneath it; which should prompt how much depends on the establishment of a certain chain of sympathy betwixt speaker and audience, and how much the establishment of such chain depends on the speaker's versatility to accommodate himself to the character, intelligence, moods, and requirements of different audiences. I state this, having since my debut in the Sonora Court-house learned these things, and learned also that Nature has not given me the power to surmount all these difficulties. I am not a good speaker, as many doubtless discovered before I did. However, my friends whom I consulted said by all means give the lecture in public, knowing, of course, that I wanted them to encourage me, and feeling this to be the best way of getting rid of me. So I had posters printed and commenced public life on a small field. I hired a hall; admittance twenty-five cents. I felt guilty as I read this on the bills. I read one alone furtively by moonlight, because after they were posted and the plunge taken I was ashamed to appear by daylight on the streets. It seemed so presumptuous to ask respectable, God-fearing citizens of that town to sit and hear *me*. This was a result of the regular oscillations of my mental and temperamental seesaw.

I was always too far above the proper scale of self-esteem one day and too far below it the next. The real debut was not so easy as the preliminary, borrowed, bogus one. There were the hard, stern, practical people present, who counted on receiving their regular "two bits" worth of genuine, solid fact, knowledge and profitable information, who discounted all nonsense, didn't approve of it and didn't understand it. I felt their cold and withering influence as soon as I mounted the platform. Not many of such hearers were present, but that was enough to poison. I saw their judgment of my effort in their faces. I weakly allowed those faces, and the opinions I deemed shadowed forth on them, to paralyze, psychologize and conquer me. I allowed my eyes, numberless times, to wander and meet their stony, cynical gaze, and, at each time, the basilisk orbs withered up my self-assertion and self-esteem. Becoming more and more demoralized, I sometimes cowardly omitted or forgot what I deemed my boldest matter and best hits. However, the large majority of the audience being kindly disposed toward me, heard, applauded and pronounced the lecture a "success." Some ventured, when it was over, to advise me that the subject-matter was much better than the manner of its delivery. Of that there was not the least doubt. In speaking, I had concentrated matter enough for two hours' proper delivery into one, and a part of the mental strain and anxiety during the lecture was to race my words so as to finish within the limits of an hour on time. I feared wearying the audience, and so took one of the best methods of doing so. The next day self-esteem, going up to fever-heat, and my comparative failure not being so bad as the one I had anticipated when my estimates of myself were at zero, I determine on pressing my newly-found vocation and "starring" Tuolumne County. Carried by this transient gleam of self-conceit beyond the bounds of good judgment, and overwhelmed with another torrent of composition, I wrote still another lecture, and advertised that. The curiosity, complaisance, and good-nature of my friends I mistook for admiration. Indeed, during the fever, I planned a course, or rather a constant succession of lectures which might, if unchecked, have extended to the present time. But, on the second attempt, I talked largely to empty benches. A character of audience I have since become accustomed to, and with whom I am on terms of that friendship and sympathy only begotten of long acquaintance. The benches were relieved here and there by a discouraged-looking hearer who had come in on a free ticket, and who, I felt, wanted to get out again as quickly as possible. Then, I knew that my friends did not care to hear me any more. This was bitter, but necessary and useful. People will go often to church and hear dull sermons because of custom, of conventionality, and of religious faith and training. They will attend political meetings during an exciting campaign and hear equally dull political speeches because of patriotic or partisan sympathy or fealty. They will go also to hear noted people because of curiosity, but they will not hear more than once a mere man unbolstered by any of these outside influences. I next gave the lecture at Columbia. Columbia, though but four miles distant, was then the rival of Sonora as the metropolis of Tuolumne County, and it was necessary to secure a Columbian indorsement before attempting to star it through the provincial cities of Jimtown, Chinese Camp, Don Pedro's, and Pine Log. I billed Columbia, hired the theatre for two dollars and a half, and, after my effort, had the satisfaction of hearing from a friend that the appreciative and critical magnates of the town had concluded to vote me a "success." Then I spoke at Jamestown, Coulterville, Mariposa, Snelling's and other places, with very moderate success. Perhaps I might have arisen to greater distinction or notoriety than that realized on the Tuolumne field had I better known that talent of any sort must be handled by its possessor with a certain dignity to insure respect. Now, I travelled from town to town on foot. I was met, dusty and perspiring, tramping on the road, by people who knew me as the newly-arisen local lecturer. I should have travelled in a carriage. I posted my own bills. I should have employed the local bill-sticker. I lectured for ten cents per head, when I should have charged fifty. Sometimes I dispensed with an admittance fee altogether and took up contributions. In Coulterville, the trouser-buttons of Coultervillians came back in the hat, mixed with dimes. Looking back now on that experience, I can sincerely say to such as may follow me in any modification of such a career, "Never hold yourself cheap." If you put a good picture in a poor frame, it is only the few who will recognize its merit. Don't let your light shine in a battered, greasy lamp. It's all wrong. We all know the dread that genius inspires when clad in a seedy coat. Lecturing frequently tries a man's soul; especially when the lecturer's career is not a very successful one. If his path be strewn with roses and success, there may not be much of a story to tell. But it is different when his path is strewn with thorns and he steps on them. It is sad to hire a hall in a strange village and wait for an audience which never comes. It is ominous to hear your landlord, just before supper, remark, "Our people don't go much on lecters. But they'll pile into a circus or menagerie or anything else that isn't improvin'." They say this all over the land. It is sadder when you offer him a handful of your free tickets for himself and family to hear him, "Guess the folks hain't got time to go to-night. There is a ball over to Pappooseville, and everybody's goin'." I never did bill myself yet in a village for a lecture, but that I happened to pitch on the night of all nights when some great local event was to take place. Or else it rained. It is sad to speak to thirty-two people in a hall large enough to hold a thousand and try to address those thirty-two people scattered about at the thirty-two points of the mariner's compass. Once in New York I spoke to a fair audience in a hall on the ground floor. Things went on beautifully till 9 o'clock, when a big brass band struck up in the bigger hall over my head and some fifty couples commenced waltzing. It was an earthquake reversed. It ruined me for the night. None can realize until they enter the lecture field what trivial occurrences may transpire to upset the unfortunate on the platform and divert and distract the attention of an audience. On one occasion a cat got into a church where I was speaking, and trotted up and down a course she had laid out for herself before the pulpit. She did this with an erect tail, and at times made short remarks. It is singular that a single cat acting in this manner is more effective in interesting and amusing an "intelligent audience" than any speaker. Under such conditions Cicero himself would have to knock under to the cat. He might go on talking, but the cat would capture the house. And then the awful sensation of being obliged to keep on as though nothing had disturbed you; to pretend you don't see such a cat; that you are not thinking of it; and knowing all the while that your audience are getting their money's worth out of the cat and not out of you! On another fearful occasion I was speaking at Bridgehampton, Long Island, on the subject of temperance. I lectured on temperance occasionally, though I never professed teetotalism—for any length of time. One can lecture on temperance just as well without bring a total abstainer—and perhaps better. Now, I was born and they attempted to bring me up properly near Bridgehampton. Every one knew me and my ancestors, immediate and remote. I had not spoken over ten minutes when a man well-known in the neighborhood and much moved by the whiskey he had been drinking all day, arose and propounded some not very intelligible queries. I answered him as well as I could. Then he put more. Nay, he took possession of the meeting. No one ventured to silence him. They are a very quiet, orderly people in Bridgehampton. Such an interruption of a meeting had never before been heard of there, and the people seemed totally unable to cope with the emergency. The wretch delivered himself of a great variety of remarks, but ever and anon recurred to the assertion that "he'd vouch for my character, because he not only knew me, but my parents before me." "He was present," he said, "at their wedding, which he remembered well from the fact of wine being served there, as well as rum, gin, and brandy." That for me was a laborious evening. Sometimes I spoke, and then the inebriate would get the floor and keep it. He rambled about the aisles, allayed a cutaneous disturbance in his back by rubbing himself against one of the fluted pillars, and, when I had at last finished, made his way up to the choir and, interpolating himself between two damsels, sang everything and everybody out of tune from a temperance hymn-book.

CHAPTER XXX.

RUNNING FOR OFFICE.

THIS is the confession of a political villain; not, however, a perjured political villain. I never swore to run for office for my country's good. I did run once for an office for my own good. I was unsuccessful. Virtue has its own reward; so has vice. The wicked do not always flourish like green bay trees. Indeed, judging from a home experience, I am not prepared to say that they flourish at all. The fall political campaign of 1866-67 came on while I was carrying my comic lecture about the camps of Tuolumne, Stanislaus, and Mariposa. A thought one day took possession of me, "Why not run for the Legislature?" I belonged to a political party. My frozen toes troubled me a good deal and the lecture did not pay much over expenses. I consulted with one of the pillars of our party. He belonged in Oak Flat. I took the pillar behind Dan Munn's store on Rattlesnake Creek and avowed my intention. The pillar took a big chew of tobacco, stared, grinned, and said: "Why not?" I consulted with another pillar behind Bob Love's store in Montezuma. He was throwing dirt from a prospect-hole with a long-handled shovel. He leaned on the shovel, blew his nose *au natural* without artificial aid, grinned, and after some deliberation said: "Why not?" I found another pillar of our party slumming out a reservoir near Jamestown. He was enveloped in yellow mud to his waist, and smaller bodies of mud plastered him upward. A short pipe was in his mouth and a slumgullion shovel in his hand. He said: "Go in for it and win."

With less assurance and more fear and trembling I consulted with other and more influential party pillars in Sonora, the county town. Some hesitated; some were dignified; some cheered me on; some said, "Why not?" I made the same remark to myself, and replied, "Why not?" The Assembly was a good gate for entering the political field. My ideas of its duties were vague. Of my own qualifications for the post I dared not think. They may have been about equal to those with which I entered the *Henry's* galley as a sea cook. But what matter? Other men no better qualified than I had gone to Sacramento, received their $10 per diem and came back alive. I could do that. They seemed to stand as well as ever in the estimation of their constituents. Then "Why not?" The die was cast. I announced myself in the county paper as a candidate for the State Assembly. The County Convention assembled at Sonora. It was a body distinguished for wisdom and jurisprudence. Judge Ferral of our city was there. He was then a bright-eyed, active, curly-haired youth, and had already given much promise of his successful career. Judge Leander Quint was there. H. P. Barber presided. Tuolumne County had not then been shorn of its brightest lights by the necessities of the rest of the State and the world. Somebody nominated me. I arose and paid somebody else five dollars. This was the first price of ambition. Then I found myself making my nominating speech. It was a very successful speech. I left out politics altogether, made no pledges, discussed no principles and talked no sense. At first the audience stared. Then they laughed immoderately. So did I. Then they nominated me by acclamation. It was one of the proudest moments of my life, although I did not know it at the time. Taken for all in all, it was no wonder they laughed. I was obliged to laugh myself at the whole affair behind the Court-house when the Convention adjourned. And "Why not?"

It was the laugh of a fiend! I wanted the position for the per diem. I was buried in turpitude. My colleagues were all running on principle to save the country. It is singular that the motive of such a wolf in sheep's clothing as I was at that time was not detected. The great and good men, secure in their own rectitude and purity of purpose, by whom I was surrounded, never once guessed at the presence of the snake in their grass. Looking back at this occurrence after the lapse of nearly twenty-five years, I am more and more astonished that the party should have risked taking such a load as myself on its shoulders. I had no position, no standing, next to no reputation, no property, no good clothes, no whole shoes, no fixed habitation and three sore toes. I had not nor did not realize the responsibilities of a citizen. I had no family and could not realize the duties and responsibilities of those who were rearing young citizens for the great Republic. Should such a man be sent to the State Legislature? Of course not. Are such men ever sent? Of course not. I do not think now that at the period spoken of I was even incorruptible. Should a person who seldom saw over ten dollars in his possession at any one time be sent where he might be "approached" by designing men? Of course not. Was such an one ever sent? Never! The commonwealth of California ran a fearful risk in my nomination.

Few, probably none, suspected the mental misery I endured during this campaign. Because I knew and felt my turpitude. I knew my unfitness for the position to which I aspired. I knew where lay the snake in the grass. Could I meet daily a trusting, credulous constituency, who believed that my mind was full of projects for the relief of the State and nation, without remorse? Of course not. I had remorse—bad, but I dared not back out and off the track. So I kept on, and the vultures gnawed my vitals. Those who think the wicked have such a good time are sadly mistaken. Our party was firmly grounded on one grand belief. It was that nothing the other party could do was right, and nothing that we did was wrong. This at that time I did not believe. But I pretended to. Or rather I stifled all thought on the subject. This was the first great sin. Unlike my colleagues, I was untrue to my own convictions. They——but how I wished for their faith. It could move mountains of doubt. Mine couldn't. How I hated my conscience. It tormented me worse than a chronic colic. There I was standing shoulder to shoulder with patriots—battling bravely for a cause, a principle, while I—I cared for naught save a seat in the Assembly at $10 a day.

It was a stirring campaign, that of 1866, in and about Tuolumne County. The antagonism was of the bitterest character. Political opponents reviled each other in print and sometimes peppered each other with pistols. Bullets flew about night and day. It was dangerous in Sonora to sleep in a clapboarded house in the average line of aim. The papers left nothing unsaid which could taunt and irritate. Editors went about the streets weighed down by masked batteries. It was calculated that 500 pounds of iron were daily packed about the streets in the shape of derringers, knives, and revolvers. The champions of the opposing parties never met on the highway but that people peered and squinted from door and window for the bombardment to commence. Knives were bathed in gore. Barroom floors showed bloody stains. Men died with their boots on. Loaded shotguns lay in ambush behind front and back doors. The atmosphere smelt of blood and possible killing. Saloon plate-glass mirrors showed the track of pistol bullets. Mass meetings were assemblages of men from town and country, secretly armed. People spent most of their time hating each other. Ministers went behind the orthodox returns and preached sectional and partisan politics. The more vital tenets of religion were suspended for the time being with the writ of habeas corpus. I canvassed the county with my comic lecture. It took. It was popular with both parties. It was a pleasant relief from the heavier logic and argument used by heavier and more solid speakers. It was like the farce after the tragedy. It sent assemblies and mass meetings home in good humor. Nobody asked if such a candidate was fit to make laws. But there Tuolumne showed wisdom.

They didn't want any more laws made. Everybody who had been sent to the Legislature since California was created a State had been busy putting more laws on the statute books. There was an overplus. People couldn't keep count of the laws already made. Tuolumne then showed wisdom in its endeavor to send one man to the Legislature of 1866-67 who, not being able to draw up a bill, could not have added a single new law to the mass already made. I gave my party a great deal of trouble. Once in a private conversation with one I deemed a friend, although he belonged to the opposition, I committed myself in favor of greenbacks as a legal tender. Our party did not approve of greenbacks. Ours was the old-fashioned hardmoney dollar of our dad's party. I was hardly aware of this, through a lamentable ignorance of what we really did advocate. The County Central Committee, hearing of my treason, sent after me a messenger with a missive calling on me to explain. I saw then the horrible blunder I had made, and wished the earth would open and swallow me. Then I concluded to resign or to run away. But a man bolstered me up and advised me to deny the report, which I did in an open mass meeting. The use of paper then would have doubled the amount of money in circulation, and that seemed to me just what the people needed. Every mother's son of them on being questioned said they wanted more money, and here seemed a means of relieving that want. But the party refused to put in a plank which might have doubled the dollars in everybody's pockets.

Feeling that I had not done justice to the party in making an active canvass of the county, principally because I had no money to make a canvass with, by treating long lines of ever-ready patriots at every bar in Tuolumne, I concluded I would hold a series of private mass meetings in the day time on horseback. I would do this on election day. I would gallop from poll to poll and make a speech at each poll. I had a route laid out embracing half the county. I made the initial equestrian speech at Jamestown. Thence I galloped to Shaw's Flat. Shaw's Flat upset me. The pillar of our party there, at whose saloon the polls were held, came to his door while I was speaking, took one look at me and walked off in disgust. I saw the disgust on his face an inch thick. It smote me. It threw a wet blanket over all this newly-roused enthusiasm. I started for Columbia, but all the way that man's face peered into mine. It robbed me of all courage and confidence. I had no further heart to continue the work. It was not at all the regular thing. It was an innovation on old party usages. The country even then was too old for such politico-equestrian heroics. I rode back to Jamestown, put the horse in his stable, and hid myself. The people did not agree to send me to Sacramento. Perhaps it was fortunate for them they did not. Probably it was for me. Whatever happens to a man in this life is probably the best thing for him, inasmuch as nothing else can happen to him. I had the profit of an experience in making a semi-political debut, and the people profited by sending another man.

Could the past but be recalled, with all its conditions, contingencies, and accessories; could I once more renew this episode with the advantage of years of experience and accumulated wisdom, I might succeed and fill the post of legislator. But the future is apt to come too late. To be sure it was for me a period of folly and weakness. My soul even now squirms with shame to think of it. "And it should," I hear my fellow-human judges saying. Of course it should. Man's first duty to himself is to hide his follies and bear himself as though he never committed any. Only I can afford to tell what a wretch I have been. Were I a candidate for office I could not.

Some day, when the world is wiser, will men cease strutting about in their masks of propriety and wisdom, and publish their own past errors as freely as now they do those of their fellows? Is it a good preliminary previous to entrance into that world where "all things shall be revealed," where each action lies in its true nature, and where each one of us must "even to the teeth and forehead of our faults give in evidence." "Why not?"

CHAPTER XXXI.

AN EARLY CALIFORNIA CANVASS.

PREVIOUS to this election which did not elect me, Williams and I canvassed the county together. He aspired to the office of Sheriff. We mounted our horses, and with long linen dusters on our backs and bottles of whiskey in our pockets, rode first to Spring Gulch, consisting of two groceries, six saloons, an empty hotel, twenty miners' cabins, a seedy school-house, a seedier church, the hillsides around denuded of earth, torn and scarred by years of hydraulic washing, and showing great patches of bare yellow ledge covered with heaps of boulders. The few men met were in coarse, ragged, gray shirts and mud-stained duck pants, had a worn, worked-out look; over all shining the hot afternoon sun, the heated atmosphere quivering and rising, behind the hill-bounded horizon, a snow-white mass of cloud which, at precisely the same hour every afternoon, attains the same altitude, then gradually sinks. The eye gazes steadily upon it; there are seen great hollows and depths of shining whiteness. It is the vapor coming from the melting snow on the Sierra peaks eighty miles away. The few loungers about the Washington Saloon see William Saunders and myself riding down the hill. Our dusters and clean linen proclaim us as "candidates." Candidates means drinks. There is a gradual concentration of unemployed seediness at the Washington. We dismount; soon the coveted and cheering bottle is placed on the bar; a line of tumblers in skirmishing order form behind it; every one within sight and hearing is called up; a pause of glad anticipation ensues while the glasses are being filled; the precision of bar-room etiquette is strictly observed, that not a drop be swallowed until all are ready; then the dozen tumblers are simultaneously raised; the standing toast "Here's luck," and the reviving alcohol fulfils its mission. This is electioneering.

Sam White is the Bismarck of our interests in Spring Gulch. He is the standing delegate to the County Convention from this precinct. He goes by virtue of a paying claim, a capacity for venturing among the rocks and shoals of saloons, gaming tables and innumerable calls to drink, without losing his head. He can drink deeply, quietly, and fearfully; he can drink himself into noise and turbulence and still keep a set of sober faculties in reserve underneath. We hold a short cabinet meeting with Sam behind the barn. He sees clearly the political complexion of Spring Gulch. Bob O'Leary is doubtful, but may be bought; Jack Shear and Tom Mead must be braced up to allegiance by whiskey; Miles and O'Gorman are mad because a favorite of theirs could not get the nomination for Supervisor last year, and won't vote anyhow; Bob Jones is favorable to us, but wants to leave before the primary meeting comes off; the rest are sure for us or sure against us.

We visit the Franklin House just opposite. The political candidate's money must not all be spent in one house. This is one of the fundamental principles in electioneering. Every saloon controls a few votes, or rather a few whiskey-sodden organizations, who are voted like machines. The solemn ordeal of an American treat is again witnessed. Jim Brown becomes affectionately and patriotically drunk, and as we ride away loudly proclaims himself a "white man and in favor of a white man's government."

We feel that Spring Gulch is secure. We carry it in our pocket. We ride a couple of miles over the ridge to Six-Bit Gulch. Red crags tower upward for hundreds of feet; a rivulet flows along, and on a little flat under a spreading live-oak is an old log cabin. In front is a bit of vegetable garden inclosed by old sluice lumber. High up in the branches overhead a gauze-covered meat-safe; on the trunk is nailed a coffee-mill; under it hangs a frying-pan; close by the washtub and wash-board a few fowl peck about; the quail in a clump of chaparral near by are querously twittering, scolding and fluttering, and making the preliminary arrangements for their night's rest.

Sam Lugar, gray and worn, resident in this gulch for the last sixteen years, sits outside the door smoking his evening pipe.

A hundred yards above is the residence of the "Judge," another hard-working, whiskey-drinking hermit. A glance within shows the Judge eating his evening meal. A child is playing about on the mud floor, whose creamy complexion and bright bead-like eyes indicate its Indian origin. Hanging above the fire-place are a gun, an Indian bow, a quiver full of glass-tipped arrows; on the shelf bits of gold-studded quartz, a bunch of crystals, petrifactions, and curiously-shaped stones found by the "Judge" from time to time in his diggings. There are boxes full of old magazines and newspapers; on the rude window-sill a coverless, well-worn copy of Shakespeare. The Judge is tall, straight, and sallow in complexion. He has lived on this spot since 1849. Six-Bit Gulch was very rich. He has torn up virgin gold in the grass roots. He lives now on recollections of the flush times. Present failures and long past successes form the staple of his conversation. His mining is merely secondary to another occupation, the great aspiration of his life—to beat a poker game over in Spring Gulch. He has been unsuccessfully trying this for the last seven years. A bundle of aboriginal duskiness enveloped in a bright calico gown, hanging about her adipose proportions, stirs as we enter. That is the Judge's wife—a squaw.

Her family down to the third generation, are camped in the brush hard by. They visit the Judge at stated intervals, and at such times the family expenses are trebled. The gray shirt and duck pants tied at the waist with a string constitute the Judge's only dress-suit. On the floor near him is a shapeless, wet mass of India rubber boots, shirt and pants, drenched and splashed with yellow mud. This man was once a spruce clerk in a New England store. At seventeen, the set and whiteness of his collars, the fit of his boots, the arrangement of hair and neck-tie were subjects of long and painful consideration before the mirror. He had his chosen one among the village girls; he saw her regularly home from the Sunday-evening prayer-meetings. The great gold fever of 1848 seized him. He saw a vision: A few months picking up nuggets in California; a triumphant return home; a wedding; a stylish mansion; a fast horse; a front pew; termination, a marble monument in the Terryville cemetery: "Beloved and respected by all who knew him, he sleeps in hope of a still brighter immortality."

We stop at the "Judge's" for the night. Wife and child are sent off to the Indian camp in the chaparral. Sam Lugar drops in after supper. The Judge is an incessant talker. The bottles and glasses are placed on the table. The Judge becomes fatherly as to counsel and admonition against excess in drink. Also against gambling. He has peculiar theological views. Moses, he says, was a keen old miner. He and Aaron put up a plan to gain all the gold in the Israelites' possession. While Moses was on Mount Sinai receiving the stone tables, Aaron was counselling the making and worship of the golden calf. By such means did he concentrate in a lump all the Jews' jewelry. What then? Moses comes down, sees the calf, gets angry, breaks into pieces, burns it up. But what becomes of the gold? Didn't Moses and Aaron sneak around that night and "pan it out" of the ashes?

The Judge is his own theologian.

We visit Price, of Hawkins' Bar. Price is now the sole constituency of Hawkins'. He ran this bar in its golden infancy; he saw it in its youth; he is steadfast to it in its decay. Thirty-four years ago, eight hundred men lived here; the Tuolumne banks were lined with them, shaking their cradles. From the top of yonder red hill the combined grating of the pebbles shaken in hundreds of rocker-sieves sounded like the crash of machinery in a cotton mill.

Old Hawkins first discovered gold here. Price tells of the pickle-jars full he had buried under the floor of his cabin. The secret could not be kept. They came trooping down the steep Red Mountain trail, blankets and tools on their backs, footsore, weary, thirsty, hungry—but hungrier still for gold. They put up tents and brush houses, or crept, slept and cooked under projecting rocks; they stood all day in ice-cold water; they overworked bodies hitherto unused to manual labor; they blistered delicate hands; they lived on bacon and heavy bread of their own making; they drank raw whiskey by the quart; they died, and were buried almost where they died, in nameless graves. Up yonder, but a few yards in the rear of Price's cabin, is the old camp graveyard. The fence is rotting away and stands at various angles. The inscriptions on the headboards are half effaced by time and the elements. Some are split and have fallen down. Read "Jacob Peiser, æt. 27." He died close by in the gulch hard by, with a pistol-bullet through him. A dispute over a claim. "Samuel Purdy, 31." Drowned trying to cross the river during a freshet. "John Wilkins, æt. 35." Killed by a cave in the bank claim about a hundred yards away. "Samuel Johnson, æt. 25." He dove with a sand bag to stop a great leak in the Ford Chann's head wall, and he stopped the leak in part with his own body, for the stream sucked him in the crevice and he never came up alive. "John Weddell, 35." Blown up by the premature explosion of a blast in the Split Rock quartz claim. "Abram Hewison, 45." Delirium tremens, stark mad at midnight, jumped into the river from the point yonder, where the stream whirls round the bend with tremendous force and then rushes down toward the long deep cañon a mile away in a succession of great white crested billows, whose sad, never-ceasing murmur seems an eternal requiem for those lying here.

Price has seen all this. That was the climax of his life. Price's heaven is not in the future. It is in the past. It is embraced in a period about twenty-five years ago, when he made "an ounce per day." Those, he remarks, were times worth living for. Eight hundred souls then at Hawkins'; five gambling houses in full blast every night; music, dancing, and fandangos at either end of the bar.

The river roars unvexed toward the sea. It has burst through its dams and choked the races with sand. The scars and furrows on the hill sides are quite hidden by the thickly growing vegetation; young oaks and pines are coming up in the place of the old. Trail and road are overgrown with brush. Among the rank weeds we stumble on traces of man's former presence— the top of a saloon counter, the mahogany leg and faded green cushion of a billiard table, rusty tin ware, broken picks and shovels, a few rude stone chimneys, about whose blackened fire-places years ago gathered the hopeful, sanguine men of "'49." It is so still. The declining afternoon sun is throwing long shadows from the mountains on the other bank. Slowly they creep up and shade the steeps on our side. Every moan and babble of the Tuolumne falls distinctly on the ear.

"Civilization" here put in a transient appearance. It scarred the hill sides with pits and furrows dug for gold. It cut down the wide-spreading symmetrical oaks. It forced the Tuolumne through race and flume from its channels. It built gaudy temples dedicated to the worship of Bacchus, resplendent with mirrors, pictures, and cut-glassware, located on the very site where a few months previous stood the Indian's smoking wigwam. It brought toiling men, hard-fisted, awkward, ungainly, clumsy, with all grace and suppleness worked out of them and strong only to lift and dig. It brought all manner of men, educated and ignorant, cultivated and coarse, yet for whom Christian training, Christian Church, Christian Bible, Christian spire in city, town, and village pointing heavenward, had failed to convince that gold was not the chief aim and end of all human effort. By day there was labor drudging, labor spasmodic, a few prizes, many blanks, some hope, much more discouragement. By night, revelry, carousal, gambling, oaths, recklessness, pistol shots, knife thrusts, bloodshed, death. Bird and beast fled affrighted to lonelier and more secure retreats before the advent of the raging, cruel animal man.

But now civilization has flown and nature seems easier and somewhat improved by its absence. Price is ours. He will walk nine miles on election day to Chinese Camp, the nearest precinct, to deposit a ballot for us. An order on the proprietor of the Phœnix Saloon for a generous supply of whiskey stimulates his devotion to his country. What a glorious land of liberty is this! See in the clear azure sky above us, floating a mere speck, the eagle, the bird of freedom! He poises himself for a swoop. He comes rushing down on quivering pinion. Nearer! nearer! It is a turkey buzzard, who has scented a dead horse.

Constituencies can only be found where civilization rages.

CHAPTER XXXII.

ANOTHER CHANGE.

THE world seemed coming to an end, I mean my world. I had "ran for office" and was not elected, I had lectured and the people did not call for more, my mines and all they contained were still under ground. The cities I had planned were still unbuilt, I had written for our county paper and gained a small county, but cashless reputation. The fall of 1866 was at hand, and I was saying "Vanity of vanities, all is vanity," when one day I received an unexpected letter from the publisher of a San Francisco weekly paper (*The Golden Era*). He said in substance, "Come to San Francisco and try your chances on the *Era*. We will do the best we can for you."

I went and was met by the good and great-hearted Joseph Lawrence, the principal publisher, and up to that time an entire stranger to me.

The transformation in my life was sudden and startling. It was from the mountain solitudes to the bustle of a great city, from the miner's cabin to the elegancies of the first-class hotel in which my friend positioned me; from the society of the "boys" to that of artists, actors, editors, and writers, some since of world-wide reputation.

It was the sharpest corner I had ever turned in my life. It led into a new road, a new life, new associations, new scenes, and eventually new countries.

And this change came sudden, unexpected at the "darkest hour" and like "a thief in the night."

San Francisco had changed greatly since I had left it eight years previous. Much of the old "'49" characteristic had disappeared or was disappearing. The roughness in garb and manner had abated, the high silk hat topped more masculine heads, the afternoon feminine promenade on the main shopping streets was more elegantly attired, "society" was classifying itself into sets and "circles" more or less pretentious, many more men had homes to rest in at night, the glare and splendor of the openly public gambling house had gone, the revolver as an outside garniture of apparel had disappeared.

I could write with some facility. In other respects, I was awkward, unassimilative with the new element about me, and what is called "shy and retiring" which really implies a kind of vanity demanding that the world shall come and pet you without your having the courage to boldly face it and assert your place in it or whatever you may think your place. I was afraid of being quizzed or made a mark of ridicule by others, and any pretentious fop could with ease make me take a back seat and make me keep my mouth shut. One night Mr. Lawrence invited me to call with him on a noted actress. I refused out of pure dread. Dread of what? Of an opinion I had previously manufactured in my own mind of what the actress might think of me; when I should probably have been of about as much importance to her as a house fly. The consequence which we shy and retiring people attach to ourselves in our secret mind is ridiculously appalling.

Mr. Lawrence remained in San Francisco but a few months after my advent on the *Era*. While he stayed he did all in his power to give me, socially and otherwise, a good "send off." He introduced me to aspiring and successful people, placed me in good material surroundings and opened for me the door to a successful element. That was all he could do, and in my estimation about all one person can do to really advance the fortunes of another.

But when he left I descended, hired the cheapest lodgings, lived on the cheese-paring plan, and was thereby brought mainly into contact with that cheap element in human nature which longs for the best things in the world, is willing even in some way to beg for them, looks on the prosperous with envy and aversion and expends most of its force in anxiety or grumbling, instead of devising ways and means to push forward.

So for the most part I did. I accepted the lowest remuneration for my services, deeming it the inevitable, went figuratively hat in hand to those who bought my articles, and brought my mind at last to think they had done me a great favor on paying me my just dues. I was always expecting starvation or failure of some sort and for that very reason got a near approach to it. My cheap lodgings brought me a sneak thief who stole the first decent suit of clothes I had worn for years in less than forty-eight hours after I had put them on. My associations brought me people who were always moaning over their luck, living mentally in the poorhouse, and therefore we mutually strengthened and supported each other on the road to what was little better than the poorhouse.

Like them, I never thought of being else than a worker for wages, and ran away mentally at any idea of taking responsibilities. Like them I regarded the class who did, as living in a world I never could reach. Like them I regarded the only sure and safe haven was a "job," or situation at steady, regular wages.

So, for years I had indifferent luck, and lived a good deal on the threadbare side of life. The cause and the fault lay entirely in myself. Industriously, though unconsciously I sat down on myself, punched myself into corners; as I in mind accepted the bottom of the heap as the inevitable I stayed near the bottom.

If I should live that and previous portions of my life over again, I should probably do the same thing. Because I believe there is a truth in predestination. In other words, when you are in a certain mental condition your physical life and fortune will be an exact correspondence or material reflection of that condition. When you grow out of that condition and get a different mind your surroundings, fortunes, and associations will be in accordance with that state of mind. Thank Heaven, we can grow. But the I that existed twenty-five years ago was predestined to meet the fortunes it did twenty-five years ago, and those fortunes could only change as the mind of that "I" changed.

CHAPTER XXXIII.

EDITING VS. WRITING.

IN course of time I came temporarily to the occupancy of an editorial chair. I became a "We." Because on becoming an editor you cease to be an "I," you are more. You are several persons rolled into one. You are then the publisher, the proprietor, the paper's biggest paying advertisers, the political party you represent, and the rest of your brother editors. Under these circumstances it is impossible for you to say what "I" think. Because in some cases you may not know what your own private opinions really are, or if they should assert themselves strongly you might not want to know them. You are a "we," one advantage of which is that as in a sense you have ceased to exist as a personality. You are no longer personally responsible for what you say in print. The responsibility of the "we" can be distributed among so many that it need not stick anywhere and the bigger the paper the larger the area over which it can be distributed.

I knew there was a difference between "editing" a paper and writing for one, but how much of a difference I did not realize until my destiny placed me temporarily in charge of the Sunday supplement of a city daily, which, in accordance with the regulations, or rather exactions, of modern journalism, published a Sunday paper, or rather magazine, of sixteen pages. I had about forty-six columns to "edit."

To "edit" is not to write. I speak thus plainly for the benefit of the many young men and maidens who are to swell the ranks of the great army now industriously engaged in sending contributions to the editor's waste basket, and who still imagine that the editor does nothing but write for the paper.

I pause here a moment to ask where, at the present increase of size and amount of matter published, are our Sunday papers to stop. Already the contents of some Sunday issues amount to more than that of the average monthly magazine.

While this competition is going on at such a lively and increasing rate between newspaper publishers to give the most reading matter for the least money, I wonder if the idea may not in due course of time strike them that they may be giving to those who read more than they can really read and digest.

Our business men to-day do not read one-half the contents of the daily paper. They have only time to glance at them. They would really be much better suited could some device of journalism give them their news in readable print in the compass of a handkerchief, and give them no more.

I entered on my duties in a blissful ignorance of the trials that awaited me. I did not know how to "put a head" on an article or a selected "reprint." I know nothing of the hieroglyphics necessary to let the printer know the various kinds of typo in which my headings should be set up. I did not realize that the writer's manuscript must be, in a sense, ground through the editor's mill and go through a certain process before being put in the printer's hands. I did know that something was to be done, but the extent of that something I did not know. Of the signs to be placed on manuscript to show whether the type used should be "brevier" or "minion" or "agate," or those to designate "full-face caps" for my upper headings and "full-face lower case" for my lower headings, of a "display heading," of "balancing the columns," nor that the headings on a page should not be jammed up together or too far apart. I was in that condition of ignorance that the smallest part of a printer was justified in looking down on me with contempt.

—

N. B.—In the composing room a printer is a much larger-sized Indian than a mere writer.

—

You who read the instructive and entertaining columns of ghastliness, accident, and crime in your morning paper—you who are unfortunately or otherwise neither writers nor printers, you think you could easily write one of those staring sensational headings over the article which tell all about it before you read it and whet your appetite for reading it. But you might not. It is not so much the literary ability needed. It is the printer who stands in the way. It is the printer who must have just so many words for one kind of "head" and so many for another. You must get your sense, sensation, and information condensed into say twenty-four or twenty-six words for one part of the "head" and ten or twelve for another part, and these must neither run over nor run under these numbers. If they do and the spaces are uneven that issue of the paper would, in that printer's estimation, be ruined. If you, the editor, do not "make up" your pages so that the columns "balance," the paper, for him, would be a wreck. The foreman of the composing room values a newspaper for its typographical appearance. This is right. A paper, like a house, should look neat. Only the foreman need not forget that there is something in the articles besides types. The magnate of our composing room called all written matter "stuff." "What are you going to do with this stuff?" he would remark, and he used to put such an inflection of contempt on that word "stuff" that it would have made any but an old tough writer sick to hear him. Poems literally perspiring with inspiration, beautiful descriptive articles reeking with soul and sentiment, lively humor, manuscript written and re-written so lovingly and carefully—children of many a brilliant brain—all with him was but "stuff"!

During all the years that I had been writing I had bestowed no attention on the "making up" of a paper. I had a vague idea that the paper made up itself. I had passed in my articles, and had seen them in their places a few hours later, and never dreamt that the placing of these, so that the columns should end evenly or that the page should not look like a tiresome expanse of unbroken type, required study, taste, and experience.

I was aroused from this dream when first called on to "make up" my eight-page supplement. Of course, the foreman expected me to go right on like an old hand, and lay out in the printed form where the continued story should be and how many columns it should fill, where the foreign correspondence and illustrated articles should appear, where the paste pot and scissored matter, shorter articles, and paragraphs should be, so that the printer could place his galleys in the form as marked out per schedule.

I was confronted within a single week with all this mass of my own editorial and typographical ignorance, and even more than can here be told. It had not before dawned upon me that an editor should be—well, we will say, the skeleton of a printer. I was not even the ghost of one. I was not before aware that in the recesses of editorial dens and composing rooms the printer stood higher than the writer. "Everybody" writes nowadays. But "everybody" does not set type or "make up" papers.

I saw then what I had done. I saw that I had rashly assumed to govern a realm of which I was entirely ignorant. I made a full and free confession to our foreman. I put myself before him as an accomplished ignoramus. He was a good fellow and helped me through. It was tough work, however, for several weeks. As Sunday came nearer and nearer, my spasms of dread and anxiety increased. I was seized in the dead of night with fears lest I had not sent up sufficient "stuff" to fill my forty-six columns. Then I would be taken with counter fears lest I had sent up too much, and so run up an overplus on the week's composing bill. I worried and fretted so that by Saturday night I had no clear idea at all or judgment in the matter, and let things take their own course.

But the hardest task of all was dealing with the mourners—I mean the manuscript bearers. I found myself suddenly inside of the place, where I had so often stood outside. I was the man in the editorial chair, the arbiter of manuscript destiny, the despot who could accept or reject the writer's article. But I was very uncomfortable. I hated to reject anybody's writings, I felt so keenly for them. I had so many times been there myself. I wished I could take and pay for everybody's manuscript. But I could not. The requirements of the paper stood like a wall 'twixt my duty and my sympathy. The commands from the management allowed only a certain amount to be expended weekly for original articles. I felt like a fiend—an unwilling one—as I said "No" time after time and sent men and women away with heavy hearts. In cases I tried even to get from the rejected a little sympathy for myself. I told them how hard it was for me to say "No." I tried to convince them that mine was a much harder lot than theirs, and that mine was by far the greater misery.

And how many times after I had suffered and rejected the MSS. did I try to answer in a manner satisfactory to them this question: "Did I know of any newspaper or magazine that would be likely to accept their matter?" How I tried to say that I did not, in a cheerful, consoling, and encouraging manner, in a manner which would convey to them and fill them with the idea that the town was full of places yawning and gaping for their articles, until they were outside of my office themselves, when I was willing that the cold unwelcome truth should freeze them.

Then I received letters asking for the return of manuscript. On entering on my duties I found the shelves piled with them—legacies left me by various predecessors—whether read, accepted, or rejected, I could not find out. But there they lay roll on roll—silent, dust covered. It seemed a literary receiving vault, full of corpses.

It was a suggestive and solemn spectacle for a young writer to look upon. Those many pounds of manuscript—articles which might make a sensation if printed—truths, maybe, which had not yet dawned on the world—all lying unread, dead, cold and unpublished.

Lone, lorn ladies came to me with the children of their brains. I referred them at times to the editor of the daily up-stairs. He referred them to me back again. Sometimes this shuttlecock process was reversed. The daily editor fired the applicant down at me. I fired him up again. The trouble in all these cases lay in the inability of these people to recognize a rejection when it was mildly and sympathetically applied. It was necessary in some cases for us to fire these people up and down at each other a dozen times before their weary legs gave them a hint of the true state of the case.

I saw more than once the man who thought to clinch an acceptance of his matter by giving me a long explanation of his article, and its value to this or that interest. I had the traveller from distant lands, who wanted to tell in print over again what he had seen. I received copies of verses, accompanied by modest notes from the senders that they might find a place "in some corner" of the paper. I was beset by a delusionist who had a theory for doing away with death, and who left me, as he said to "prefer death" and die in my sins, because I told him I had really no desire to obtain information on the subject.

Then I had the "space grabber" to deal with—the poor fellow who writes to live at so much per column, who tries to write as many columns as possible, and half of whose mind while writing is working more to fill up his columns with words rather than ideas. But our modern system of elephantine journalism is in a measure responsible for the "space grabbing" tendency, since our daily and weekly journalistic mammoths and megatheriums gape ever for more and more matter. There is so much space which must be filled, and if not filled stuffed. Every demand brings some sort of supply, and as the paper must be stuffed, the "space grabber" is developed to stuff it.

I had also to cope and meet with the literary rehasher. The rehasher is another journalistic brother who writes the same story, experience, description, etc., over and over again in different ways. He wrote it years ago. It proved a success. He has been writing it ever since. He serves it up roast, baked, boiled, broiled, fried, stewed.

These processes may endure for several years. Then he shoves it on your table, covered with a thin disguise—a gravy, so to speak—of his more recent opinion or experience. But it is about the same dish. The older and more experienced journalistic nose detects it by the same old smell. Finally it comes up as hash, plain hash, dry hash, wet hash, baked hash, but after all the same old hash.

Our papers and magazines even to-day abound with the work of the rehasher. It is just as good for the young readers. Every ten years a generation comes along for whom the rehash is quite new. They do not know that it is the same old hash written and read years and years ago by people dead and gone. The pretentious magazines dish up more or less of this hash. It is served up in style, garnished with sprigs of fine language and sentiment and has often a "dressing" of elegant illustrations poured over it. But it's the same old hash for all that. If you look over the magazines for a period say of twenty years, you will find these rehashes—articles descriptive of Rome, Egypt, London, the Bayeaux tapestry, travels in countries worn footsore by travellers for generations, the essay on Dante, Shakespeare, Goethe. As for the frontier romance and "Wild Injun" story, that has been ground and reground into hash so fine that it has become "spoon victuals," and is eaten only by the young and callow of the reading brood.

A literary colleague, who commands an editorial chair, says that he allows his rehashers to serve him the same article four times, providing the garnishing and dressing of the dish show artistic cookery. But he shuts down after that. This is not only charitable on his part, but possibly a great benefit to the rehasher, for if he is allowed to go on unchecked, the mental rehashing process will become automatic, the result of which will be the unconscious rehashing of the same article through all eternity.

This experience gave me, in certain respects, an entire change of heart. I will never think hard again of an editor though he does not return my manuscript even if I send stamps. I will still continue to think kindly of him though he "declines with thanks." For I realize now that the "editor" who would do his duty must have nerves of steel and a heart of stone.

CHAPTER XXXIV.

OPINIONS JOURNALISTIC.

FOR five years I wrote for many papers in San Francisco and wrote some things good, some bad, some indifferent. I attacked and ridiculed the errors and foibles of others with the miraculous confidence and inferred self-righteousness of a man who had not as yet begun to realize his own shortcomings. I assailed abuses and was sometimes disgusted at what then I deemed the timidity and lack of nerve on the part of newspaper publishers, when they refused to print my tirades, reproofs, and sarcasms. As a champion I was very brave to speak on paper in the privacy of my own room. As a man with no capital at stake, I was very wise in showing others where to put their money.

I was rated in San Francisco as a "Bohemian" and deserved the name. I was largely in sympathy with the idea that life being short should be worked at a rapid pace for all that could be got out of it, and that we the dwellers on the top floor of intellect were justified in regarding with a certain scorn the duller and generally wealthier plodders on the lower floors of business. We were as proud of our comparative poverty and disregard of money because we held in some way we never could explain that such poverty argued for us the possession of more brains, though we were very glad to receive our money from people we deemed ourselves so far above. I think this is all nonsense.

I think now that the ability to express ideas well on paper is a vastly over-rated and over-praised talent. A man may write well and not have sufficient executive ability to build a hen coop or govern one after it is built, and brains play a very important part in any kind of managerial ability, be the field large or small.

Bohemianism as it existed thirty years ago is nearly dead. It has been discovered that late hours, gin, and nocturnal out-pourings of wit, brain, and brilliancy, do not increase the writer's originality, or fertility of idea, and that a great deal of force is wasted at such times which should be turned into dollars and cents.

A man or woman to-day who succeeds permanently with the pen will not only live well-ordered lives, but possess a business ability outside of the pen, in order to get their ideas before the public. Never before were there so many writers, and never before so many able writers. The literary mediocrity of to-day would have made a brilliant reputation sixty years ago. But of those who are merely writers, even if good writers, three-fourths as regards compensation are almost on the same relative plane as the type-writer. The supply is greater than the demand. People must write even if not paid for the pleasure of seeing their ideas in print, and for this reason to-day do we find country weeklies furnished regularly free of expense with interesting correspondence from abroad by the editor's travelling friends.

As a newspaper man and correspondent, I was not always very particular in writing about people, and dragging their personality before the public. I wanted subjects and something or somebody to write about. These were my capital stock in trade.

I don't wonder that a certain unpopularity with a class attaches itself to "newspaper men," "correspondents" and reporters. The tendency and temptation is to become social Paul Pry's, especially when family or individual secrets will swell a column and bring dollars. Of all this I did my share, and regard myself now with small favor for so doing.

The freedom of the Press has developed Press freebooters male and female, and the Press has now all the freedom of the village gossip.

On the other hand a great many people like to see their names in print. The remark "don't put my name in the paper" often means "do put my name in the paper," with little care as to the accompanying comment.

Many people have a terrible and I think needless fear of what the newspaper can do and say to make or unmake them, to give a book or a play a reputation or kill it outright. I notice that a play often becomes very popular when its first critics condemned it, and the same can be said of books. Uncle Tom's Cabin, Mark Twain's Innocents Abroad, Helper's Irrepressible Conflict and Bret Harte's Heathen Chinee were not advertised into notice by the Press. Their force made the Press advertise them.

The Press, which so often claims to "mould popular opinion" is in reality moulded by popular opinion and follows it, while sometimes claiming to lead it. There is a power which brings men and movements for greater or lesser periods into public notice, which the Press does not manufacture.

The Press which claims indirectly to have so much of the public morals and the public good in its care and keeping—this "lever of civilization" which will deluge its columns for days and weeks with the preliminaries of a prize fight or parades for a similar time the details of a scandal, places a great deal before the eyes of every boy and girl which seems to me neither civilized nor civilizing.

I object here neither to the prize fight nor its publication. But I can't think the man who spreads it all broadcast day after day before the community as a promoter of the highest refinement or civilization.

The Press of to-day is either ridiculing ideas or ignoring them entirely, which the Press of a near Future will treat as most important realities, just as fifty years ago, nine-tenths of the American newspapers treated the subject of human slavery. Did the Press of America mould public opinion in this respect or was it the idea that moulded public opinion first and as a necessary consequence the Press followed. Not that I advocate the idea that the editor should express himself far in advance of public opinion or rather of public knowledge. It is a very unwise thing to do. The inevitable result is the kick instead of the copper. Martyrdom is not the business of a newspaper. Many a leading editor of to-day deemed conservative and old fogyish is really more liberal and progressive than those who rail at him. But he is wiser than they and has learned that ideas which may be accepted and in full sway a century hence, cannot be argued as if in full fruition to-day. He may know also how to pave the way for a new idea, and is often doing it while his readers never realize his intent.

CHAPTER XXXV.

RECENT ANTIQUITY.

I WAS soon to leave for the Eastern States. When I realized that I was going, I found to my surprise that I had made a home in California, that it was an old home and about it clung all the memories and associations of an old home.

I wanted to visit the mines and take a farewell look at the camps where I had lived and worked in a period now fast becoming "old times," and I went.

The term antiquity is relative in its character. Twenty years may involve an antiquity as much as 200 or 2,000. Indeed, as regards sensation and emotion, the more recent antiquity is the more strongly is it realized and more keenly felt. Standing to-day on the hillside and looking down on the site of the camp where you mined twenty-five years ago, and then going down that hill and treading over that site, now silent and deserted, and you realize, so to speak, a live antiquity. So far as ancient Greece or Rome are concerned, their histories would make no different impression on us if dated 600 years ago or 6,000. We are imposed upon by these rows of ciphers. They convey really no sense of time's duration. They are but mathematical sounds. We know only that these nations and these men and women lived, ate, slept, drank, quarrelled, coveted, loved, hated, and died a long time ere we were born and that of it all we have but fragments of their history, or rather fragments of the history of a few prominent individuals.

But when you stand alone at Dry Bar, where you mined when it was a lively camp in 1857, with its score of muddy sluice streams coursing hither and thither, its stores, its saloons, its hotel and its express office, and see now but one rotting pine-log cabin, whose roof has tumbled in and whose sides have tumbled out; where all about is a silent waste of long-worked-off banks or bare ledge and piles of boulders in which the herbage has taken root; where every mark of the former houses and cabins has disappeared, save a mound here, or a pile of stone indicating a former chimney there, you have a lively realization of antiquity, though it be a recent one. You knew the men who lived here; you worked with them; you know the sites of the houses in which they lived; you have an event and a memory for every acre of territory hereabout. Down there, where the river narrows between those two high points of rock, once stood a rickety bridge. It became more and more shaky and dangerous, until one day Tom Wharton, the Justice of the Peace, fired by a desire *pro bono publico* and rather more than his ordinary quantity of whiskey, cut the bridge away with his axe and it floated down stream. Over yonder, on that sandy point, was the richest claim on the bar.

Will you go down to Pot-Hole Bar, two miles below? The trail ran by the river. But freshet after freshet has rushed over the bank and wiped out the track made by the footprints of a few years. There is no trace of the trail. The chaparral has grown over and quite closed it up. Here and there is a faint trace, and then it brings up short against a young pine or a buckeye, the growth of the last ten years. Yet in former days this path ranked in your mind of the importance of a town street. You had no idea how quickly nature, if left alone, will restore things to what we term "primitive conditions." If a great city was deserted in these foothills, within twenty years' time the native growths would creep down and in upon it, start plantations of chaparral in the streets, festoon the houses with vines, while winged seeds would fill the gutters and cornices with verdure. It is a hard struggle through the undergrowth to Pot-Hole Bar. No man lives there now. No man goes there. Even the boulder piles and bare ledges of fifteen years ago, marking the scarifying work of your race on mother earth's face, are now mounds overgrown with weeds. What solitude of ancient ruined cities equals this? Their former thousands are nothing to you as individuals; but you knew all the boys at Pot-Hole. It was a favorite after-supper trip from Dry Bar to Pot-Hole to see how the "boys" were getting on, and vice versa from Pot-Hole to Dry Bar.

A cotton-tail rabbit sends a flash of white through the bushes. His family now inhabits Pot-Hole. They came back after all of your troublesome race had left, and very glad were the "cotton-tails" of the riddance. There is a broken shovel at your feet and near by in the long grass you see the fragment of a sluice's false bottom, bored through with anger holes to catch the gold and worn quite thin by the attrition of pebble and boulder along its upper surface. This is about the only vestige of the miner's former work. Stop! On the hillside yonder is a mound-like elevation and beyond that a long green raised line. One marks the reservoir and the other the ditch. It was the Pot-Hole Company's reservoir, built after they had concluded to take water from the ditch and wash off a point of gravel jutting toward the river. They had washed it all off by 1856, and then the company disbanded and went their respective ways. Pot-Hole lay very quiet for a couple of years, but little doing there save rocker washing for grub and whiskey by four or five men who had concluded that "grub and whiskey" was about all in life worth living for. A "slouchy" crowd, prone to bits of rope to tie up their suspenders, unshaven faces, and not a Sunday suit among them.

They pottered about the bar and the bank, working sometimes in concert and then quarrelling, and every man betaking himself to his private rocker, pick, and shovel for a few days or weeks and coming together again, as compelled by necessity. One of them commenced picking into a slim streak of gravel at the base of the red hard-pan bank left by the pot-holers. It paid to the pan first two cents and a little farther in three, and a little farther seven, and then the gold became coarser and heavier and it yielded a bit to the pan. The blue ledge "pitched in," the gravel streak grew wider and richer, the crowd took up the whole face of the bank, 150 feet to the man, and found they had struck fortunes. And then they worked at short intervals and "went it" at long ones, and all save four drank themselves to death within four years.

They have all long since gone. They are scattered for the most part you know not where. Two are living in San Francisco and are now men of might and mark. Another you have heard of far away in the Eastern States, living in a remote village, whose name is never heard of outside the county bounds. One has been reported to you as "up North somewhere;" another down in Arizona "somewhere," and three you can locate in the county. That is but seven out of the one hundred who once dwelt here and roundabout. Now that recollection concentrates herself you do call to mind two others—one died in the county almshouse and another became insane and was sent to Stockton. That is all. Nine out of the one hundred that once resided at Dry Bar. It is mournful. The river monotonously drones, gurgles, and murmurs over the riffle. The sound is the same as in '58. A bird on the opposite bank gives forth, at regular intervals, a loud querulous cry. It was a bird of the same species whose note so wore on the nerves of Mike McDonald as he lay dying of consumption in a big house which stood yonder, that, after anathematizing it, he would beseech his watcher to take a gun and blow the "cussed" thing's head off. Perhaps it is the same bird. The afternoon shadows are creeping down the mountain side. The outline of the hills opposite has not at all changed, and there, down by the bank, is the enormous fragment of broken rock against which Dick Childs built his brush shelter for the summer and out of which he was chased by a sudden fall rise of the river. But it is very lonesome with all these people here so vivid in memory, yet all gone, and never, never to come back.

You wonder if any of the "old crowd" now living, live over as you do the past life here; if a single one within the last ten years has ever revisited the spot; or if any of them have any desire to revisit it. Some of them did so once. There was Jake Bennett. As late as '62, Jake, who had removed to the next county, would come every summer on a pilgrimage to "see the boys," and the boys at Dry Bar were even then sadly reduced in number, for the camp ran down very quickly within the four years dating from '58. But Jake was faithful to old memories and associations, and proved it by the ten-miles' walk he was obliged to take to reach Dry Bar. Dry Bar was never on a regular stage route. Jake was an ex-Philadelphian and called rest "west" and violin "wiolin." But no one comes here now, at least on any such errand. It's a troublesome and rather expensive locality to reach and mere sentiment does not pay. The nearest resident is a Missouri hog-rancher, whose house is above on the hill a couple of miles away. He neither knows nor cares for Dry Bar's former history. He came here but ten years ago. His half-wild swine are ambushed about in the shelter of the elder and buckeye bushes, and frightened at your approach plunge snorting into the deeper thickets.

Here it is. The remains of your own cabin chimney, a pile of smoke-blackened stones in the tall grass. Of the cabin every vestige has disappeared. You built that chimney yourself. It was an awkward affair, but it served to carry out the smoke, and when finished you surveyed it with pleasure and some pride, for it was your chimney. Have you ever felt "snugger" and more cozy and comfortable since than you did on the long, rainy winter nights, when, the supper finished and the crockery washed, you and your "pard" sat by the glowing coals and prepared your pipes for the evening smoke? There were great hopes and some great strikes on Dry Bar in those days; that was in '52. Mining was still in the pan, rocker and long tom era; sluices were just coming in. Hydraulicking 100-foot banks and washing hills off the face of the earth had not been thought of. The dispute as to the respective merits of the long vs. the short-handled shovel was still going on. A gray or red shirt was a badge of honor. The deep river-beds were held to contain enormous store of golden nuggets. River mining was in its wing and coffer-dam phase.

Perhaps the world then seemed younger to you than now? Perhaps your mind then set little store on this picturesque spot, so wrapped were you in visions of the future? Perhaps then you wrote regularly to that girl in the States—your first heart's-trouble—and your anticipation was fixed entirely on the home to be built up there on the gold you were to dig here? Perhaps the girl never married you, the home was never built and nothing approaching the amount of *oro* expected dug out. You held, then, Dry Bar in light estimation. It was for you only a temporary stopping place, from which you wished to get its gold as quickly as you could and get away from as soon as possible. You never expected Dry Bar, its memories and associations thus to make for themselves a "local habitation and a name" in your mind. We live sometimes in homes we do not realize until much of their material part has passed away. A horned toad scuttles along the dry grass and inflates himself to terrify you as you approach. Those rat-like ground squirrels are running from hole to hole, like gossiping neighbors, and "chipping" shrilly at each other. These are old summer acquaintances at Dry Bar.

Is it with a feeling of curiosity you take up one of those stones handled by you thirty-one years ago and wonder how like or unlike you may be to yourself at that time? Are you the same man? Not the same young man, certainly. The face is worn; the eyes deeper set; the hair more or less gray and there are lines and wrinkles where none existed then. But that is only the outside of your "soul case." Suppose that you, the John Doe of 1883, could and should meet the John Doe of 1853? Would you know him? Would you agree on all points with him? Could you "get" along with him? Could you "cabin" with him? Could you "summer and winter" with him? Would the friends of the John Doe of '53, who piled up that chimney, be the friends of the present John Doe, who stands regarding its ruins? Are the beliefs and convictions of that J. Doe those of this J. Doe? Are the jokes deemed so clever by that J. Doe clever to this J. Doe? Are the men great to that J. Doe great to the present J. Doe? Does he now see the filmly, frothy fragments of scores of pricked bubbles sailing away and vanishing in air? If a man die shall he live again? But how much of a man's mind may die out and be supplanted by other ideas ere his body goes back to dust? How much of this J. Doe belongs to that J. Doe, and how much of the same man is there standing here?

CHAPTER XXXVI.

GOING HOME.

AFTER sixteen years of exile in California, I found myself rolling seaward and homeward through the Golden Gate in the Panama steamer Sacramento. The parting gun had been fired, the captain, naval cloak, cap, eye-glass and all, had descended from his perch of command on the paddle-box, the engine settled steadily to its work, Telegraph Hill, Meigg's Wharf, Black Point, Alcatraz, Lime Point, Fort Point, one by one receded and crept into the depressing gloomy fog, the mantle in which San Francisco loves so well to wrap herself. The heave of the Pacific began to be plainly felt, and with it the customary misery.

The first two days out are devoted to sea and homesickness. Everybody is wretched about something. No sooner is the steamer a mile beyond the Heads than we, who for years have been awaiting a blessed deliverance from California, are seized with unutterable longings to return. All at once we discover how pleasant is the land and its people. We review its associations, its life, its peculiar excitements, and the warm friendships we have made there. And now it is all fading in the fog: the Cliff House is disappearing, it is going, it is gone. Heart and stomach are contemporaneously wretched: we bury ourselves in our berths; we call upon the steward and stewardess; we wish ardently that some accident may befall the ship and oblige her to put back. No! Not more inexorable, certain and inevitable is the earth in its revolution, the moon in its orbit, or one's landlord when the rent is overdue, than is the course of the stately vessel south. South, day after day, she plunges; the North Star sinks, the sky becomes fairer, the air milder, the ocean of a softer blue; the sunsets develop the tints of Fairyland; the sunrise mocks all human ornamentation in its gorgeousness. Light coats and muslin dresses blossom on the promenade-deck; the colored waiters develop white linen suits and faultless neckties. The sea air on the northern edge of the tropic zone is a balm for every wound, and forces us into content against our perverse wills.

We had a medley on board. There was a batch of sea-captains going East, some with wives, some without; one of the maritime madams, they said, could navigate a vessel as well as her husband; she certainly had a sailor balance in walking the deck in rough weather. There was a tall Mephistophelic-looking German youth, who daily took up a position on deck, fortified by a novel, a cigar, and a field-glass, never spoke a word to any one, and was reported to be a baron. There were a dogmatic young Englishman with a heavy burr in his voice, who seemed making a business of seeing the world; a stocky young fellow, one of Morgan's men during the war, and another who had seen his term of service on the Federal side; a stout lady, dissatisfied with everything, sick of travelling, dragging about with her a thin-legged husband well stricken in years, who interfered feebly with her tantrums; and a young man who at the commencement of the trip started out with amazing celerity and success in making himself popular. This last was a cheery, chippery young fellow; his stock in trade was small, but he knew how to display it to the best advantage. It gave out in about ten days, and everybody voted him a bore. He took seriously to drinking brandy ere we arrived in New York. And then came the rank and file, without sufficient individuality as yet developed to be even disagreeable.

But there was one other, a well-to-do Dutchess County farmer, who had travelled across the continent to see "Californy," and concluded to take the steamer on his way home to observe as much as he might of Central America; a man who had served the Empire State in her legislature; a man mighty in reading. Such a walking encyclopædia of facts, figures, history, poetry, metaphysics and philosophy I never met before. He could quote Seward, Bancroft, Carl Schurz, Clay, and Webster by the hour. His voice was of the sonorous, nasal order, with a genuine Yankee twang. I tried in vain to spring on him some subject whereof he should appear ignorant. One might as well have endeavored to show Noah Webster a new word in the English language. And all this knowledge during the trip he ground out in lots to order. It fell from his lips dry and dusty. It lacked soul. It smelt overmuch of histories, biographies, and political pamphlets. He turned it all out in that mechanical way, as though it were ground through a coffee-mill. Even his admiration was dry and lifeless. So was his enthusiasm. He kept both measured out for occasions. It is a pleasant sail along the Central American coast, to see the shores lined with forests so green, with palms and cocoanuts, and in the background dark voltanic cones; and this man, in a respectable black suit, a standing collar and a beaver hat, would gaze thereon by the hour and grind out his dusty admiration. Among the steerage passengers was a bugler who every night gave a free entertainment. He played with taste and feeling, and when once we had all allowed our souls to drift away in "The Last Rose of Summer," the Grinder in the midst of the beautiful strain brought us plump to earth by turning out the remark that "a bewgle made abeout as nice music as any instrument goin', ef it was well played." Had he been thrown overboard he would have drifted ashore, and bored the natives to death with a long and lifeless story of his escape from drowning.

Dames Rumor and Gossip are at home on the high seas. They commence operations as soon as their stomachs are on sea-legs. Everybody then undergoes an inspection from everybody else, and we report to each other. Mrs. Bluster! Mrs. Bluster's conduct is perfectly scandalous before we have been out a week: she nibbling around young men of one-half—ay, one-fourth—her age! The young miss who came on board in charge of an elderly couple has seceded from them; promenades the hurricane-deck very late with a dashing young Californian; but then birds of a feather, male and female, will flock together. Mr. Bleareye is full of brandy every morning before ten o'clock; and the "catamaran" with the thin-legged and subjected husband does nothing but talk of her home in ———. We know the color and pattern of her carpets, the number of her servants, the quality of her plate, and yesterday she brought out her jewelry and made thereof a public exhibition in the saloon. All this is faithfully and promptly borne per rail over the Isthmus, and goes over to the Atlantic steamer. I am conscientious in this matter of gossip: I had made resolutions. There was a lady likewise conscientious on board, and one night upon the quarter-deck, when we had talked propriety threadbare, when we were both bursting with our fill of observation, we met each other halfway and confessed that unless we indulged ourselves also in a little scandal we should die, and then, the flood-gates being opened, how we riddled them! But there is a difference between criticism of character and downright scandal, you know; in that way did we poultice our bruised consciences.

On a voyage everybody has confidences to make, private griefs to disclose, to everybody else. This is especially the case during the first few days out. We feel so lone and lorn; we have all undergone the misery of parting, the breaking of tender ties; we seem a huddle of human units shaken by chance into the same box, yet scarcely are we therein settled when we begin putting forth feelers of sympathy and recognition. There was one young man who seemed to me a master in the art of making desirable acquaintances for the trip. He entered upon his work ere the Golden Gate had sunk below the horizon. He had a friendly word for all. His approach and address were prepossessing. He spoke to me kindly. I was miserable and flung myself upon him for sympathy. The wretch was merely testing me as a *compagnon de voyage*. He found me unsuitable. He flung me from him with easy but cold politeness, and consorted with an "educated German gentleman." I revenged myself by playing the same tactics on a sea-and love-sick German carriage-maker. "An eye for an eye, a tooth for a tooth," you know.

We touched at Magdalena Bay and Punta Arenas. We expected to stay at Punta Arenas twelve hours to discharge a quantity of flour. Four times twelve hours we remained there. Everybody became very tired of Costa

Rica. The Costa Rican is not hurried in his movements. He took his own time in sending the necessary lighters for that flour. A boat load went off once in four hours. The Costa Ricans came on board, men and women, great and small, inspected the *Sacramento*, enjoyed themselves, went on shore again, lay down in the shade of their cocoanut palms, smoked their cigarettes and slept soundly, while the restless, uneasy load of humanity on the American steamer fretted, fumed, perspired, scolded at Costa Rican laziness and ridiculed the Costa Rican government, which revolutionizes once in six months, changes its flag once a year, taxes all improvements, and acts up to the principle that government was made for the benefit of those who govern. Many of the passengers went on shore. Some came back laden with tropical flowers, others full of brandy. The blossoms filled the vessel the whole night with perfume, while the brandy produced noise and badly-sung popular melodies.

The Grinder went on shore with the rest. On returning he expressed disgust at the Costa Ricans. He thought that "nothing could ever be made of them." He had no desire that the United States should ever assimilate with any portion of the Torrid Zone. He predicted that such a fusion would prove destructive to American energy and intelligence. We had enough southern territory and torpor already. The man has no appreciation of the indolence and repose of the tropics. He knows not that the most delicious of enjoyments is the waking dream under the feathery palm, care and restlessness flung aside, while the soul through the eye loses itself in the blue depths above. He would doom us to an eternal rack of civilization and Progress-work—grind, jerk, hurry, twist and strain, until our nerves, by exhaustion unstrung and shattered, allow no repose of mind or body; and even when we die our bones are so infected by restlessness and goaheaditiveness that they rattle uneasily in our coffins.

Panama sums up thus: An ancient, walled, red-tiled city, full of convents and churches; the ramparts half ruined; weeds springing atop the steeples and belfries; a fleet of small boats in front of the city; Progress a little on one side in the guise of the Isthmus Railroad depot, cars, engines, ferry-boat, and red, iron lighters; a straggling guard of parti-colored, tawdry and most slovenly-uniformed soldiers, with French muskets and sabre bayonets, drawn up at the landing, commanded by an officer smartly dressed in blue, gold, kepi, brass buttons and stripes, with a villainous squint eye, smoking a cigar. About the car windows a chattering crowd of blacks, half blacks, quarter blacks, coffee, molasses, brown, nankeen and straw colored natives, thrusting skinny arms in at the windows, and at the end of those arms parrots, large and small, in cages and out, monkeys, shells, oranges, bananas, carved work, and pearls in various kinds of gold setting; all of which were sorely tempting to some of the ladies, but ere many bargains were concluded the train clattered off, and we were crossing the continent.

The Isthmus is a panorama of tropical jungle; it seems an excess, a dissipation of vegetation. It is a place favorable also for the study of external black anatomy. The natives kept undressing more and more as we rolled on. For a mile or two after leaving Panama they did affect the shirt. Beyond this, that garment seemed to have become unfashionable, and they stood at their open doors with the same unclothed dignity that characterized Adam in the Garden of Eden before his matrimonial troubles commenced. Several young ladies in our care first looked up, then down, then across, then sideways: then they looked very grave, and finally all looked at each other and unanimously tittered.

Aspinwall! The cars stop; a black-and-tan battalion charge among us, offering to carry baggage. They pursue us to the gate of the P. M. S. S. depot; there they stop; we pass through one more cluster of orange, banana, and cigar selling women; we push and jam into the depot, show our tickets, and are on board the *Ocean Queen*. We are on the Atlantic side! It comes over us half in awe, half in wonder, that this boat will, if she do not reach the bottom first, carry us straight to a dock in New York. The anticipation of years is developing into tangibility.

We cross the Caribbean. It is a stormy sea. Our second day thereon was one of general nausea and depression. You have perhaps heard the air, "Sister, what are the wild waves saying?" On that black Friday many of our passengers seemed to be earnestly saying something over the *Ocean Queen's* side to the "wild, wild waves." The Grinder went down with the rest. I gazed triumphantly over his prostrate form laid out at full length on a cabin settee. Seward, Bancroft, politics, metaphysics, poetry, and philosophy were hushed at last. Both enthusiasm and patriotism find an uneasy perch on a nauseated stomach.

But steam has not robbed navigation of all its romance. We find some poetry in smoke, smoke stacks, pipes, funnels, and paddles, as well as in the "bellying sails" and the "white-winged messengers of commerce." I have a sort of worship for our ponderous walking-beam, which swings its many tons of iron upon its axis as lightly as a lady's parasol held 'twixt thumb and finger. It is an embodiment of strength, grace, and faithfulness. Night and day, mid rain and sunshine, be the sea smooth or tempestuous, still that giant arm is at its work, not swerving the fractional part of an inch from its appointed sphere of revolution. It is no dead metallic thing: it is a something rejoicing in power and use. It crunches the ocean 'neath its wheels with that pride and pleasure of power which a strong man feels when he fights his way through some ignoble crowd. The milder powers of upper air more feebly impel yon ship; in our hold are the powers of earth, the gnomes and goblins, the subjects of Pluto and Vulcan, begrimed with soot and sweat, and the elements for millions and millions of years imprisoned in the coal are being steadily set free. Every shovelful generates a monster born of flame. As he flies sighing and groaning through the wide-mouthed smokestack into the upper air, he gives our hull a parting shove forward.

A death in the steerage—a passenger taken on board sick at Aspinwall. All day long an inanimate shape wrapped in the American flag lies near the gangway. At four P.M. an assemblage from cabin and steerage gather with uncovered heads. The surgeon reads the service for the dead; a plank is lifted up; with a last shrill whirl that which was once a man is shot into the blue waters; in an instant it is out of sight and far behind, and we retire to our state-rooms, thinking and solemnly wondering about that body sinking, sinking, sinking in the depths of the Caribbean; of the sea monsters that curiously approach and examine it; of the gradual decay of the corpse's canvas envelope; and far into the night, as the *Ocean Queen* shoots ahead, our thoughts wander back in the blackness to the buried yet unburied dead.

The Torrid Zone is no more. This morning a blast from the north sweeps down upon us. Cold, brassy clouds are in the sky; the ocean's blue has turned to a dark, angry brown, flecked with white caps and swept by blasts fresh from the home of the northern floe and iceberg. The majority of the passengers gather about the cabin-registers, like the house-flies benumbed by the first cold snap of autumn in our northern kitchens. Light coats, pumps and other summer apparel have given way to heavy boots, over-coats, fur caps and pea-jackets. A home look settles on the faces of the North Americans. They snuff their native atmosphere: they feel its bracing influence. But the tawny-skinned Central Americans who have gradually accumulated on board from the Pacific ports and Aspinwall, settle inactively into corners or remain ensconced in their berths. The air which kindles our energies wilts theirs. The hurricane-deck is shorn of its awnings. Only a few old "shell-back" passengers maintain their place upon it, and yet five days ago we sat there in midsummer moonlit evenings.

We are now about one hundred miles from Cape Hatteras. Old Mr. Poddle and his wife are travelling for pleasure. Came to California by rail, concluded to return by the Isthmus. Ever since we started Cape Hatteras has loomed up fearfully in their imaginations. Old Mr. Poddle looks knowingly at passing vessels through his field-glass, but doesn't know a fore-and-aft schooner from a man-of-war. Mrs. Poddle once a day inquires if there's any danger. Mr. Poddle does not talk so much, but evidently in private meditates largely on hurricanes, gales, cyclones, sinking and burning vessels. Last night we came in the neighborhood of the Gulf Stream. There were flashes of lightning, "mare's tails" in the sky, a freshening breeze and an increasing sea. About eleven old Mr. Poddle came on deck. Mrs. Poddle, haunted by Hatteras, had sent him out to see if "there was any danger;" for it is evident that Mrs. Poddle is dictatress of the domestic empire. Mr. Poddle ascended to the hurricane-deck, looked nervously to leeward, and just then an old passenger salt standing by, who had during the entire passage comprehended and enjoyed the Poddletonian dreads, remarked, "This is nothing to what we shall have by morning." This shot sent Poddle below. This morning at breakfast the pair looked harassed and fatigued.

The great question now agitating the mind of this floating community is, "Shall we reach the New York pier at the foot of Canal street by Saturday noon?" If we do, there is for us all long life, prosperity and happiness: if we do not, it is desolation and misery. For Monday is New Year's Day. On Sunday we may not be able to leave the city: to be forced to stay in New York over Sunday is a dreadful thought for solitary contemplation. We study and turn it over in our minds for hours as we pace the deck. We live over and over again the land-journey to our hearthstones at Boston, Syracuse, and Cincinnati. We meet in thought our long-expectant relatives, so that at last our air-castles become stale and monotonous, and we fear that the reality may be robbed of half its anticipated pleasure from being so often lived over in imagination.

Nine o'clock, Friday evening. The excitement increases. Barnegat Light is in sight. Half the cabin passengers are up all night, indulging in unprofitable talk and weariness, merely because we are so near home. Four o'clock, and the faithful engine stops, the cable rattles overboard, and everything is still. We are at anchor off Staten Island. By the first laggard streak of winter's dawn I am on the hurricane-deck. I am curious to see my native North. It comes by degrees out of the cold blue fog on either side of the bay. Miles of houses, spotted with patches of bushy-looking woodland—bushy in appearance to a Californian, whose oaks grow large and widely apart from each other, as in an English park. There comes a shrieking and groaning and bellowing of steam-whistles from the monster city nine miles away. Soon we weigh anchor and move up toward it. Tugs dart fiercely about, or laboriously puff with heavilyladen vessels in tow. Stately ocean steamers surge past, outward bound. We become a mere fragment of the mass of floating life. We near the foot of Canal street. There is a great deal of shouting and bawling and counter-shouting and counter-bawling, with expectant faces on the wharf, and recognitions from shore to steamer and from steamer to shore. The young woman who flirted so ardently with the young Californian turns out to be married, and that business-looking, middle-aged man on the pier is her husband. Well, I never! Why, you are slow, my friend, says inward reflection. You are not versed in the customs of the East. At last the gangway plank is flung out. We walk on shore. It is now eighteen years since that little floating world society cemented by a month's association scattered forever from each other's sight at the Canal street pier.
